The Complete Guide to

Pre-Employment Testing

PERSONALITY & APTITUDE TEST PREPARATION

Job Test Prep

Copyright © 2006 by jobtestprep

Email: info@jobtestprep.com

http://www.jobtestprep.com

ISBN: 965-91038-0-8

Contents

Part 2 – Aptitude Test Preparation

INTRODUCTION

In the current job market, being invited to a job interview almost always entails taking pre-employment tests (also called selection/screening tests). Employers use these tests to select the most suitable applicant for the job out of a pool of candidates. Your scores on these selection tests are always analysed relative to the other applicants' scores. Candidates with the highest scores will be offered the position. Research has repeatedly shown that preparation for selection tests dramatically boosts performance and self-confidence, and therefore increases the likelihood of getting the position. This book will prepare you for two critical elements of the selection process – personality tests and aptitude (IQ) tests.

Your personality and aptitude test results are crucial in determining your chances of getting the job. Receiving a personality profile that does not fit the job requirements or scoring below a certain threshold on the aptitude tests will seriously minimise your chances of obtaining the position.

There are many books on the career shelf that aim to prepare you for pre-employment tests. Normally, these focus on aptitude or intelligence test (IQ) preparation. There are no books that really prepare candidates for a personality test. Some authors claim that their books prepare job seekers for personality testing, but none actually do so in practice. In addition, most of the preparation books argue that it is impossible to prepare for a personality test, recommending that you should, "just be yourself and answer as truthfully as you can". Besides being untrue, this advice can be misleading. The authors of these books have chosen to align themselves with the test publishers and recruiters rather than with the job applicant.

This is the first and only book on the market that really deals directly with personality tests. It explains how personality tests actually work, introduces you to the most popular tests on the market and teaches you ten golden rules for approaching a personality test. We reveal the secrets and hidden traps behind personality tests, teach you the specific traits that are important for the position you are seeking, and finally provide you with practice using two actual personality tests. On the whole, our preparation system helps you to build a coherent strategy for tackling any personality assessment tests. We provide you with a general strategy for approaching personality assessment rather than preparing you for a specific test. This approach will help you coping with any personality test with confidence and practical knowledge. Besides its practical value, this personality test preparation also significantly decreases the stress that usually accompanies personality assessment.

This book is also the most thorough guide to aptitude test preparation on the market. It includes a preparation course for the vast majority of the common and less common aptitude tests, including those that are profession-specific.

The aptitude section of this book will enable you to focus only on those tests that are applicable to the position you are applying for. Accompanying each sample test is a training section that explains the underlying principles and teaches you concrete strategies for approaching the tests – so you do more than just practice. In addition, a detailed step-by-step solution is provided for each question, including the method used to reach the solution.

Once you've seen the tests, practiced them and received useful feedback on how to improve your score, you'll find the real tests much easier to cope with. Consequently, you'll feel much more focused, knowledgeable and relaxed during the actual testing situation.

Good luck!

Part 1

Personality Test Preparation

1

PERSONALITY TESTS – WHAT ARE THEY ALL ABOUT?

While it's clear that the job interview and other selection methods are a major source of concern for most job applicants, personality tests are the most mystifying element of the selection process. Most people don't know much about them. Many applicants believe that personality tests are inaccurate and a psychologists' caprice. Many personality test-takers are convinced that the results don't truly reflect their behaviour. This attitude toward personality tests is often a reason for failure. If you approach a test with resistance, cynicism or anger you minimise your chances of success.

Most job selection processes, such as the job interview, examine overt behaviour. In contrast, personality tests reach deeper and aim to reveal personal characteristics that are less obvious. The information provided by these tests, as well as by the interview and the aptitude tests, helps the evaluator to put the pieces together and get an overall impression of the applicant.

A claim we hear over and over again by candidates in our *Job Test Prep* courses is that personality tests are invalid and unreliable, that they cannot really extract true information about one's personality and that only psychologists believe in them. Our experience tells us that this claim is false. Personality tests may not be a perfect predictor of future job performance, but they are certainly reliable tools that assist substantially in the job selection process.

> **Psychologist's Case Study:**
> Recently, I interviewed a psychologist who had applied for a position at *Job Test Prep*. During the interview, I was convinced that she was a perfect candidate for the job. She looked very presentable, made me feel at ease, showed focus and interest in my questions and had impressive work experience. However, her personality test results undermined the good impression that she'd made. They revealed information that I couldn't see in the interview. Specifically, the test indicated that the candidate had difficulty handling stressful situations and that she had an innate need to make a good impression, even at the cost of bending the truth. Needless to say, she didn't get the job.

As the above example indicates, one of the main reason personality tests are used is that they provide insight that is often lacking in the interview process. One known weakness of the interview is that the interviewer's personal preferences can prevent him/her from having impartial judgment. Research has shown, for example, that physically attractive candidates have a better chance of succeeding in the interview compared to less attractive candidates. Unlike the interview, personality tests are both more objective and more resilient to the assessors' biases. This is a clear advantage for you, the test-taker. It means that you'll face the personality test without any judgmental bias from others.

The Veil of Secrecy Behind Personality Tests

Assessment centres and other test administrators keep a veil of secrecy with regard to personality tests. Their reason is obvious: they are interested in obtaining the most spontaneous response possible from the test-taker. Their assumption is that the less the examinee knows about the personality test the more honest and sincere their answers will be, so the test results will indicate a more accurate reflection of their personality. The problem with the 'veil of secrecy' is that it provokes a wave of inaccurate rumours about the nature of the test, which in turn results in increased tension, anger and anxiety towards the tests and the evaluators. Many rumours, like the idea that you have to "be consistent at all times", are simply not true and may cause candidates to make mistakes and consequently fail to get the position they seek.

Why keep a veil of secrecy?

Unlike aptitude and other types of tests that are updated on an annual basis (the GMAT and GRE, for example), personality tests very rarely change. Some of these tests have maintained the same format since the 1940s. Personality tests are rarely updated because the process of ensuring validity is long and expensive. Changing the content may undermine the validity of the test, and therefore reduce its accuracy. Clearly, if the content of personality tests remains unchanged, the test developers have to keep both the questions and the method of analysis a secret.

Here are some examples of how recruiters implement the 'veil of secrecy':

1. Before your assessment, try to research useful information about the personality test you're going to take. We're confident that this information will be very difficult to find. First of all, most assessment centres will avoid telling you the actual name of the test you're taking. Assessment centres and tests administrators usually do give some information about the tests they administer on their websites, but this information is very limited and won't help you improve your test performance. The information may also be misleading. If a job applicant thinks that this is all the information required to prepare for the test, he/she might be very surprised during the actual testing situation.

2. If you ask the recruiter or the evaluator at the assessment centre if you should prepare for the personality test, the answer will always be a resounding 'NO'. This is despite the fact that everyone who has ever gone to an assessment centre claims that preparation would have helped them to complete the test more successfully.

3. Candidates' test results are kept secret. This is because the assessors want to minimise the amount of test-related information disclosed in general. They usually justify the decision not to release the candidates' full report by claiming that they don't want to offend people who have done poorly. In actual fact, they just want to keep the testing information a secret.

4. Some candidates, after doing poorly on the selection test, approach the assessment centre asking for feedback so that they can understand the reason for their poor performance. In most cases, the feedback session is expensive and includes a very general explanation of the results. Candidates will not receive any information suggesting what would have led them to succeed.

Bad Advice: Just Be Yourself

The worst advice you'll ever get before taking a personality test is,

"On the day of the test, just be yourself".

This advice usually comes from recruiters and tests administrators. It assumes that if job candidates behave as they normally do during the job selection process, it will increase their chances of success. According to this philosophy, if you're generally a shy person you should be shy during the job interview and selection tests, and if you're impulsive by nature you should answer impulsively on the test.

Let's analyse: what does it really mean to "be yourself"? Our day-to-day behaviour is strongly influenced by the situation we're in. The nature of the situation influences our stress level, which in turn has an impact on our behaviour. For example, you can be aggressive in one stressful situation but courteous in another. Which side of your personality do you want to show on the test?

Our experience at ***Job Test Prep*** tells us that the recommendation to "just be yourself" is potentially harmful. On the day of the test you should emphasise your strengths, not your weaknesses. A spontaneous, natural response is not necessarily the best one, neither in life nor on a selection test. For example, if your boss has treated you rudely at work, telling him or her off would likely be a foolish mistake that might cost you your job. It's usually best to swallow the insult, cool down and approach the situation in a more rational manner later on. This rule applies to selection tests – do the smart thing and be calculated.

Both occupational psychologists and recruiters often argue that people cannot really prepare for a personality test because:
1. if a person is aggressive, he/she will always be aggressive.
2. if a person is introverted, he/she will always be introverted.
3. if a person is polite, he/she will always be polite.

At ***Job Test Prep***, the experience we've gained from preparing thousands of job applicants since 1992 tells us that the facts are different:

1. A person who tends to be aggressive can be polite if he/she is made aware of the behaviour and understands the benefits of behaving more courteously.
2. A person who is typically shy can be more assertive if he/she is made aware of the fact that shyness may impede his/her chances of moving up the ladder.

Stress and the Personality Test

Feeling stress and discomfort before taking a personality test is a completely understandable and natural response; you are being asked to take an unfamiliar psychological test without understanding the evaluation criteria. The only thing you do know is that the test is supposed to reveal hidden sides of your personality, and that can be very intimidating.

Feelings of stress associated with test-taking can influence your behaviour in four ways:

Carelessness

Personality tests are long and tiring, and they often contain a number of repetitive questions. After answering a myriad of questions, you may become careless and start answering quickly and systematically. For example, you may take hasty decisions and choose the first response that sounds reasonably "like" you rather than reading each question in full and selecting the most appropriate answer. This type of carelessness can occur with many types of questions.

Here's a tricky question as an example:
- *People do not understand my good intentions.*
   A. Sometimes true
   B. Never true

If you don't consider the two options carefully, you may be tempted to answer B. However, almost everybody has been in a situation where they weren't properly understood, so the answer *Never true* is inappropriate. It is absolutely vital to read both the question and each of the possible responses carefully and to pay close attention to words like ***always***, ***never***, ***sometimes*** and ***usually***.

Over-investment

Generally, there is no specific time limit for completing a personality test. Some applicants take this instruction too literally and spend too much time on the test. You should know that in many assessment centres and on some computer applications, the time factor does play a hidden role. The overall time taken to complete the test and the hesitations between answers are often noted. If you are too worried about the outcome of the test you may invest extra time pondering over each question, re-thinking your answers over and over again, erasing and re-completing and ultimately taking way too long to finish the test. The evaluators will make a note of any hesitant behaviour and may conclude that you have difficulty dealing with stressful situations. This aspect of the evaluation is kept well hidden from applicants, as the evaluators want to observe your natural pace of work.

Indecisiveness

Some candidates, overwhelmed by stress, become very indecisive. For example, imagine that you are asked the following question:

- *I don't mind being interrupted while I'm working.*
  A. true
  B. ?
  C. False

When deciding how to answer this question, you may debate whether you should show that you like to be very focused when you do your job, or whether you should show that you're approachable even when concentrating on other things. After some contemplation, you may be tempted to choose an indecisive answer (B. ?). Responding indecisively throughout the test can lead the evaluators to conclude that you're an indecisive person and that you didn't handle the testing situation well. Indecisiveness won't help your application, nor will employers appreciate it. In cases where you are tempted to select the *neutral* option (?), we recommend that you reconsider and evaluate which answer more appropriately represents qualities that are suited to the position you applied for. For example, if you're going to work as a customer service representative, you need to show that you are very approachable. Conversely, if you are a computer programmer, focus and concentration are more relevant qualities.

Irritating Behaviour

Stress can also influence your behaviour towards the examiners. Some applicants are so concerned about their test results that they repeatedly harass the examiners by asking questions and demanding clarifications. This behaviour can make you appear needy and unable to perform effectively in an ambiguous situation.

In summary, we've seen how a high level of stress can impede your performance on the personality assessment. Conversely, when your stress level is low and you know what's expected of you, your attitude towards the test will be more focused and determined.

<u>When applicants come prepared for a personality test:</u>
1. they complete tasks in an efficient, calculated manner.
2. they deal with the task at hand, and complete it within a reasonable amount of time.
3. they don't waste precious time worrying about the nature of the test.

Stress plays an important role in the outcome of a personality test. It influences your responses and reveals to the examiners whether you tend to be focused or panicked in a stressful situation. The secret to alleviating stress is to come prepared. When your stress level is under control you will display a sound, coherent personality profile that amplifies your strengths rather than your anxiety.

2

THE MOST POPULAR PERSONALITY TESTS ON THE MARKET

Many types of personality tests are used for selection purposes, but it would be fair to say that the world of job selection assessment is dominated by four major personality tests:

1. Occupational Personality Questionnaire 32 (OPQ32)
2. 16 Personality Factors (16PF)
3. NEO Personality Inventory (NEO PI)
4. California Personality Inventory (CPI)

These tests share many similar features, but they differ in two major ways. First of all, the answering formats on these tests vary (e.g., true/false questions, rating scales from 1 to 5). Secondly, the quantity of personality traits the tests measure also varies. Each of these tests measures between 16-32 different traits. The 16 PF measures 16 traits, the CPI measures 20 traits, the NEO measures 30 traits and the OPQ measures 32 traits.

In your assessment you'll probably be taking one of these four tests in your assessment session. In the following sections, you'll learn how to identify each test and the personality traits they measure.

Occupational Personality Questionnaire (OPQ 32)

The Occupational Personality Questionnaire (OPQ32) is the flagship of SHL, a leading test publisher in the field of job selection testing. The OPQ is one of the most popular and widely used personality assessment tests on the market, and is available in many languages. Unlike a number of other personality questionnaires that were developed for the general population, the OPQ was developed specifically for vocational testing and its goal is to predict important aspects of an individual's personality in the workplace.

As its name indicates, the OPQ measures 32 personality dimensions that relate to job performance. It usually takes between 45 minutes to an hour to complete.

How do you recognise the OPQ 32?

The OPQ 32 comes in two different formats.
1. OPQ32i: This format is used most often in Internet or computer-based assessment. For each question, you'll be given four statements. You'll be asked to choose only two of the four statements: the statement that most describes your personality and the statement that least describes your personality.

    Example:

	Least	Most
I don't usually get annoyed if my plans change unexpectedly.	☐	☐
I have a natural talent for influencing people.	☐	☐
I'm a talkative person.	☐	☐
I feel that group discussions are very important.	☐	☐

2. The second and less common format of OPQ is the OPQn. On this questionnaire, you'll be asked to rate a single statement on a scale from 1 to 5, with 1 indicating that you *strongly disagree* (1) and 5 indicating that you *strongly agree* (5).

    Example:

    I'm modest about my accomplishments.

❶	❷	❸	❹	❺
Strongly Disagree	Disagree	Neutral	Agree	Strongly Agree

<u>The OPQ measures 32 characteristics.</u>

1. Persuasive	12. Evaluative	23. Relaxed
2. Controlling	13. Behavioural	24. Worrying
3. Outspoken	14. Conventional	25. Tough Minded
4. Individualist	15. Conceptual	26. Optimistic
5. Outgoing	16. Innovative	27. Trusting
6. Affiliative	17. Variety Seeking	28. Emotionally Controlled
7. Modest	18. Adaptable	29. Socially Confident
8. Democratic	19. Forward Thinking	30. Vigorous
9. Caring	20. Detail Conscious	31. Competitive
10. Data Rational	21. Conscientious	32. Achieving
11. Decisive	22. Rule Following	

16 Personality Factors (16PF)

The 16PF is one of the oldest, respected and well-documented commercial personality tests on the market. It's owned and distributed by OPP, a leading British test publisher. Developed in 1949 by Raymond Cattell, the 16PF is widely used for both vocational testing and for psychology-related research. It's available in many languages. It has a total of 185 questions, including 15 questions that measure aptitude (the last 15 question of the test). It takes between 25-50 minutes to complete.

How do you recognise the 16PF?

It's quite easy to recognise the format of the 16PF. The test has a three-choice response format and the middle option is always a question mark.

<u>Examples:</u>
- *When I daydream I find myself drifting off.*
  A. True
  B. ?
  C. False

- *When building something, I prefer*
  A. working in a team.
  B. ?
  C. working by myself.

The PF measures 16 characteristics.

1. Warmth	9. Openness to Change
2. Emotional Stability	10. Self-reliance
3. Dominance	11. Apprehension
4. Vigilance	12. Abstractness
5. Rule-consciousness	13. Perfectionism
6. Privateness	14. Reasoning
7. Sensitivity	15. Social Boldness
8. Tension	16. Liveliness

California Personality Inventory (CPI)

The CPI, which includes 434 questions, is the longest personality test on the market. There's a shorter version of the test that has 260 questions, but it's rarely used for job selection purposes. It was first published in 1956 and is used globally in several languages. Compared to the personality tests described so far, the CPI is a much more "psychological" tool that tries to dig deeper into the personality of the candidate. Because it contains such a large number of questions, it's difficult for the candidate to figure out which characteristics are being examined.

How do you recognise the CPI?

The CPI is a true/false questionnaire with no neutral option. This response format, along with the substantial length of the test, makes it easy to recognise.

The CPI measures 20 different characteristics:

1. Achievement via Conformance	11. Femininity/Masculinity
2. Self-Acceptance	12. Self-Control
3. Achievement via Independence	13. Dominance
4. Independence	14. Good Impression
5. Intellectual Efficiency	15. Capacity for Status
6. Empathy	16. Communality
7. Psychological Mindedness	17. Sociability
8. Responsibility	18. Well Being
9. Flexibility	19. Social Presence
10. Socialisation	20. Tolerance

NEO Personality Inventory (NEO PI)

The NEO was developed in 1992, making it the most current of the personality tests discussed so far. The test is based primarily on the **"Big 5"** theory of personality, which is the most widely accepted theory in the field of personality psychology today. According to this theory, an individual's entire personality can be described using five broad personality dimensions. As the NEO PI (and most other personality tests) is largely based on and influenced by this theory, we'll elaborate on the **"Big 5"** theory in the next chapter.

How do you recognise the NEO PI?

Similar to the OPQn, the NEO has a 5-point scale response format that ranges from *strongly disagree* to *strongly agree*. It's fairly easy to recognise.

Example:

I rarely feel sad or blue.

❶	❷	❸	❹	❺
Strongly Disagree	Disagree	Neutral	Agree	Strongly Agree

The NEO-PI measures 30 different characteristics:

Neuroticism
1. Anxiety
2. Angry Hostility
3. Depression
4. Self-consciousness
5. Impulsiveness
6. Vulnerability

Agreeableness
1. Trust
2. Straightforwardness
3. Altruism
4. Compliance
5. Modesty
6. Tender-mindedness

Openness
1. Fantasy
2. Aesthetics
3. Feelings
4. Actions
5. Ideas
6. Values

Extroversion
1. Warmth
2. Gregariousness
3. Assertiveness
4. Excitement Seeking
5. Positive Emotions
6. Activity

Conscientiousness
1. Competence
2. Order
3. Dutifulness
4. Self Discipline
5. Deliberation
6. Achievement Striving

3

THE "BIG 5" MODEL

In chapter 2, you learned that there are four main personality tests on the market. If you do take a personality test, you'll very likely be taking one of these four tests. Because there is considerable overlap between the tests, it wouldn't be particularly helpful to teach you the specific traits each one measures. At any rate, you probably won't know which test you'll be taking. To tackle this problem, we're going to prepare you for ALL of the major tests at once. Overall, it's very important that you understand the rationale behind them rather than focusing on a specific test or question type.

All of the leading personality tests either adhere to or at least are influenced by the "**Big 5**" model of personality. The "**Big 5**" model argues that every human personality can be completely understood by looking at only five broad traits: *neuroticism, extroversion, agreeableness, conscientiousness and openness*. In this chapter, we'll examine each of these traits and learn how they're measured. When you've completed the chapter, you'll have all the information you need to handle most personality tests. Understanding the "**Big 5**" model of personality will increase your chance of success on the personality portion of the job selection tests considerably.

In this chapter we will:
1. describe each of the **"Big 5"** personality dimensions.
2. explain the sub-traits personality tests use to evaluate the **"Big 5"** dimensions.
3. describe how each trait relates to specific positions and jobs.
4. explain how to recognise typical questions that measure traits within the model.

Neuroticism

Neuroticism is an umbrella term that focuses on the way people tend to cope with their own emotions. To evaluate neuroticism, the test measures feelings of apprehension, restlessness, vulnerability and the extent to which the individual can manage his/her own emotions. In general, high neuroticism signifies sensitivity and emotionalism while low neuroticism represents emotional security, resilience and calm. Obviously, a low neuroticism score is preferred in the workplace.

Neuroticism is commonly measured by examining a sub-trait called *emotional management*. In simple terms, people who are high in emotional management don't get easily overwhelmed by transient emotions; they are more rational and capable of handling their emotions.
While being emotionally stable is an advantage, you don't want to come across as robotic! In extreme situations, it's acceptable to show some level of emotion at work if the situation calls for it.

Here are a few typical questions that measure emotional management:
- *I don't usually pay attention to my own transient emotions.*
- *I always keep my feelings under a tight lid.*
- *I rarely act on impulse.*

Another trait that is looked at to measure neuroticism is *apprehension*. Although apprehension is a natural emotional response that most people experience from time to time, most employers won't hire job candidates that come across as highly anxious. High apprehension indicates difficulty handling pressure. As a general rule, a personality test is not the forum to confess your tendency to get anxious. Having said that, you should answer the questions sensibly. If the situation described in the question would naturally lead to a stressful response, answer accordingly. You don't want to give an unrealistic picture of yourself.

Here are a few typical questions that measure apprehension:
- *After a meeting, I mull over the things I've said.*
- *It's easy for me to just kick back and relax.(reversed[1])*
- *I usually get annoyed if my plans change unexpectedly.*
- *I worry before important meetings.*

---

[1] *Reversed* means that answering 'true' to the question will result in a low score on the trait.

Neuroticism is also measured by examining the sub-trait ***vulnerability***. People who score high on vulnerability take criticism poorly, are easily offended and feel uncomfortable in social situations. High vulnerability is an undesirable quality in an employee because it indicates that he/she might not respond well to criticism, even if it's constructive. The ability to handle criticism well is essential to every position. On the other hand, scoring very low on the vulnerability dimension may indicate that you are too thick-skinned and don't take criticism seriously. Ideally, you want to try to score in between the two extremes. For example, if you are asked whether being mocked in public offends you, it's acceptable to show that you're human and answer "true". However, if the question asks if you often get offended, it would be best to answer "false". You don't want to give the impression that you're easily insulted.

Here are a few typical questions that measure vulnerability:
- *When I sense that people dislike me I usually feel offended.*
- *When I'm criticised I avoid taking it personally. (reversed)*
- *What others think of me is no concern of mine. (reversed)*
- *I have a tendency to take things personally.*

Extroversion

Most of us are familiar with the words ***extroversion*** and ***introversion*** and use them freely. Every personality test on the market includes measures for identifying your position on the extroversion-introversion scale. The extent to which you're either extroverted or introverted can determine your suitability for certain careers.

In broad terms, extroverts tend to be people-oriented individuals who actively seek out relationships with others. They're outgoing, dynamic and have a need for companionship. On the other hand, introverts tend to be reserved, serious and have minimal need for the company of others.

On all of the common personality tests, there are a number of sub-traits that assess your position on the extroversion-introversion scale. In the next few pages, we will examine each sub-trait individually and discuss how each one relates to specific occupations.

One sub-trait that measures extroversion is *social energy*. People high in social energy have a strong social presence and are lively and talkative. They enjoy social gatherings and quite often initiate conversation. High social energy is important in fields that require frequent interaction with people, such as sales, line management, customer service and call centre service.

Here are a few typical questions that measure social energy:
- *I enjoy being the centre of attention.*
- *I'm a talkative person.*
- *Starting a conversation is easy for me.*
- *I'm better at talking than at listening.*

Another sub-trait that commonly measures extroversion is *companionability*. Extroverts generally don't enjoy being on their own and have a deep need to be around other people. High companionability indicates an extrovert's need for companionship.

Psychologist's Case Study:

Not long ago, I prepared a solicitor who had applied for a very solitary position in public office for a series of selection tests. Her personality test results indicated a very high score on companionability (10/10). This was problematic. Her score showed a profound need for the company of others, while the job she'd applied for demanded working alone most of the time. I asked her if this score was an accurate reflection of her personality, and she replied that although she enjoyed being around people she had no objection to working alone. She explained that she'd answered in a way that would lead to a high score because she'd assumed that the recruiter would prefer a friendly person in the position. I explained that the recruiter would be unlikely to select a person with such a high need for companionship, as he/she would get bored quickly and be unhappy with the position. Naturally, I advised her to tone down her responses to the companionship questions.

Generally, if you're applying for a position where you're going to spend most of your time working alone (e.g., technical positions, IT, industry professionals and senior managers) you don't want to come across as a person who *really* needs to be around people. You also don't want to present yourself as a person who is extremely solitary, because this might mean that you have trouble working with people. Try to aim for an average score in this area.

For team-based jobs, sales and service-oriented positions like social workers, doctors, hospitality workers and customer support staff, scoring high on companionability is definitely an advantage. You don't want a low score if you are applying for a position in these fields, because it may indicate potential difficulties in dealing with people.

Here are a few typical questions that measure companionability:
- *I enjoy having lots of people around me.*
  A. True
  B. False
- *After being by myself for a while, I:*
  A. really feel the need to be around other people.
  B. can continue being by myself.
- *The best hours of the day are when:*
  A. I have people around me.
  B. I'm reading or doing something by myself.

Another sub-trait associated with being an extrovert is ***social comfort***. People that are socially comfortable feel at ease when speaking in forums and giving lectures. Being socially comfortable in formal meetings is a key factor in the success of sales personnel and managers at all levels. It's also important, to some extent, for customer service representatives and other positions that require frequent interaction with senior staff.

Here are a few typical questions that measure social comfort:
- *I feel at ease when my boss or other senior managers are around.*
  A. True. It gives me a good opportunity to discuss current work issues.
  B. False. I'd prefer that they go somewhere else.
- *I usually fit in pretty quickly when I join a new group.*
  A. True. It's easy for me to fit in.
  B. False. It usually takes me a while to fit in.
- *It's difficult for me to speak in front of an audience.*
  A. Rarely
  B. Often

Important:

For those of you who tend to feel socially uncomfortable, don't readily admit it on the test. There are probably some situations where you do feel very comfortable around people. Don't ignore these situations. Ask yourself the following question: regardless of how you feel inside, could you stand in front of an audience and lecture on subject matter that you were knowledgeable about? Could you do it if you were thoroughly prepared? I imagine that for most of you, the answer would be yes. You may not feel as comfortable as you would like, but most of you would face up to the challenge. That's the only thing the recruiter really wants to know.

Another sub-trait that indicates extroversion is the tendency to be ***dynamic***. Dynamic people are active and vigorous. On a day-to-day basis, they tend to be very busy and highly visible individuals. Sales people have to be very dynamic, and should receive a high score on this trait. Being dynamic is also a real advantage for project managers, line managers and graduate roles. Scoring extremely low on this trait is never an advantage, as it indicates an inability to self-motivate to the point of laziness.

Here are a few typical questions that measure whether an applicant is dynamic:
- *I often feel full of energy.*
- *My life is fast-paced.*
- *I like being busy.*

Dominance is another common sub-trait that's used to measure extroversion. Dominance is an essential quality for managers, because dominant people naturally take on leading roles and tend to take charge of situations. This means that if you're applying for a managerial role, you want to show dominance but not extreme dominance. You don't want to come across as a dictator. In some cases, people applying for graduate and senior sales positions would also benefit from a high dominance score.

Psychologist's Case Study:

Being extremely dominant is not helpful in every position. At ***Job Test Prep***, I often see candidates for customer service roles that present themselves, via a personality test, in a very dominant light. When I explain to them that the role they are applying for doesn't require a high dominance score, they often answer that they want the recruiter to see their potential so that they'll be promoted in the future. My answer to them is that they won't have a future if they insist on displaying such high dominance! Scoring high on dominance when applying for a non-leadership role may imply an inability to work as a team player or the desire to be promoted too quickly.

For certain roles, any sign of extreme dominance might actually harm your chance of getting the position. This is especially true for clerical positions, customer service representatives and call centre personnel. On the other hand, a very low dominance score might suggest low self-confidence. Try to aim for an average dominance score.

Here are a few typical questions that measure dominance:
- *I naturally take control of most situations.*
- *When other people are involved, I find it hard to take control of the situation. (reversed)*
- *I usually let others do the talking. (reversed)*

Selling and negotiating effectively are also qualities that indicate extroversion, and are commonly measured on personality tests. Obviously, these traits are essential for sales personnel and we recommend that those seeking positions as sales representatives try to score high on this trait. However, make sure not to score too high as you don't want to come across as overconfident.

Effective sales and negotiation skills are important not only for salespeople but for managers and graduates as well. The ability to influence, negotiate and sell a product, concept or idea is definitely an advantage for these roles, even if they aren't specifically sales positions. A person applying for a position at a call centre would also benefit from an average or above score in this area, as persuasiveness is important in this profession. Computer programmers, engineers and clerical workers can score low in selling and negotiating.

Here are a few typical questions that measure sales and negotiation skills:
- *I feel comfortable selling.*
- *I have a natural talent for influencing people.*
- *I feel comfortable when I have to negotiate.*

Extroversion is also measured by looking at the test-taker's degree of ***optimism***. Optimistic people are generally content and fulfilled in life, and tend to have a positive outlook. Optimism is a desirable quality, particularly for those seeking service-oriented jobs and sales positions. However, it's important to note that employers will not always be looking for an extreme optimist. For some managerial jobs, an extremely high score in optimism might work against the candidate. Showing excessive optimism may signify naivety, an unrealistic view of the world or the need to constantly make a good impression. However, you also don't want to come across as a full-blown pessimist. The bottom line is that optimism is important in moderate amounts. Try to be realistic and aim for an average score.

Here are a few typical questions that measure optimism:
- *I generally anticipate that things will turn out for the best.*
- *I generally feel that the future will be bright.*
- *I'm not usually considered to be a cheerful optimist.*

Agreeableness

A person who is high in *agreeableness* is friendly, empathic and kind by nature. Agreeable people tend to be cooperative, accommodating and helpful. People that score low on agreeableness are usually rather shrewd, and aren't afraid of confronting others. Although agreeableness sounds intuitively like a good quality, how agreeable you should be at work depends on your occupation. There are several sub-traits that personality tests look at to measure agreeableness.

The first trait that indicates agreeableness is *empathy*, meaning the extent to which a person is caring, helpful and merciful. Being empathic and attentive to the needs of others is, to some extent, important for service-oriented positions like customer service representatives, clerical workers and call centre staff. However, too much empathy might suggest that the person is too compassionate and not practical or rational enough.

Consider the following example:

Psychologist's Case Study:
A couple of years ago, a woman came to *Job Test Prep* after losing her job. She'd been working as a customer service representative for a large insurance company, and she wanted to prepare for selection tests so she could find a similar position. During the initial interview, she admitted that she'd lost her job because she identified too closely with clients and often argued in their favour with her supervisors. I explained to her that while her actions were empathic and admirable, her focus on the clients was at the expense of the organisation. At the end of the day, she was a representative of the organisation and the organisation was the one paying her bills. I recommended that in the future she try to be more realistic with clients, or at least to think twice before confronting her supervisors.

For most positions, with the exception of social workers and psychologists, we recommend some degree of caution when answering empathy questions. If you're in a senior position, too much empathy may harm your ability to function. At this level, the needs of the organisation have to come first. Senior executives have to be somewhat colder and more practical and rational in their analysis of situations than those in lower positions. Having said that, you don't want to receive too low a score on empathy, as this would indicate a lack of sensitivity to others, distance and emotional detachment.

<u>Here are a few typical questions that measure empathy:</u>
- *I believe that all people, without exception, are entitled to respect.*
- *I would rather be known as a compassionate person than as a moral person.*
- *If I had to choose, I would rather be a psychologist than an engineer.*

Another sub-trait used to measure agreeableness is ***adaptability***, meaning the ability to "fit-in" and adapt to new situations. Adaptability is one of the few qualities that is relevant to all positions. A high degree of adaptability shows that you can adapt to new surroundings with ease. Adaptive people often adjust their behaviour to fit in with their peers. Adaptive people also tend to follow the rules and regulations of the workplace. A low score on adaptability in general, and specifically on questions that ask about acceptance of rules, is a turn-off for most employers. A high score on adaptability is especially important for those looking for consultancy roles, graduate roles, service-oriented positions, semi-skilled positions and clerical jobs.

<u>Here are a few typical questions that measure adaptability:</u>
- *I believe that it's important for people to adjust their behaviour to fit their surroundings.*
  A. True
  B. False
- *In primary school, I gave my teachers a hard time. (reversed)*
  A. True
  B. False
- *I like to break the rules. (reversed)*
  A. Sometimes
  B. Rarely
- *In my home, the rules are clear to everyone.*
  A. True
  B. False

- *I respect polite and obedient people more than those who are carefree.*
  A. True
  B. False

On the high end of the agreeableness continuum are qualities like cooperativeness and the tendency to be accommodating. On the low end are traits like ***directness*** and ***individualism***. People who are highly direct tend to speak freely and express their views without much regard for the consequences. People who are highly individualistic tend to stick to their principles regardless of the views of others. These qualities are valuable primarily for managers and professionals who need to defend and follow through on their ideas.

Although directness and individualism are important traits for managers and professionals, scoring too high on these traits might indicate stubbornness, inflexibility and difficulty working with others. At ***Job Test Prep***, we generally tell candidates for managerial positions: "show that you've got a backbone, but not that it's made of steel!"

If you are applying for a position as a graduate, salesperson, clerical worker, customer service representative or call centre worker, you don't want your directness and individualism scores to be too high. In these positions, workers are usually expected to follow instructions and be cooperative, patient and considerate.

Here are a few typical questions that measure directness and individualism:
- *I have no problem telling people if they are mistaken.*
- *I regard the right to speak my mind as very important.*
- *I am cautious to express my anger even when it's appropriate. (reversed)*
- *I refuse to do things I disagree with.*
- *I rarely change my opinion, even when other people disagree.*

Another sub-trait that indicates agreeableness is modesty. ***Modesty*** is generally a good quality. Most people try to present themselves as modest on a personality test, regardless of the position they're seeking. This isn't always a good strategy. For sales and managerial positions, we recommend the opposite. Being too modest can indicate a poor ability for 'self-promotion', which is a quality salespeople and managers need to do their jobs successfully. A high modesty score may also indicate low self-confidence. So, it isn't necessarily negative for managers and salespeople to sometimes "sing their own praises", as long as they don't overstate their accomplishments too much!

Here are a few typical questions that measure modesty:

- *I don't usually share my accomplishments with others.*
- *I tend to conceal my strengths.*
- *I'm humble about my accomplishments.*

Another sub-trait used to measure agreeableness is ***trust***. Being trusting is primarily important in service-oriented roles, because people with a trusting nature find it easier to work with others. However, you don't want to come across as too naïve, for example, by answering "never" to the question, "I am suspicious of people's motives".

For positions outside of the service industry, being trusting is not a particularly relevant quality. However, you certainly don't want to give the impression that you are either too naïve (high score) or too paranoid (low score). Aim for an average score. For management and business-oriented positions, some sense of mistrust can indicate experience.

Psychologist's Case Study:

There are few jobs where a high score on *trust* may not be beneficial to applicants. I recall preparing a young female police officer that had applied for a detective position and was about to go through a series of screening tests within the police force. In her prep course at ***Job Test Prep*** her personality test results indicated that she was a very trusting person. I confronted her with her "trust" score, telling her: "Your job will require that you try to catch criminals. When working against criminals, it doesn't make sense to have "trust" as a strong personality characteristic. Are you really that naïve?" She replied that she was not naïve at all. She had answered honestly to one "trust" question and then had continued to answer positively because she was worried about keeping her answers consistent. Her test anxiety confused her and led her to reply in a naïve manner. This is a good example of how stress can affect one's judgment when taking a personality test.

Here are a few typical questions that measure trust:

- *I usually believe what people tell me and see no reason to doubt them.*
- *People often take advantage of honest, friendly people. (reversed)*
- *To be honest, every other person I meet can't be trusted. (reversed)*

Conscientiousness

If there is one single quality we recommend that you adopt, it's ***conscientiousness***. People who are conscientious have a need to complete tasks, meet deadlines and fulfil commitments. It is the most sought after quality in every position. Research has repeatedly shown that there is an association between conscientiousness and job performance, regardless of the job itself. We cannot stress this point enough. Conscientiousness is associated with organisational skills and order. A low score on conscientiousness indicates a lack of self-discipline and a tendency to give up when faced with difficulty and stress. These are qualities employers do not want to see.

Here are a few typical questions that measure conscientiousness:
- *I derive personal pleasure from completing tasks at work.*
- *I work at a pace that allows me to finish things on time.*
- *It takes me some time before I actually get down to work. (reversed)*
- *I would have to be very ill to miss a day of work.*

One sub-trait used to measure conscientiousness is ***planning***. Planning is a frame of mind that guides both leisure and work behaviour. It's about having a long-term strategy and deriving a sense of confidence from planning your life. Planning skills are considered important for most roles - unless the position requires flexibility, like in certain sales positions. Planning is especially important for management and clerical positions. If you're a person who likes to plan, we recommend that you do indicate this on your test. However, don't stress the quality too much as it may show that you don't cope well with change and ambiguity.

Here are a few typical questions that measure planning:
- *I like to plan ahead so that I won't waste time.*
- *I enjoy planning things in advance.*
- *I usually plan every detail of my vacation.*

Conscientiousness is also indicated by the ability to keep things in order and to be logically organised. ***Order*** is important for most roles, although too high a score indicates the tendency to become stressed and a fear of failure. Conversely, a low score on the dimension of order is also not recommended, as it suggests a tendency to lose things and be messy and absent-minded.

Here are a few typical questions that measure order:
- *I keep everything in its place so that I'll know exactly where it is.*
  A. True. I always do.
  B. False. I'm not particularly tidy.
- *Quite often, I have to look for things that I've misplaced. (reversed)*
  A. True
  B. False
- *I keep my belongings in excellent condition.*
  A. True
  B. False

Another trait that indicates conscientiousness is the tendency to be a ***critical thinker***. A critical thinker is good at analysing situations and data and spotting errors and flaws. Critical thinkers have an eye for detail, as well as the ability to read the fine print. Being a critical thinker is especially important for accountants, solicitors and people in IT and technical positions. Graduates and managers, particularly those in senior positions, should also possess fine-tuned critical-thinking skills. Being a critical thinker is less important for people in customer service and support-oriented roles.

Here are a few typical questions that measure the ability to be a critical thinker:
- *I usually notice the hidden pitfalls involved in a plan.*
  A. True
  B. False
- *In a lecture, it's easy for me to identify a weak argument.*
  A. True
  B. False
- *If I'm presented with new information, I take the time to critically analyse it.*
  A. True
  B. False

Finally, most personality tests measure conscientiousness by looking at the candidate's level of ***ambition***. To ambitious people, career is the top priority. Ambition is an important quality for anyone who wants to advance in their profession, but it's especially important in graduate, managerial and sales positions. In clerical positions and in certain customer service jobs, showing excess ambition is negative because it may indicate that you'll be looking for a higher position quickly. This means that if you're applying for a job with limited future career prospects, you should try to send the message that although you're hard working, you intend to stay in the position for a long time. An average score on ambition is ideal if you're applying for this type of position. A very low score on ambition may indicate a lack of motivation, so try to avoid it.

Here are a few typical questions that measure ambition:
- *My career is high on my list of priorities.*
- *I set ambitious goals for myself.*
- *I aim to become a leading persona in my community.*
- *I don't usually feel driven to succeed. (reversed)*

Openness

People who receive a high score on the *openness* dimension of the **"Big 5"** model are open to life's experiences, have a broad range of interests and tend to possess a vivid imagination. People that receive a low score are less open, and tend to be practical, traditional and set in their ways. Let's look at the sub-traits that measure openness on personality tests and examine how they apply to different fields of work.

One common trait that is examined when assessing the ability to be open is the extent to which a person is *conservative*. Conservative people have a clear, set view of the world. They don't feel the need to innovate and explore, preferring to be in situations where things have been previously tried and tested. Conservativeness is not a desirable quality for candidates applying for graduate, IT, sales and managerial positions, since these positions demand the ability to be broadminded, flexible and open to change. However, be cautious in the way you present yourself. You don't want to appear too forward thinking, as people like this usually find it hard to work within a set of rules and regulations.

If you're applying for a position in a very well established organisation, (e.g., a manufacturing plant or an established financial institution) you'll be expected to follow the existing protocol rather than initiate change. In this case, you want to appear more rather than less conservative. In addition, semi-skilled workers, clerical and technical staff should try to show some level of conservativeness on their personality profile, as this will indicate discipline.

Here are a few typical questions that measure conservativeness:
- *Well-established routines are usually the most effective way of doing things.*
  A. True. If it works, why change it?
  B. False. Every procedure can be challenged and improved upon.
- *I really enjoy going back to my old, favourite place when I'm on holiday.*
  A. True. Why change a good thing?
  B. False. I usually don't go back to the same place twice.
- *I must admit that it would be pretty hard for me to change the way I do things.*
  A. True
  B. False
- *In a restaurant, I enjoy ordering new and unfamiliar dishes. (reversed)*
  A. True
  B. False

Openness is also measured by looking at one's ***intellectual ability***. Intellectual people enjoy theoretical and philosophical discussions and try to understand underlying concepts. Being intellectual is important in positions where thinking per se plays a key role. These include IT jobs, professional roles and senior management positions. You don't want to come across as too intellectual if you're applying for a fast-paced position that involves intensive decision making, such as customer service, sales, technical, clerical and some junior/line manager positions.

Here are a few typical questions that measure your intellectual ability:
- *If something is unclear to me, I try to get a deep and thorough understanding of the underlying concepts.*
- *I often enjoy thinking about theories and conceptual ideas.*
- *If a discussion becomes too theoretical, I usually lose interest. (reversed)*

The level of creativity people posses is also an indicator of openness. ***Creativity*** sounds like an attractive quality, but for many fields of work it is not necessarily desirable. Here's a good example:

Psychologist's Case Study:
A couple of years ago, I prepared a candidate to apply for a position in a call centre. She was a very energetic and talkative person, and I felt she would be a good candidate for a position as a call centre representative. However, her personality test results showed a very high score in creativity. Later, during the interview, she told me that she usually has plenty of good ideas and suggestions for improvement. I explained to her that in a call centre position, there is usually very little room for innovation. There is a standard text to be used in discussions with clients and not much flexibility in terms of the content. In general, having <u>plenty</u> of suggestions for improvement, especially from someone new to a position, is not necessarily positive. I recommended that she tame her creativity score on the test.

Overall, people in clerical, customer service, call centre and semi-skilled positions are expected to cope with repetitive tasks. The ability to initiate and innovate is not necessarily a desirable skill in such positions, so people applying for these types of jobs should try to keep their creativity scores average. In contrast, people in IT, technical, sales and managerial positions are expected to be able to improvise and "think outside of the box" on a regular basis. People applying for these roles should try to show a high level of creativity.

<u>Here are a few typical questions that measure creativity:</u>
- *I have plenty of original ideas.*
- *I find that original ideas come to me easily.*
- *I think outside of the box.*

Openness is also measured by examining the applicant's level of ***tolerance***. A high level of tolerance suggests patience and an even-temper. This trait is especially important in service and sales-oriented positions (call centre staff, customer service representatives and clerical workers), because tolerant people are helpful and don't get frustrated easily. Frustration is something that service people encounter on a day-to-day basis, and being tolerant helps them succeed in their jobs.

<u>Here are a few typical questions that measure tolerance:</u>
- *People who don't know what they believe in by the time they're 30: (reversed)*
  A. are perfectly normal.
  B. have a problem.
- *I get frustrated with people quickly. (reversed)*
  A. Sometimes
  B. Rarely

Another trait that's commonly used to assess openness is the tendency to ***daydream***. Daydreaming is one of the few qualities that employers don't want to see for any position. No one wants an employee that tends to drift off and daydream, or who is very impractical. We strongly encourage you to refrain from presenting yourself as a person who often daydreams. People with high scores in the daydreamer domain may find it hard to get a job.

<u>Here is a typical question that measures daydreaming:</u>
- *I enjoy daydreaming.*
  A. Often
  B. Rarely
- *I'm usually considered very practical (reversed)*
  A. Often
  B. Rarely
- *I sometimes wander off in my fantasies and lose track of time*
  A. Often
  B. Rarely
- *I seldom let my thoughts wander(reversed)*
  A. Often
  B. Rarely

Summary Table: The Traits Required for Specific Roles

Position		Ideal Traits
All Positions	High	conscientiousness, adaptability, rule acceptance
	Low	apprehension, daydreaming
Senior Manager	High	dominance, ambitiousness, sales and negotiation skills, creativity, critical thinking and intellectual skills, social comfort, planning skills, directness, individualism, competitiveness
	Low	conservativeness, consulting skills, vulnerability, empathy, companionability, humbleness
Middle Manager	High	dominance, ambitiousness, sales and negotiation skills, planning skills, dynamic nature, directness, creativity, social comfort, decisiveness, competitiveness
	Low	humbleness, conservativeness, vulnerability
Junior/Line Manager	High	dominance, ambitiousness, social comfort, planning skills, dynamic nature, ambitiousness, decisiveness, sales and negotiation skills, competitiveness
	Low	vulnerability
Professional	High	individualism, critical thinking skills, intellectual ability, social comfort, planning skills
Graduate	High	dynamic nature, ambitiousness, social comfort, the ability to be a team player, intellectual ability, sales and negotiation skills, dominance
	Low	vulnerability
Clerical	High	planning skills, orderliness
	Low	dominance, directness, aversion to routine, individualism
IT / Engineer	High	individualism, critical thinking skills, creativity, planning, intellectual ability
	Low	conservativeness, companionability

Position		Ideal Traits
Salesperson	High	sales and negotiation skills, dynamic nature, ambitiousness, social energy, social comfort, competitiveness, decisiveness, tolerance, creativity, dominance, companionability, empathy, aversion to routine
	Low	conservativeness, individuality, humbleness, vulnerability
Customer Service Staff	High	consulting skills, empathy, faith, the ability to be a team player, tolerance, companionability
	Low	individualism, vulnerability, dominance, directness, aversion to routine
Call centre Staff	High	sales and negotiation skills, consulting skills, empathy, faith, the ability to be a team player, companionability, tolerance
	Low	dominance, directness, aversion to routine, vulnerability, individualism
Semi-skilled Workers	High	the ability to be a team player, conservativeness
	Low	dominance, directness, creativity, aversion to routine, individualism
Technical Staff	High	critical thinking skills
	Low	aversion to routine

4

10 GOLDEN RULES OF PERSONALITY TESTING

There are ten golden rules you need to know to be really prepared for a personality test. These rules are crucial to your overall understanding of personality tests and we strongly encourage you to memorise the information revealed in this chapter.

Rule 1: You have the power.
Rule 2: Personality tests are not naïve.
Rule 3: It's about how you behave at work.
Rule 4: Each question focuses on a trait.
Rule 5: Try not to get an extreme score.
Rule 6: There are "right" and "wrong" answers.
Rule 7: Your personality profile has to make sense.
Rule 8: You're not perfect.
Rule 9: Be honest but sensible.
Rule 10: Believe in Yourself.

Let's review these general rules in more detail.

Rule 1: You have the power.

This is an important point to clarify right from the start. Personality tests are not sophisticated x-ray machines that can penetrate your soul to see who you really are. The most popular tests on the market are based on self-reporting. You will sit alone and complete either a computer-based test or a pen and paper questionnaire. The nature of self-reporting is that that YOU report how YOU perceive yourself. How you come across to the evaluators is entirely YOUR decision.

When you understand the nature of personality tests and the hidden traps they include, you'll have the power to influence your test results and increase your chances of getting the job you want.

However, make no mistake. Although personality tests are based on self-reporting, they are sophisticated tools. Most of them include hidden traps to prevent you from trying to manipulate the results. The second rule will teach you about these traps.

Rule 2: Personality tests are not naïve.

There are three main built-in traps included in most personality tests:

Trap # 1: Impression management questions
Trap # 2: Consistency checks
Trap # 3: The middle/neutral option

Lets discuss these traps in detail.

Trap # 1: Impression Management

Most personality tests include built-in scales that measure the extent to which you are trying to make a good impression. Obviously, it's acceptable to try to make a good impression when you're applying for a job. However, the items that measure *impression management* examine to what extent you're willing to be dishonest to make that impression. To give an example, someone who answers "true" to the question, "I've never told a lie" or "never" to the question, "Occasionally I am in a bad mood" is clearly trying too hard to make a good impression.

If you score high on the impression management scale, it indicates that you've lied about your true beliefs and behaviour in order to project the image that you felt the recruiter was seeking. A high score on the impression management scale throws your entire personality profile into question. In extreme cases, a high score may lead the recruiter to disregard your personality test and reject your application. A low score on the impression management scale, on the other hand, indicates that you're a loyal person who will be honest even if it may reduce your chance of success.

Here are a few typical impression management statements (True/False):
- *Sometimes I find it hard to motivate myself.*
- *Occasionally, I feel the need to get away from my family.*
- *I've never lied to someone I know.*
- *I can recall a time that I was unkind to someone.*
- *If I get extra change in a shop I always return it.*
- *Sometimes I pretend to look in a different direction just to avoid meeting someone.*
- *I sometimes laugh at dirty jokes.*
- *I'm always willing to help people.*
- *I've taken advantage of others.*
- *My looks don't concern me at all.*
- *Sometimes I feel like cursing.*
- *I enjoy gossiping from time to time.*
- *Sometimes I feel like getting back at someone who's hurt me.*
- *I recall times that I've felt disheartened.*
- *I've said offensive things to people.*

When you look at this group of question it might seem obvious that they have a "hidden agenda". However, when you will be in the real test, taking a series of gruelling tests for hours, sitting next to other worthy candidates who are competing for the same job, you're stressed, tired and keen to excel, you might fall into the ***impression management*** traps.

> **Important:**
> Study the list and try to get the general idea so you can recognise new questions and avoid the traps. When you come across an ***impression management*** question, be honest. If you're honest, you aren't likely to fall at the far low end of the scale.

Trap # 2: Consistency

The issue of consistency is something we need to clarify, as people often make grave mistakes because they feel they have to be very consistent on their personality test. Sometimes, when taking a personality test it feels like questions repeat themselves. Test takers usually believe that if they've answered a question one way they have to answer the same way on similar questions. This is a mistake! Questions are never identical. They stress different strengths and vary slightly. You need to judge each question on its own rather than thinking about how you answered previously.

Some tests do measure consistency, but only in terms of content. If you answer one question one way, and then answer differently to a completely opposite question this may present a problem.

Here's an example of inconsistent responding:
- *I'm always the dominant person in the group and enjoy taking the lead: true*
- *I have no problem letting others take the lead: true*

If these two questions were placed one after the other, it would be easy to spot the contradiction and answer consistently. However, the challenge appears when there are possibly 100 questions between each.

Dealing with the consistency check is fairly simple: just come prepared. Make sure you've researched which of your strengths are relevant to the position you want. When you're answering questions that relate to traits that are irrelevant to your profession, simply answer the questions truthfully without trying to exaggerate.

Important:
Know this: If you answer <u>very</u> consistently on a particular trait, that is, answering basically the same to 100% of the questions regarding the same trait, it will lead to an extreme score on that particular trait. If, on the other hand, you want a high score on a certain trait but not extreme, you can answer to the same direction to 8 or 10 questions and this will lead to a high and acceptable score.

To illustrate this point, let's look at someone who has applied for a position in a call centre. Working as a call centre operator does not require a high degree of dominance. This means that the applicant should aim for an average score on the dominance scale. Let's see how the call centre applicant should handle the dominance questions:

- *If I was the leader of a group, I would feel comfortable giving orders: true*
- *I always enjoy leading people: false*
- *I would be a good leader if given the chance: true*
- *I usually tell people off when they do things I disagree with: false*

These examples illustrate the response pattern of a person who is capable of dominance, but isn't overly dominating. This pattern of responding is not considered inconsistent.

Trap # 3: The Neutral Option

One method of assessing your personality without asking about it directly is by observing the way you choose your answers. The middle option (often called "neutral") reveals a lot about your personality. This is applicable only for answering formats that include a middle option.

Examples 1:

❶ Strongly Disagree	❷ Disagree	❸ Neutral	❹ Agree	❺ Strongly Agree

Example 2:

A. True
B. ?
C. False

Selecting the middle option is not recommended. It shows the assessors that you:

...have difficulty making decisions.

The questions on a personality test are often difficult to answer, but recruiters do expect that a candidate will rise to the challenge. Choosing the neutral response too frequently indicates that you're trying to avoid answering the question. If you can't answer the test questions confidently, how will you make real decisions in the workplace?

...might have answered randomly.

Selecting the middle option too often may indicate that you didn't really take the test seriously and completed it without actually reading the questions.

...had a particular reaction to specific items.

Choosing the middle option for certain types of items can indicate that you were sensitive to the content of those questions. This could indicate a weakness in your personality.

Clearly, it's not always easy to reach a decisive answer on certain questions. Try to minimise the number of times you select the neutral option. When you encounter a question that you could comfortably answer either way, choose the answer that most accurately represents what you would actually do, or select the response that would lead to a personality profile suitable for your profession.

Rule 3: It's about how you behave at work.

Personality tests usually ask questions about your general life preferences, about how you typically behave, about how your friends would describe you and about how people should behave in general.

The recruiter isn't interested in knowing how you really behave in life; the sole purpose of these questions is to assess how you would behave at work. Your future on-the-job behaviour is the only thing that interests the recruiter.

Here are a few examples of questions that ask about your personal life, but really aim to understand your work behaviour:

- *I aim to become a leader in my community.*
- *I have no problem telling people they're wrong.*
- *I read at least one book a month.*

Recruiters assume that the way you act with friends and family and what you generally think of people is indicative of the way you behave at work. They usually think that people's behaviour is stable across situations, and that by asking about your general conduct and attitudes they will be able to predict your on-the-job behaviour.

Our experience at *Job Test Prep* has shown us that this assumption isn't always true. People can be warm and empathic at home and rational and assertive at work, if the roles demand it of them. People can be lively and talkative with friends but if the role requires it, they can be reserved and calculated. One of the beautiful things about human beings is that they can learn and adapt their behaviour to fit different roles and situations.

Psychologist's Case Study:
I recently prepared an army officer who was getting ready to be assessed for a possible promotion to a senior position. After analysing his personality test, my first reaction was, "Excuse me, are you applying for a position as Mother Teresa?" He had scored extremely high on the 'warmth' scale, indicating that he was a warm, sensitive person who was very attentive to others. When I confronted him he said, "Look, the personality test asked me how I behave with my friends and family, and the truth is, I'm pretty warm with them. But with my soldiers it's a different ball game, I'm pretty tough".

This case perfectly exemplifies how a personality test can be deceiving if you answer the questions naïvely. When you answer, you have to think about your work behaviour rather than your general behaviour. More importantly, you have to consider the demands of the job you're applying for and answer accordingly.

To give an additional example, consider this question. Choose the sentence that best describes you:
* *My friends would describe me as:*
  A. warm-hearted and empathic
  B. reserved and objective

You should approach this question as if it were asking you how your work colleagues, rather than your friends, would describe you. In addition, if you really are generally warm with colleagues at work but the job you're applying for demands formality, you should look into your heart and ask yourself if you actually can be formal with colleagues. If you can, answer accordingly – select option B.

Going back to the army officer from the above example, without the preparation provided by *Job Test Prep* the excessive warmth that he displayed on his personality test would possibly have prevented his promotion. Coming unprepared to a personality test and displaying the wrong characteristics for the specific job you want can seriously harm your career.

Rule 4: Each question focuses on a trait.

Personality tests contain long lists of questions that ask about your typical behaviour and feelings in different situations. Every personality test measures several traits. For example, the famous 16PF questionnaire examines 16 traits. Each of these traits is measured using 10-14 randomly presented questions.

Let's take one trait as an example, and show how the following eight questions ask for almost the same information.

1. *When I sense that people dislike me, I usually feel offended.*
2. *If I sense that people dislike me, I get very anxious.*
3. *When I'm criticised, I avoid taking it personally.(reversed)*
4. *When I receive concrete criticism about my work, I don't feel personally offended. (reversed)*
5. *What others think of me is no concern of mine. (reversed)*
6. *I have a tendency to take things personally.*
7. *When I'm teased, I take it in stride.(reversed)*
8. *People are generally too vulnerable and touchy and should toughen up for their own benefit. (reversed)*

Can you guess which characteristic these questions are trying to measure?
The answer is "vulnerability". It might seem obvious when the questions are grouped together, but the real test may be trying to measure more than 30 traits with the questions randomised. This makes it harder to identify the traits being measured.

Let's see what would be the result of different patterns of responding for these questions: Someone with the following response pattern would end up with a very low score on the vulnerability dimension:

1. Yes	*5. No*
2. Yes	6. No
3. Yes	7. Yes
4. *No*	8. Yes

Such a low level of vulnerability may suggest that you are too thick-skinned and don't take criticism seriously enough. However, if you answer all the questions in the opposite manner, you'll receive a very high vulnerability score. This suggests to the recruiter that you're highly sensitive and might not respond well to criticism, even if it's constructive. Obviously, neither extremes are ideal. It's best to try to aim for a score in between the two extremes. For example, if a question asks if you feel offended when mocked in public, it is acceptable to answer "true" – after all, you're only human. In general, however, try not to indicate that you're too easily offended.

It's important to realise that your answers to individual questions on the personality test are almost meaningless. Test administers don't look at the answer to any one particular question. In general, test results are analysed automatically by a computer that groups your answers to the 10-14 trait-specific questions. Your results on each specific trait are based on an average of the trait-specific questions and compared to the norms for your position.

Rule 5: Try not to get an extreme score.

Having any particular quality to the extreme is considered undesirable, no matter which position you're seeking. In general, try to avoid getting an extreme score (e.g., 10/10) on any one particular trait on the personality test unless you are certain that this trait is especially relevant to your position.

Imagine that your results on each particular trait are scored on a scale from 1 to 10. An extremely low score would be 1 out of 10. An extremely high score would be 10 out of

10. You'll get an extreme score if you answer either positively or negatively to every question that refers to the same trait. Even if you want a high score on a certain trait, you don't want to answer consistently to ALL questions that are looking at the same trait. Try to consider each question separately, and think about the specific situation asked about in the question.

Important:
1. To avoid getting an extreme score, pay close attention to words like *always, never, all the time* and *very often*. These words should warn you that you have to be cautious in the way you answer the question, even if you do want to emphasise a particular quality.
2. We certainly don't mean to suggest that you should lie about your personality characteristics on the test, obliterating any traits that you may actually have from the results. Simply try to focus on your strengths and avoid overstating your weaknesses.

Rule 6: There are "right" and "wrong" answers.

One thing test administers always say about personality tests is that there are no right or wrong answers. This is obviously not true. Personality tests are used for screening purposes, to select the best candidate for a particular job. Recruiters will, therefore, recommend candidates that best fit the required criteria and job description. This means that there are right and wrong answers that relate to specific job criteria. Recruiters have an ideal candidate in mind for each job, meaning they're looking for specific characteristics to fit each position. When recruiters analyse your test results, they try to determine whether your personality matches the personality of the ideal candidate.

Different positions require different personality characteristics. For example, the qualities required to be a sales person are very different from those required to be a clerk. Before you take the test, we highly recommend that you find out which characteristics fit the "ideal" candidate for the job you want (see table on page 34).

Once you know which characteristics are important for your position, the best way to prepare is to be able to recognise questions related to them on the test.

Rule 7: Your personality profile has to make sense.

Imagine that your personality is a puzzle with many pieces. Similar to a puzzle, some pieces will match other pieces and some won't. In the end, though, all the pieces fit together to form a picture.

Let's imagine that dominance is an important piece in your personality puzzle. Dominance usually co-occurs with other related traits such as 'social confidence'. That is, dominant people tend to feel socially confident. Dominance also often co-occurs with 'directness', (speaking your mind). On the other hand, dominance generally doesn't co-occur with traits like 'shyness' or 'social anxiety'.

To give another example, two personality traits that are commonly assessed in personality tests are ***consulting*** and ***team playing***. Consulting is the extent to which a person tends to consult with other people when making decisions and team playing is the extent to which a person enjoys working in a team. It's hard to imagine someone who's a team player making decisions alone and failing to consult with colleagues.

At ***Job Test Prep***, we've often observed job candidates trying very hard to make a good impression on the personality test. These candidates try to answer the test questions so that they will score very positively on a number of traits, even if these traits are inherently contradictory. For example, some candidates present themselves as very independent and dominant but also as very consulting-oriented, team-oriented and humble. This combination of traits simply doesn't make sense.

Your personality has to make sense! You have to make sure to avoid contradictions in your test answers. The following table describes typical, logical associations between traits.

Summary Table: Which Traits Usually Go Together?

Sales and Negotiation Skills	dominance, ambition, social energy, social comfort
Dominance and Leadership Skills	ambition, sales and negotiation skills, directness, creativity, low apprehension
Directness	dominance, individualism, social energy, low humbleness
Individualism	directness, low rule following
Social Energy	social comfort, social energy, low humbleness, directness, sales skills
Companionability	social energy, empathy
Social Comfort	low anxiety, social energy, dominance, sales and negotiation skills
Humbleness	low social energy, low directness
Consulting Skills	empathy, insight into people, tolerance
Empathy	insight into people, consulting skills, companionability, tolerance
Critical Thinking	intellectualism, dominance, directness, creativity
Insight into People	empathy, intellectualism, consulting skills
Conservativeness	low aversion to routine, low creativity
Intellectual Ability	insight into people, aversion to routine, critical thinking, artistic ability
Creativity	ambition, dominance, sales and negotiation skills, low conservativeness, critical thinking, intellectualism
Aversion to Routine	low conventionality, creativity
Adaptability	ambition, critical thinking
Planning Skills	ambition, critical thinking
Orderliness	conscientiousness
Conscientiousness	orderliness, dynamism
Rule Acceptance	conventionality
Tranquillity	optimism, low anxiety, low sensitivity
Anxiety	low social comfort, low dominance, sensitivity
Sensitivity	anxiety

Summary Table: Which Traits Usually Go Together?

Faith in People	optimism
Emotional Management	low social energy
Dynamism	conscientiousness
Competitive Drive	ambition
Ambition	competitiveness, dominance, sales and negotiation skills, creativity, planning
Tolerance	empathy, team playing, consulting skills
Artistic Ability	intellectualism, creativity
Daydreaming	tranquillity
Decisiveness	dominance
Team Playing	consulting skills, companionability, empathy, social energy, tolerance

Rule 8: You're not perfect.

The phrase "nobody's perfect" isn't just a saying. Naturally, everyone has both strengths and weaknesses. One of the most important tricks to taking a personality test is to respect your strengths, but accept that you aren't perfect. Don't try to present yourself as a perfect person, because you couldn't possibly have every desirable characteristic. In fact, it's unlikely that anyone would receive a high score in all or most of the desirable characteristics such as conscientious, intelligence and modesty.

Generally, people that are anxious and afraid of failure tend to overstate their skills. The result is an exaggerated personality profile with many scores that fall into the high range. The more relaxed you are when you take the test, the more you'll focus on the specific characteristics that are important in your profession. It's important that you believe that you actually do have the right personality for the job you seek. If you believe in yourself, you won't have to exaggerate. Focus on the traits that are relevant and answer questions about other traits realistically, and your personality profile will match the recruiter's ideal profile.

> **Psychologist's Case Study:**
> I often see anxious job candidates who try to hide their emotions by presenting themselves as very calm. For example, they answer "false" to questions like, "sometimes I worry about things". Clearly, this is not an honest response. Try to come across as neither particularly relaxed nor particularly stressed. Our experience has shown that a worried and unprepared candidate may project temporary feelings of apprehension onto the test, and consequently score extremely high or low on the apprehension scale.

Rule 9: Be honest but sensible.

It's one thing to be honest, and quite another to be too honest. Imagine that the personality test was a conversation with your boss: would you tell him/her everything about your personal life? The personality test is not the forum to mention hidden fears, doubts or occasional mood swings. The personality test is not your friend or your therapist, meaning someone that you can trust with your private thoughts. It's the place to express honest, work-related behaviour. Ultimately, that's the only thing the assessors are really interested in.

> **Psychologist's Case Study:**
> Not long ago, I prepared a 37-year-old applicant for a series of selection tests. He'd applied for a position as a job development trainer at a large international IT company. The new position had very demanding working hours and responsibilities, but the remuneration package was attractive.
>
> After analysing his personality test results, my first reaction was to ask him if this was really the job he wanted - his responses seemed to be too honest, because they indicated a severe difficulty with public speaking as well as a lack of social confidence. I asked him if he could stand up in front of people and train them. He replied that he was an excellent trainer, even though he didn't always feel comfortable. I told him that his personality test results suggested that if he were to enter a classroom to train people, he would probably faint!

Later on in the discussion, he admitted that he was very nervous about changing jobs. Up until this point, he'd worked for a large governmental organisation. He'd been very satisfied with his job and with the relaxed lifestyle it provided – it allowed him to do yoga three times a week and spend plenty of quality time with his family. Apparently, this candidate was so concerned about changing jobs that he'd unconsciously projected this fear onto the test. He'd simply chosen to be too honest.

This case is a perfect example of how doubts and fears can show up in your personality test results, with devastating consequences. Needless to say, if the recruiter had seen his personality profile as I saw it, his application would have been rejected.

You have to be sure that you want the job before you apply. At minimum, hide your doubts until you complete the selection tests and receive a job offer. Only then can you make a proper, educated decision. During the test you need to be calculated, focused and determined to do well. Be honest, but be sensible!

Rule 10: Believe in Yourself.

Before you take a personality test, you have to believe that you're the right person for the job. This isn't a cliché. If you believe in yourself, this will act as a self-fulfilling prophecy. You'll project this confidence throughout the assessment process and hopefully land the position you want.

Many people amplify their failures and minimise their successes. One of the major reasons that people don't succeed on selection tests is excessive self-criticism. If you judge yourself too harshly, you'll have difficulty presenting yourself positively on a selection test. People who are highly self-critical find it hard to convince the recruiter that they're the best candidates for the job. This is because they always find reasons why they're not good enough.

Before you take your selection tests, you have to stop looking at yourself negatively. A day before your test, take the time to sit down and make a list of your past work accomplishments. Try to remember times when you took the initiative and your ideas were accepted, times when you were promoted or commended and successes that happened as a result of your actions. Think about your personal contribution, regardless of the importance of your job. Write down anything positive you remember about your professional behaviour at work.

Before you step into the assessment centre, run through the list in your head. Visualise relevant situations and scenarios. Think about how much you've contributed in past jobs, and how much you plan to contribute in your future job. Remind yourself that you have a lot to give and that your future employer will appreciate your contribution. Even if you've made mistakes in the past and were unsuccessful, consider how you want to change and move forward in life, get a better salary, earn the respect of others and enjoy what you do. Even if you've had failures in the past see them as a chance to learn and improve your abilities in the future. We have all experienced failure at some point. Try to consider your failures a learning experience and see them as an opportunity to improve your abilities in the future. There is absolutely no reason to see failure as a disaster. You don't have to admit these past failures during the selection process.

A confident attitude will definitely help you answer the test questionnaire properly, improve your results and get the job.

5

PERSONALITY TEST PRACTICE

The following is the first of two personality tests you will practise. Practicing will help you get a real feel for taking a personality test and provide you with knowledge that you can later implement. At the end of the test, you'll find a scoring table that will help you analyse your answers.

Test 1

"Typical" **Instructions:**
1. Read each statement carefully and choose the answer that best describes you.
2. There are no "right" or "wrong" answers.
3. Be honest. Don't choose an answer just because you think it's the right thing to say.
4. Don't spend too much time thinking about any one question. Generally, the first answer that comes to mind is the one you should choose.
5. Try to give a decisive answer. Choose the neutral option only when none of the other available options suit you.
6. There is no time limit for the test.

Important:

Answer exactly as you would when taking the real selection test! Imagine that you're already in the actual selection process and that recruiters will make decisions based on your test results. That's the only way you'll receive valuable feedback from this practice. Feel free to circle your answers in the book using a pencil. This will make it easier to score your results.

Good Luck!

1. I have no problem telling people if I think they are wrong.

❶	❷	❸	❹	❺
Strongly Disagree	Disagree	Neutral	Agree	Strongly Agree

2. In a lecture, it's easy for me to identify the weak arguments.

❶	❷	❸	❹	❺
Strongly Disagree	Disagree	Neutral	Agree	Strongly Agree

3. I must admit, I'm not particularly interested in contemplating the nature of our existence or in discussing recent scientific evidence.

❺	❹	❸	❷	❶
Strongly Disagree	Disagree	Neutral	Agree	Strongly Agree

4. I work hard to achieve my goals.

❶	❷	❸	❹	❺
Strongly Disagree	Disagree	Neutral	Agree	Strongly Agree

5. It takes me some time before I actually get down to work.

❺	❹	❸	❷	❶
Strongly Disagree	Disagree	Neutral	Agree	Strongly Agree

6. I think nature is an incredible form of art.

❶	❷	❸	❹	❺
Strongly Disagree	Disagree	Neutral	Agree	Strongly Agree

7. I come across as a calm and rational person.

❶	❷	❸	❹	❺
Strongly Disagree	Disagree	Neutral	Agree	Strongly Agree

8. If something is unclear to me, I try to get a deep and thorough understanding of the underlying principles.

❶	❷	❸	❹	❺
Strongly Disagree	Disagree	Neutral	Agree	Strongly Agree

9. When reading new material at work, my first instinct is to look for mistakes.

❶ Strongly Disagree	❷ Disagree	❸ Neutral	❹ Agree	❺ Strongly Agree

10. If I disagree with somebody, I make sure I say so.

❶ Strongly Disagree	❷ Disagree	❸ Neutral	❹ Agree	❺ Strongly Agree

11. Everyone needs to 'sing their own praises' now and again.

❺ Strongly Disagree	❹ Disagree	❸ Neutral	❷ Agree	❶ Strongly Agree

12. To be honest, I'm not that keen on sitting down to learn new things.

❺ Strongly Disagree	❹ Disagree	❸ Neutral	❷ Agree	❶ Strongly Agree

13. I'm not very preoccupied with arts and aesthetics.

❺ Strongly Disagree	❹ Disagree	❸ Neutral	❷ Agree	❶ Strongly Agree

14. I strive to achieve my ambitious goals.

❶ Strongly Disagree	❷ Disagree	❸ Neutral	❹ Agree	❺ Strongly Agree

15. I tend to conceal my strengths.

❶ Strongly Disagree	❷ Disagree	❸ Neutral	❹ Agree	❺ Strongly Agree

16. I would have to be very ill to miss a day of work.

❶ Strongly Disagree	❷ Disagree	❸ Neutral	❹ Agree	❺ Strongly Agree

17. I consider the right to speak my mind very important.

❶ Strongly Disagree	❷ Disagree	❸ Neutral	❹ Agree	❺ Strongly Agree

18. I often enjoy thinking about theories and conceptual ideas.

❶ Strongly Disagree	❷ Disagree	❸ Neutral	❹ Agree	❺ Strongly Agree

19. If a series of little things goes wrong during my day, I feel frustrated and irritated.

❺ Strongly Disagree	❹ Disagree	❸ Neutral	❷ Agree	❶ Strongly Agree

20. When I listen to music, I often find myself drifting off.

❶ Strongly Disagree	❷ Disagree	❸ Neutral	❹ Agree	❺ Strongly Agree

21. I tend to have mood swings more often than other people.

❺ Strongly Disagree	❹ Disagree	❸ Neutral	❷ Agree	❶ Strongly Agree

22. I think that most people who know me would say that I have high self-esteem.

❺ Strongly Disagree	❹ Disagree	❸ Neutral	❷ Agree	❶ Strongly Agree

23. What I say is what I think.

❶ Strongly Disagree	❷ Disagree	❸ Neutral	❹ Agree	❺ Strongly Agree

24. I can be trusted to complete any assignment I've committed myself to.

❶ Strongly Disagree	❷ Disagree	❸ Neutral	❹ Agree	❺ Strongly Agree

25. I've tried to write poetry in the past.

❶ Strongly Disagree	❷ Disagree	❸ Neutral	❹ Agree	❺ Strongly Agree

26. If I'm presented with new information, I take the time to analyse it critically.

❶ Strongly Disagree	❷ Disagree	❸ Neutral	❹ Agree	❺ Strongly Agree

27. I'm persistent when it comes to completing tasks.

❶ Strongly Disagree	❷ Disagree	❸ Neutral	❹ Agree	❺ Strongly Agree

28. My career is very high on my list of priorities.

❶ Strongly Disagree	❷ Disagree	❸ Neutral	❹ Agree	❺ Strongly Agree

29. I'm cautious about expressing anger, even if it's appropriate.

❺ Strongly Disagree	❹ Disagree	❸ Neutral	❷ Agree	❶ Strongly Agree

30. I have an innate desire to succeed.

❶ Strongly Disagree	❷ Disagree	❸ Neutral	❹ Agree	❺ Strongly Agree

31. I don't pay much attention to my own transient emotions.

❶	❷	❸	❹	❺
Strongly Disagree	Disagree	Neutral	Agree	Strongly Agree

32. I often have theoretical discussions with friends.

❶	❷	❸	❹	❺
Strongly Disagree	Disagree	Neutral	Agree	Strongly Agree

33. I usually notice the hidden pitfalls involved in a plan.

❶	❷	❸	❹	❺
Strongly Disagree	Disagree	Neutral	Agree	Strongly Agree

34. I don't usually share my accomplishments with others.

❶	❷	❸	❹	❺
Strongly Disagree	Disagree	Neutral	Agree	Strongly Agree

35. Rather than dealing with people in a conventional and polite way, I prefer to be direct.

❶	❷	❸	❹	❺
Strongly Disagree	Disagree	Neutral	Agree	Strongly Agree

36. I think philosophical arguments are tedious.

❺	❹	❸	❷	❶
Strongly Disagree	Disagree	Neutral	Agree	Strongly Agree

37. I am a thorough and effective worker.

❶	❷	❸	❹	❺
Strongly Disagree	Disagree	Neutral	Agree	Strongly Agree

38. Compared to most people, I set myself ambitious goals.

❶	❷	❸	❹	❺
Strongly Disagree	Disagree	Neutral	Agree	Strongly Agree

39. I don't enjoy watching dance ensembles.

❺	❹	❸	❷	❶
Strongly Disagree	Disagree	Neutral	Agree	Strongly Agree

40. I usually keep my feelings to myself.

❶	❷	❸	❹	❺
Strongly Disagree	Disagree	Neutral	Agree	Strongly Agree

41. Every now and then, I enjoy boasting about my achievements.

❺	❹	❸	❷	❶
Strongly Disagree	Disagree	Neutral	Agree	Strongly Agree

42. I tend to see both the benefits and the shortcomings of a plan.

❶	❷	❸	❹	❺
Strongly Disagree	Disagree	Neutral	Agree	Strongly Agree

43. I almost always complete assignments that I've begun.

❶	❷	❸	❹	❺
Strongly Disagree	Disagree	Neutral	Agree	Strongly Agree

44. I lose my temper relatively quickly.

❺	❹	❸	❷	❶
Strongly Disagree	Disagree	Neutral	Agree	Strongly Agree

45. I enjoy poetry.

❶	❷	❸	❹	❺
Strongly Disagree	Disagree	Neutral	Agree	Strongly Agree

46. I'm modest about my accomplishments.

❶	❷	❸	❹	❺
Strongly Disagree	Disagree	Neutral	Agree	Strongly Agree

47. If I don't like someone, they usually know it.

❶	❷	❸	❹	❺
Strongly Disagree	Disagree	Neutral	Agree	Strongly Agree

48. I prefer a stable, administrative position even if it has limited opportunities for promotion.

❺	❹	❸	❷	❶
Strongly Disagree	Disagree	Neutral	Agree	Strongly Agree

49. Before I make a decision, I take the time to consider the issue from every angle.

❶	❷	❸	❹	❺
Strongly Disagree	Disagree	Neutral	Agree	Strongly Agree

50. I read at least one book a month.

❶	❷	❸	❹	❺
Strongly Disagree	Disagree	Neutral	Agree	Strongly Agree

51. I work at a pace that allows me to finish things on time.

❶	❷	❸	❹	❺
Strongly Disagree	Disagree	Neutral	Agree	Strongly Agree

52. I rarely give in to my impulses.

❶	❷	❸	❹	❺
Strongly Disagree	Disagree	Neutral	Agree	Strongly Agree

53. I believe that I'm more competent than the people around me.

❺	❹	❸	❷	❶
Strongly Disagree	Disagree	Neutral	Agree	Strongly Agree

54. I don't usually feel the drive to succeed.

❺	❹	❸	❷	❶
Strongly Disagree	Disagree	Neutral	Agree	Strongly Agree

55. Visiting the exhibition of an artist I admire excites me very much.

❶	❷	❸	❹	❺
Strongly Disagree	Disagree	Neutral	Agree	Strongly Agree

56. I often think of things I should have said, but didn't.

❺	❹	❸	❷	❶
Strongly Disagree	Disagree	Neutral	Agree	Strongly Agree

57. I tend to think things through before coming to a decision, regardless of the importance of the issue.

❶	❷	❸	❹	❺
Strongly Disagree	Disagree	Neutral	Agree	Strongly Agree

58. If the discussion around me becomes too theoretical, I usually lose interest.

❺	❹	❸	❷	❶
Strongly Disagree	Disagree	Neutral	Agree	Strongly Agree

59. I always keep my feelings to myself.

❶	❷	❸	❹	❺
Strongly Disagree	Disagree	Neutral	Agree	Strongly Agree

60. When I work from home, I plan a work schedule and stick to it.

❶	❷	❸	❹	❺
Strongly Disagree	Disagree	Neutral	Agree	Strongly Agree

61. If I worked for a newspaper, I would want to write the theatre review section.

❶	❷	❸	❹	❺
Strongly Disagree	Disagree	Neutral	Agree	Strongly Agree

62. I aim to become a leader in my community.

❶	❷	❸	❹	❺
Strongly Disagree	Disagree	Neutral	Agree	Strongly Agree

63. When I begin a new task, I think about all of the possible outcomes before taking action.

❶	❷	❸	❹	❺
Strongly Disagree	Disagree	Neutral	Agree	Strongly Agree

64. If the timing is appropriate, I'm likely to boast.

❺	❹	❸	❷	❶
Strongly Disagree	Disagree	Neutral	Agree	Strongly Agree

Scoring:

Now go back to the questionnaire and add up your score (in the "score" column) based on the column "question number" below:

Personality Dimension	Question Number	Score	Total
EXAMPLE Directness	EXAMPLE 01, 10, 17, 23, 29, 35, 47, 56	EXAMPLE 5+ 2+ 3+ 4+etc	e.g., 23
Humbleness	11, 15, 22, 34, 41, 46, 53, 64		
Critical Thinking	02, 09, 26, 33, 42, 49, 57, 63		
Intellectualism	03, 08, 12, 18, 32, 36, 50, 58		
Conscientiousness	05, 16, 24, 27, 37, 43, 51, 60		
Directness	01, 10, 17, 23, 29, 35, 47, 56		
Emotional Management	07, 19, 21, 31, 40, 44, 52, 59		
Ambition	04, 14, 28, 30, 38, 48, 54, 62		
Artistic Ability	06, 13, 20, 25, 39, 45, 55, 61		

Your results on the assessment scale:

Circle 1-10 according to your score. A score that falls between 1-3 is considered low, a score that falls between 4-7 is considered average and a score that falls between 8-10 is considered high.

Directness

Low scorers	1	2	3	4	5	6	7	8	9	10	High scorers
Low scorers may be subtle rather than up front. They sometimes conceal their views.	8-22	23	24-25	26	27	28	29-30	31	32	33-40	High scorers speak their minds and express their views overtly. They are outspoken and direct.

Humbleness

Low scorers	1	2	3	4	5	6	7	8	9	10	High scorers
Low scorers often "sing their own praises" and feel the need to make an impression by publicising, and often exaggerating, accomplishments.	8-17	18	19-20	21	22	23	24	25	26-29	30-40	High scorers are modest, humble and usually avoid boasting. They may have a high opinion of themselves but avoid expressing it overtly.

Critical Thinking

Low scorers	1	2	3	4	5	6	7	8	9	10	High scorers
Low scorers have trouble differentiating between plausible and less plausible arguments. They don't take enough relevant factors into consideration when reaching a conclusion. They may make decisions quickly.	8-23	24	25	26	27	28-29	30	31	32	33-40	High scorers analyse situations and have a natural tendency to look for the errors and flaws in an argument. They have an eye for detail and reading the 'fine print'. They're capable of envisioning the outcome of future scenarios.

Intellectual Ability

Low scorers	1	2	3	4	5	6	7	8	9	10	High scorers
Low scorers may get bored or be put off by theoretical discussions. They don't particularly enjoy reading books and thinking about abstract concepts.	8-22	23-24	25-26	27-28	29-30	31-32	33	34-35	36-37	38-40	High scorers are inquisitive and deep. They enjoy theoretical and philosophical discussions and like to understand the concepts that underlie different principles.

Conscientiousness

Low scorer	1	2	3	4	5	6	7	8	9	10	High scorer
Low scorers often aren't very disciplined or dutiful. They may have trouble meeting deadlines and keeping their commitments.	8-27	28-29	30	31	32-33	34	35	36	37	38-40	High scorers have the need to complete the tasks they begin. They usually meet deadlines and follow through with their commitments.

Emotional Management

Low scorer	1	2	3	4	5	6	7	8	9	10	High scorer
Low scorers have trouble concealing their feelings. They let their emotions influence their decisions. They're often prone to mood swings and may be impulsive.	8-20	21	22	23	24-25	26-27	28	29	30-32	33-40	High scorers are rational. They're less attentive to their emotions and focus on the matter at hand. They know how to conceal their true feelings and don't let them interfere with their goals.

Ambition

Low scorer	1	2	3	4	5	6	7	8	9	10	High scorer
Low scorers are not ambitious and their careers are not very important to them. Their priorities in life may lie elsewhere.	8-16	17-24	25-26	27	28	29	30-32	33-37	38-40	--	High scorers are achievement-oriented and set ambitious goals for themselves in life. Their careers are a high priority.

Artistic Ability

Low scorer	1	2	3	4	5	6	7	8	9	10	High scorer
Low scorers don't enjoy art. They seldom go to exhibitions or art galleries.	8-19	19-20	21-22	23-24	25-26	27-28	29-30	31-32	33	34-40	High scorers enjoy art and aesthetics. They enjoy various forms of art and attach a great deal of importance to artistic pursuits.

Check if your scores are compatible with the scores expected for someone in your line of work.

Trait / Position	Senior Manager	Manager	Graduate	Junior/Line Manager	Professional	Clerical Worker	IT Professional/Engineer	Salesperson	Customer Service Representative	Call Centre Representative	Semi-skilled Worker	Technical Worker
Directness	Avg-high	Avg-high	Avg	Avg	Avg-high	Low-avg	Avg	Avg	Low-avg	Low-avg	Avg	Avg
Humbleness	Low-avg	Low-avg	Avg	Low-avg	Avg	Avg-high	Avg	Avg-high	Avg-high	Avg-high	Avg-high	Avg
Critical Thinking	Avg-high	Avg-high	Avg-high	Avg	High	High	High	Avg	Avg	Avg	Avg	Avg-high
Intellectualism	Avg-high	Avg	Avg-high	Avg	High	Avg	High	Avg	Avg	Avg	Avg	Avg
Conscientiousness	High	High	High	High	High	High	High	High	High	High	High	High
Emotional Management	Avg-high	Avg-high	Avg	Avg-high	Avg	Avg	Avg	Avg-high	Avg	Avg	Avg	Avg
Ambition	Avg-high	Avg-high	High	Avg-high	Avg	Low-avg	Avg-high	High	Avg	Avg	Low-avg	Avg
Artistic Ability	Low-high	Low-high	Low-high	Low-high	Low-high	Low-high	Low-high	Low-high	Low-high	Low-high	Low-high	Low-high

Test 2

Instructions:
- The following test is somewhat different from the test you just completed, and requires further explanation.
- Each question has a group of four statements. In each group, you're required to choose only two items: the item that most describes you and the item that least describes you. The other two sentences don't need to be marked.

Example:

		Least	Most
1.1	I feel comfortable selling.		
1.2	I enjoy being the centre of attention.		
1.3	I regularly consult with others.		
1.4	I spend time trying to figure out why people behave the way they do.		

How to plan your strategy for this test:
- The sentences that you don't select will keep you in the average zone for that particular trait. If you recall, we highly recommended that you try to score in the average zone for most traits, with some exceptions – traits that you need a high score in to fit the requirements of your profession (see the table on page 34). Each time you choose *most*, it will move you above the average by one point. Each time you choose *least*, it will move you below the average by one point.
- If you want a high score on a particular trait (but not extremely high, as we recommended), choose "most" consistently to most questions relating to that trait but don't choose "most" for all questions – select 1-3 questions to ignore. Then you'll score high, but not extremely high. If you choose *least* consistently for the same types of statements, you'll end up with a very low score on that trait.

Good luck!.

		Least	Most
1.1	I feel comfortable selling.		
1.2	I enjoy being the centre of attention.		
1.3	I regularly consult with others.		
1.4	I spend time trying to figure out why people behave the way they do.		

		Least	Most
2.1	I have plenty of original ideas.		
2.2	I seldom worry about things.		
2.3	I enjoy being active.		
2.4	I enjoy planning things in advance.		

		Least	Most
3.1	I worry before important meetings.		
3.2	I'd enjoy a sports match better if there were something at stake.		
3.3	I can be very persuasive.		
3.4	I often feel full of energy.		

		Least	Most
4.1	I'm a better talker than listener.		
4.2	Original ideas come to me easily.		
4.3	I worry before important occasions.		
4.4	I like to plan ahead so I won't waste time.		

		Least	Most
5.1	I enjoy competitive games.		
5.2	I am intrigued by people's behaviour.		
5.3	I think outside of the box.		
5.4	It's easy for me to just to kick back and relax.		

		Least	Most
6.1	I take the time to listen to other people's opinions.		
6.2	I usually appear to be in a hurry.		
6.3	I think first and act later.		
6.4	I like to win.		

		Least	Most
7.1	I don't usually get annoyed if my plans change unexpectedly.		
7.2	I have a natural talent for influencing people.		
7.3	I'm a talkative person.		
7.4	I think that group discussions are very important.		

		Least	Most
8.1	In stressful times, I have trouble keeping calm.		
8.2	I ask for other people's opinions.		
8.3	I tend to analyse people.		
8.4	I think and communicate creatively.		

		Least	Most
9.1	My life is fast-paced.		
9.2	I find it easy to start a conversation.		
9.3	I'm good at understanding people.		
9.4	When I'm in a long queue, I don't get as restless as most people.		

		Least	Most
10.1	I'm very good at selling.		
10.2	I come up with new, innovative solutions to problems.		
10.3	I seldom give in to my impulses.		
10.4	I understand what motivates people.		

		Least	Most
11.1	I'm lively in a social group.		
11.2	I come up with different ways of doing things.		
11.3	I hate losing.		
11.4	I worry about the future.		

		Least	Most
12.1	Before I make a decision, I usually consult with other people.		
12.2	I'm less of a worrier than most people.		
12.3	I'm more active than most people.		
12.4	I'm motivated by a competitive drive.		

		Least	Most
13.1	I enjoy closing a deal.		
13.2	I cope with most of my problems calmly.		
13.3	I find it easy to resist temptation.		
13.4	I'm an outgoing person.		

		Least	Most
14.1	I'm too self-critical.		
14.2	I know how to sell an idea.		
14.3	I consult with others before I make a decision.		
14.4	I enjoy keeping myself busy.		

		Least	Most
15.1	I can generally see where people are coming from.		
15.2	I'm an energetic person.		
15.3	I plan ahead carefully before I go on vacation.		
15.4	Winning is very important to me.		

		Least	Most
16.1	I find it difficult to lose.		
16.2	It's easy for me to negotiate.		
16.3	I enjoy thinking up new solutions to problems.		
16.4	I ask for suggestions from other people.		

		Least	Most
17.1	I intuitively understand the way people react to situations.		
17.2	I often feel tense.		
17.3	I think long term.		
17.4	It's important to me that everybody is allowed to say what they think.		

		Least	Most
18.1	It doesn't embarrass me to be the centre of attention in a group.		
18.2	I enjoy being busy.		
18.3	I'm perceptive about people.		
18.4	I find it difficult to be calm during stressful events.		

		Least	Most
19.1	I try to be first.		
19.2	I'm easy to get close to.		
19.3	I'm able to keep a cool head in stressful situations.		
19.4	I come up with extraordinary solutions to problems.		

		Least	Most
20.1	I'm good at thinking ahead.		
20.2	Selling comes to me easily.		
20.3	I worry about things that might go wrong.		
20.4	I'm a competitive person.		

		Least	Most
21.1	I'm an easygoing person.		
21.2	I understand why people react the way they do.		
21.3	I feel comfortable when I have to negotiate.		
21.4	I like having lots of things going on in my life.		

		Least	Most
22.1	I'm usually tension-free.		
22.2	I enjoy sharing my views with others.		
22.3	I take an unconventional approach to tackling problems.		
22.4	I like my weekend full of activities.		

		Least	Most
23.1	I enjoy parties and social events.		
23.2	After a meeting, I mull over the things I've said.		
23.3	I enjoy setting long-term goals.		
23.4	Before making a decision, I need to hear what other people think.		

		Least	Most
24.1	I'm an effective negotiator.		
24.2	I find it easy to come up with new ideas.		
24.3	I get anxious before a big event.		
24.4	I enjoy analysing people.		

		Least	Most
25.1	Most of the time I feel relaxed.		
25.2	I think about my future plans.		
25.3	Competition brings out the best in me.		
25.4	It's easy for me to act naturally when I meet new people.		

Scoring:

There are two steps involved in the scoring of this test. First, go through the statements quickly and assign a score to each statement based on the following rules:

- If you chose "least" for a particular statement, give yourself 0 points.
- If you didn't choose the statement, give yourself 1 point.
- If you chose "most", give yourself 2 points.
- Once you've finished, turn to the table below and sum up the scores in the "score" column according to the "question number" column.

Personality Dimension	Question Number	Score	Total
EXAMPLE Sales and Negotiation Skills	EXAMPLE 1.1, 3.3, 7.2, 10.1, 13.1, 14.2, 16.2, 20.2, 21.3, 24.1	EXAMPLE 0+1+2+2+etc	e.g., 11
Social Energy	1.2, 4.1, 7.3, 9.2, 11.1, 13.4, 18.1, 19.2, 23.1, 25.4		
Consulting Skills	1.3, 6.1, 7.4, 8.2, 12.1, 14.3, 16.4, 17.4, 22.2, 23.4		
Insight into People	1.4, 5.2, 8.3, 9.3, 10.4, 15.1, 17.1, 18.3, 21.2, 24.4		
Creativity	2.1, 4.2, 5.3, 8.4, 10.2, 11.2, 16.3, 19.4, 22.3, 24.2		
Tranquillity	2.2, 5.4, 7.1, 9.4, 12.2, 13.2, 19.3, 21.1, 22.1, 25.1		
Anxiety	3.1, 4.3, 8.1, 11.4, 14.1, 17.2, 18.4, 20.3, 23.2, 24.3		
Dynamism	2.3, 3.4, 6.2, 9.1, 12.3, 14.4, 15.2, 18.2, 21.4, 22.4		
Planning Skills	2.4, 4.4, 6.3, 10.3, 13.3, 15.3, 17.3, 20.1, 23.3, 25.2		
Competitive Drive	3.2, 5.1, 6.4, 11.3, 12.4, 15.4, 16.1, 19.1, 20.4, 25.3		
Sales and Negotiation Skills	1.1, 3.3, 7.2, 10.1, 13.1, 14.2, 16.2, 20.2, 21.3, 24.1		

Your results on the assessed scales:

Sales and Negotiation

Low scorers	1	2	3	4	5	6	7	8	9	10	High scorers
Low scorers do not enjoy the act of negotiation, persuasion and selling. They may enjoy interaction with others, but not from the standpoint of selling.	0-3	4	5	6-7	8	9-10	11-12	13	14	15-20	High scorers are effective in negotiating, selling and persuading others.

Social Energy

Low scorers	1	2	3	4	5	6	7	8	9	10	High scorers
Low scorers are better listeners and don't typically stand out in events, gatherings and meetings.	0-6	7-8	9	10	11	12	13	14	15	16-20	High scorers are lively and talkative. They enjoy social gatherings and parties and tend to initiate conversations. They are not very good listeners.

Consulting

Low scorers	1	2	3	4	5	6	7	8	9	10	High scorers
Low scorers prefer to work alone and are more effective when doing so. They are less interested in the opinions of others and are less inclined to ask for contributions from other people.	0-5	6-8	9	10	11	12	13-14	15	16	17-20	High scorers frequently consult others and find it important to listen to other people's opinions prior to making a decision or acting. They often enjoy group discussions.

Insight into people

Low scorers	1	2	3	4	5	6	7	8	9	10	High scorers
Low scorers concentrate on the matter at hand, on the concrete rather than on the underlying motivations. They are not interested in people's behaviour or motivations.	0-5	6-7	8-9	10-11	12-13	14	15	16	17-18	19-20	High scorers are interested in the human psyche and in what motivates people.

Creativity

Low scorers	1	2	3	4	5	6	7	8	9	10	High scorers
Low scorers follow suit and tend to be more practical.	0-6	7-8	9	10	11	12	13	14	15-16	17-20	High scorers are creative and innovative. They tend to be inventive and generate many new ideas. They might have difficulty following conventional routines.

Tranquillity

Low scorers	1	2	3	4	5	6	7	8	9	10	High scorers
Low scorers tend to be restless and fidgety. They tend to worry.	0-4	5	6	7	8	12	13	14	15-16	17-20	High scorers are relaxed by nature. They enjoy sitting still and kicking back. They usually don't experience much tension.

Apprehension

Low scorers	1	2	3	4	5	6	7	8	9	10	High scorers
Low scorers are more relaxed and less sensitive. They are quite often more optimistic by nature and tend to be positive.	0-1	2	3	4	5	6	7	8-9	10-13	14-20	High scorers tend to have fears and worries. They are nervous prior to events and often have morbid thoughts.

Dynamism

Low scorers	1	2	3	4	5	6	7	8	9	10	High scorers
Low scorers are slower paced. They are more relaxed, and not as active as those with high scores.	--	0-5	6	7	8	9	10	11	12-13	14-20	High scorers are active and vigorous. They tend to have a lot of things to do and quite often a high presence. They often seem hurried and very energetic.

Planning

Low scorers	1	2	3	4	5	6	7	8	9	10	High scorers
Low scorers tend to be more impulsive and often act rather than plan.	--	0-5	6	7-8	9	10	11	12	13	14-20	High scorers have the need to plan ahead both in business and pleasure. They seek a long term approach and derive a sense of confidence from having plans set up.

Competitive Drive

Low scorers	1	2	3	4	5	6	7	8	9	10	High scorers
Low scorers are not competitive. They tend to be more at bay than high scorers. They are less driven for success and put less emphasis on winning.	0-1	2	3	4-5	6	7	8	9-11	12-14	15-20	High scorers are competitive. They are quite often career-minded. They enjoy competition both at work and for pleasure. Life is about winning.

Check if your scores are compatible with the scores expected for someone in your line of work.

Trait \ Position	Senior Manager	Manager	Graduates	Junior/Line Manager	Professional	Clerical Worker	IT / Engineer	Salesperson	Customer Service Representative	Call Centre Worker	Semi-skilled Worker	Technical Worker
Sales and Negotiation	Avg-high	Avg-high	Avg-high	Avg-high	Avg	Low-avg	Low-avg	High	Low-avg	Avg-high	Low-avg	Low-avg
Social Energy	Avg-high	Avg-high	Avg-high	Avg-high	Avg	Avg	Avg	High	Avg-high	Avg-high	Avg	Avg
Consulting	Avg	Avg	Avg-high	Avg	Avg	Avg	Avg	Avg	Avg-high	Avg-high	Avg	Avg
Insight into people	Avg	Avg	Avg	Avg	Avg	Avg	Avg	Avg	Avg	Avg	Avg	Avg
Creativity	Avg-high	Avg-high	Avg-high	Avg	Avg-high	Avg	Avg-high	Avg-high	Avg	Avg	Avg	Avg-high
Tranquillity	Avg	Avg	Avg	Avg	Avg	Avg	Avg	Avg	Avg	Avg	Avg	Avg
Anxiety	Low-Avg	Low-Avg	Avg	Avg	Avg	Avg	Avg	Avg	Avg	Avg	Avg	Avg
Dynamics	Avg-high	Avg	High	Avg-high	Avg	Avg	Avg	High	Avg-high	Avg-high	Avg-high	Avg
Planning	High	Avg-high	Avg-high	Avg	Avg-high	Avg-high	High	Avg	Avg	Avg	Avg	Avg-high
Competitive Drive	Avg-high	Avg-high	Avg-high	Avg-high	Avg	Avg	Avg	Avg-High	Avg	Avg	Avg	Avg

Final Words

In the first section of this book, we expanded your knowledge of personality tests. You now know that personality tests are often a very important part of the job selection process, and that they aren't to be taken lightly. You also learned that most of the common personality tests on the market are based on self-reporting. This means that you, the candidate, have the power to influence your personality profile results.

The secret to success on any selection test is to come prepared. You need to know what characteristics are required for your position. You also have to believe that you possess these characteristics and that you are well-suited to the job you want.

When you take the personality test, make an effort to emphasise your <u>relevant</u> strengths. Try to refrain from emphasising strengths that aren't related to the position you seek. For example, if you aren't applying for a managerial position there's no reason to highlight your leadership skills.

You've learned how to recognise the questions that relate to each personality characteristic, as well as how to obtain a high score on desirable traits. You've also learned how to avoid scores that fall into the extreme range. Remember, consistency is not that important, and you must pay attention to words that express extremes like "never" and "always". When you see these types of words, it gives you a chance to avoid falling into the extremes of any particular trait.

You've learned how to recognise hidden traps that are embedded into most personality tests, such as impression management questions. You've also learned how to avoid these traps.

Now that we've exposed the veil of secrecy surrounding personality tests, you can see that, although they are quite complex, with proper preparation these tests shouldn't cause you much concern. Plan your strategy beforehand and come to the test relaxed and focused. In this state of mind, there's no reason why you shouldn't excel on your personality test. For more practice on personality assessment, visit our website at: **www.jobtestprep.com**

Good luck!

Part 2

Aptitude Test Preparation

INTRODUCTION

One of the most common uses of aptitude tests (also known as IQ, intelligence or ability tests) in the world today is for job selection and recruitment. Aptitude tests measure a range of skills that are required in the working environment, and are often administered as a matter of course. These tests usually fall into three broad skill categories: verbal, numerical and abstract (or diagrammatic). Additional skills are assessed in specific fields and for specific positions. For example, in IT, advanced numerical and technical cognitive skills are tested using specifically designed tests. We'll present and practice all of these tests thoroughly in this chapter.

When you apply for a specific job, you profess to have certain educational and professional skills. Different positions may require varying degrees of aptitude. The use of objective measurement tools like aptitude tests can assess the degree of skill you claim to have in different areas.

Aptitude tests are typically administered in three environments and formats:
1. In a classroom with a test booklet and an answer sheet, using pen and paper.
2. In a computer lab at the recruiting agency and/or at the recruiting organisation.
3. At home or long-distance, completing the test online.

The scoring for the aptitude test is simple. Most questions are of multiple-choice format, and the number of questions you answer correctly determines your final score. Whether or not you pass an aptitude test depends on the purpose of the test and the administering organisation. Some recruitment organisations require that applicants achieve a minimum threshold score in order to move on to the next stage of the selection process. Other organisations pass only a pre-determined percentage of all job applicants applying for a certain position. For example, the top 10% of applicants may be moved forward to the next stage. Your aim is to get as many questions correct as possible so you can increase your chances of passing the aptitude testing stage.

Aptitude tests are usually timed, and may take anywhere from 10 to 40 minutes per test depending on the skill being measured. Some tests measure speed and accuracy and these may be shorter. Advanced numerical reasoning tests are complex and may take longer to complete. However, keep in mind that in most cases you'll be asked to sit more than one test in any given session.

Important:
Some academics argue that it's impossible to prepare for some aptitude tests, specifically for abstract reasoning tests because they are based on innate abilities. This is not something **you** should accept at face value.

Your chances of doing well on any test increase if you:
- are familiar with the test format.
- have practiced solving aptitude questions.
- improve your verbal and numerical skills.

You will practice an extensive variety of tests in this book. While it may be generally beneficial for you to review and improve your skills using the entire selection of tests, it's more important that you focus your efforts on those specific tests that are geared towards your profession as shown in the following position guide table. We also recommend you review the tests marked under the *All Positions* category.

Position guide table

Position	Test Name	Page
All Positions		
	Logic	235
	Numerical Critical Reasoning	171
	Diagrammatic Series (reasoning)	83
	Diagrammatic Reasoning IQ	101
	Following Instructions	260
Senior Management		
	Verbal Critical Reasoning	206
	Verbal Critical Reasoning – Business	220
	Numerical Estimation	163
	Advanced Numerical Critical Reasoning	181
Junior Management		
	Verbal Critical Reasoning	206
	Verbal Evaluation	227
	Word Relationships	252
	Numerical Estimation	163
	Numerical Reasoning	167
Graduates		
	Verbal Critical Reasoning	206
	Verbal Critical Reasoning – Business	220
	Verbal Evaluation	227
	Word Relationships	252
	Numerical Estimation	163
	Advanced Numerical Critical Reasoning	181
Professionals		
	Verbal Critical Reasoning	206
	Verbal Critical Reasoning – Business	220
	Advanced Numerical Critical Reasoning	181
	Diagrammatic Thinking	146
	Spatial Reasoning	282

Position	Test Name	Page
Sales & Marketing		
	Verbal Critical Reasoning	206
	Verbal Evaluation	227
	Advanced Numerical Critical Reasoning	181
Engineering		
	Number Series	198
	Diagrammatic Reasoning	131
	Diagramming	139
	Diagrammatic Thinking	146
	Mechanical Reasoning	288
	Fault Finding	299
IT (Programming, QA, Engineering)		
	Numerical Reasoning	167
	Number Series	198
	Diagrammatic Reasoning	131
	Diagramming	139
	Diagrammatic Thinking	146
	Computer Checking	264
	Spatial Reasoning	282
	Fault Finding	299
Technological		
	Word Relationships	252
	Numerical Reasoning	167
	Diagrammatic Thinking	146
	Mechanical Reasoning	288
Administrative & Customer Service		
	Verbal Evaluation	227
	Verbal Application	248
	Word Relationships	252
	Numerical Estimation	163
	Numerical Reasoning	167
	Basic Checking – Numbers	267
	Basic Checking – Words	272
	Clerical Checking	277

1

ABSTRACT REASONING TESTS

Abstract/diagrammatic reasoning tests assess logical and analytical thinking. They <u>do not</u> require prior numerical and/or verbal knowledge, and they use various shapes, patterns and diagrams only. Since these tests do not require numerical, verbal or any other acquired skills, they are often regarded as good and viable tests for measuring general intelligence (IQ). As such, tests like the Diagrammatic Series and Diagrammatic Reasoning Tests are given to most job applicants regardless of the position they are applying for. The skills assessed by diagrammatic tests are considered extremely important for computer programming and for various types of engineering positions.

Since it is generally believed that diagrammatic tests measure IQ, the type of intelligence we are born with, most people assume that you can't prepare for these tests or improve your results. We disagree! Although certain aspects of intelligence may be innate, our years of experience preparing candidates for pre-employment tests tells us that preparation can significantly improve your results on abstract reasoning tests.

First and foremost, if you review and familiarise yourself with the tests that are on the market, you will become accustomed to the types of questions asked and how to approach and solve them. This will give you more confidence, reduce your tension and save you precious time in the actual testing situation. In addition, the different question types tend to repeat themselves, which limits the number of rules and techniques for solving them. This means that if you familiarise yourself with some of the common rules, there is a good chance that you'll be able to apply them when you are taking the actual test.

In this section, there are a number of different test types provided for you to practice. Each test has a time limit, and we suggest that you adhere to it.

Important:
Diagrammatic tests often include more questions than the average person can answer within the given time limit. The large number of questions is intended to put pressure on you. Don't be discouraged if you fail to complete all of the questions. However, we do recommend that you work as quickly and as accurately as possible.

Test 3 Diagrammatic Series (Reasoning)

This test assesses your reasoning and logical analysis skills. It is one of the most common types of tests used to evaluate abstract reasoning skills. It's used to evaluate candidates seeking wide range of positions, from secretarial and administrative jobs to supervisory and managerial positions, including technological and programming positions.

Instructions
Each question consists of a series of diagrams shown in a logical sequence. The goal is to choose the next diagram in the series out of the five options presented.
Try to work through the example below.

Example:
Choose the diagram that should follow logically in the following sequence of diagrams.

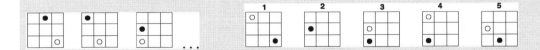

Solution:
The black dot moves one step anti-clockwise in each diagram. The white dot moves one step clockwise in each diagram.

<u>The answer is 3.</u>

Remember
Work as quickly and as accurately as you can.
The test consists of 30 questions and you have 15 minutes to solve them.

Good Luck!

1.

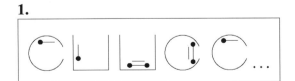 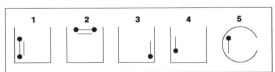

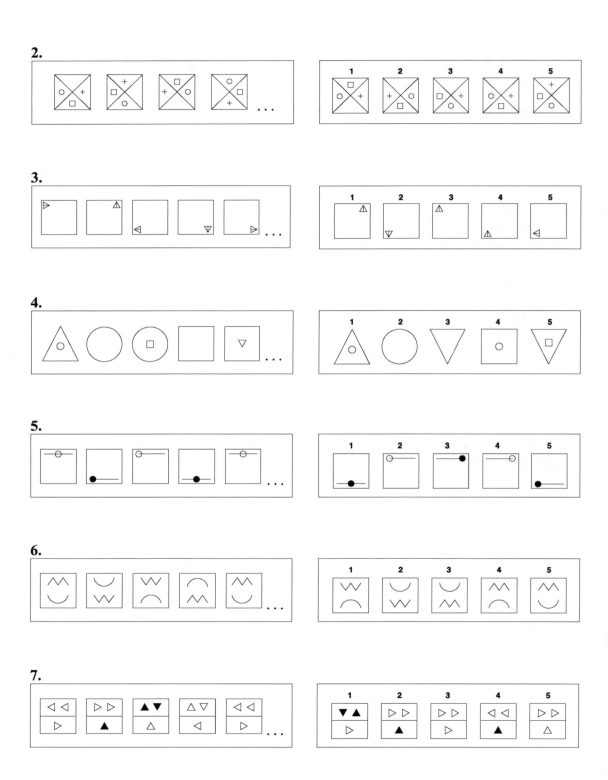

8.

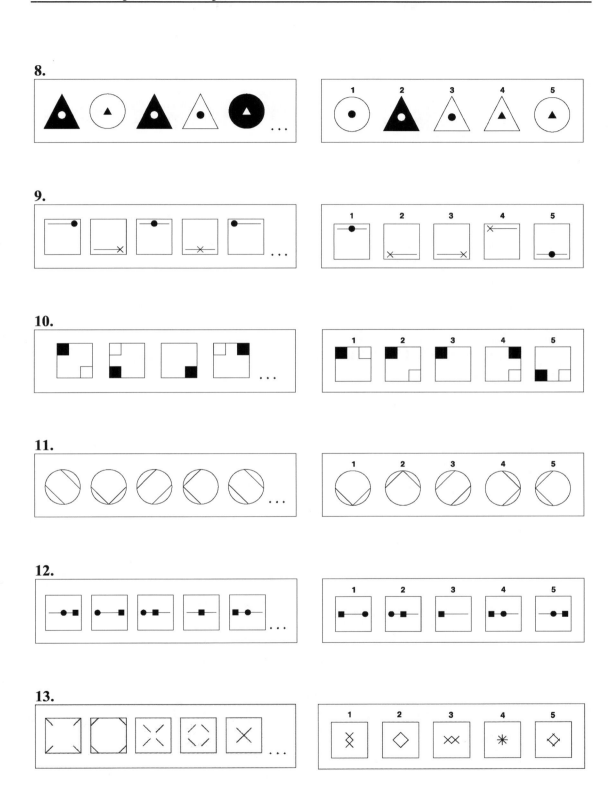

9.

10.

11.

12.

13.

14.

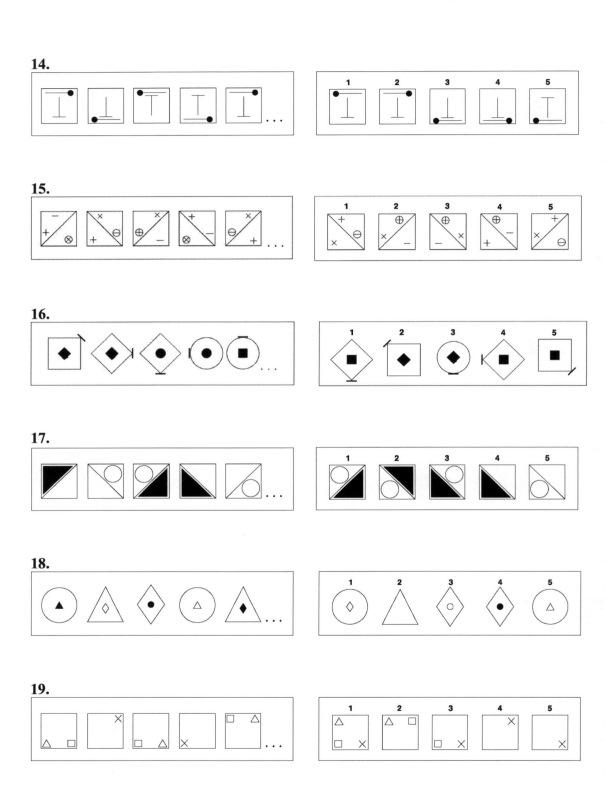

15.

16.

17.

18.

19.

20.

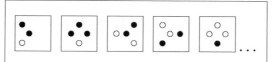 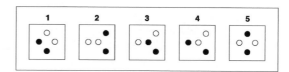

21.

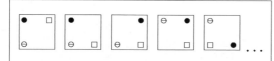 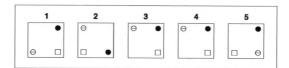

22.

 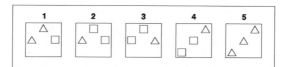

23.

24.

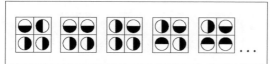 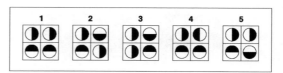

25.

 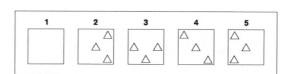

26.

 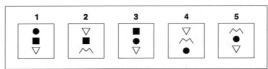

27.

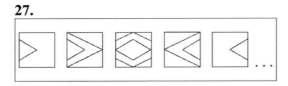 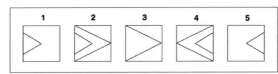

28.

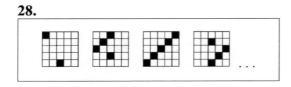 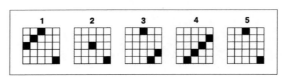

29.

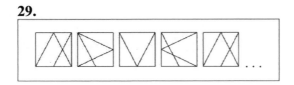 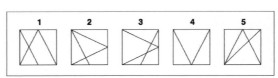

30.

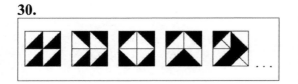 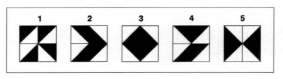

Test 3 General Tips:

- If there are a number of shapes within each object, try to isolate them and identify the progression of each shape separately.
- Check to see whether the shapes rotate clockwise or anti-clockwise in a particular pattern.
- Check whether the shapes alternate between outlined/hollow and filled-in shapes.
- Check whether the shapes increase or decrease in size.
- Check whether the shapes seem to be in motion, entering from one side of the diagram and exiting from the other as the series progresses.
- If you are unsure of the answer, try eliminating possible options. The logical sequence may become obvious.

Test 3 Answers:

1.

 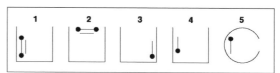

This series consists of open circles and open squares. Notice that the first and last items are identical. This means that the next item in the series should be identical to the second item in the series.

The answer is 4.

2.

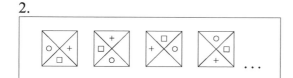 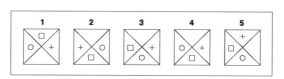

Each diagram in the series has three shapes: a square, a circle and a 'plus' sign. The circle and the 'plus' sign move in an anti-clockwise direction. The square moves in a clockwise direction. The next diagram in the series should have a circle on the left, a square at the bottom and a 'plus' sign on the right.

The answer is 4.

3.

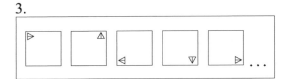　　　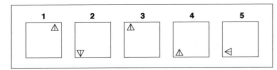

Each diagram contains a triangle. The triangle moves in two different ways:

1. It moves clockwise in the corners of the square. It makes one movement from one diagram to the next. Between the first and the second diagram the triangle moves clockwise one corner, between the second and the third diagram the triangle moves two corners, and so on. This means that the triangle should move five corners in the missing diagram.
2. The triangle rotates 90 degrees anti-clockwise around its own axis between diagrams.

<u>The answer is 4.</u>

4.

The series is made up of pairs of geometric shapes. The first, third and fifth items in the series consist of two shapes – a big one and a smaller one within it. The second and fourth items contain a shape which has nothing inside it. The smaller shape within the bigger shape indicates what the next shape in the series will be. For example, the small square within the circle indicates that the next shape in the series will be a large square. Following this logic, the next diagram in the series should be a large triangle with its tip facing down.

<u>The answer is 3.</u>

5.

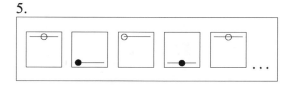 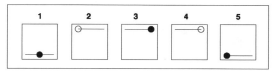

In this series, squares that contain white circles alternate with squares that contain black circles. This means that the next diagram in the series should be a square with a line and a black circle going through it (this eliminates options 2 and 4). In addition, the lines with the black circles are always located at the bottom of the square. This should also be the case in the next diagram (this eliminates option 3). We can now choose between option 1 and option 5. The black circle moves on the line from the left to the centre and then back. This means that the black circle, which is at the centre of the line in the fourth diagram, should now move back to the left.

The answer is 5.

6.

Each diagram contains a W shape and a U shape. The two shapes switch places from (top to bottom and vice versa) one diagram to the next. In addition, in every other diagram they turn in the opposite direction (facing up or down). In the next diagram in the series, the W should be facing up and situated in the bottom of the square. The U should be facing up and located in the top of the square.

The answer is 2.

7.

 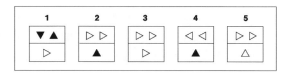

Notice that the first and last items are identical. This means that the next item in the series should be identical to the second item in the series.

The answer is 2.

8.

 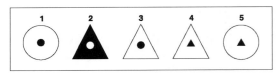

The first three shapes are in a logical pattern. Notice that the first and third diagrams are identical, and the second diagram is different. Following this logic, the missing diagram should be identical to the fourth diagram. This is because the fourth, fifth and sixth diagrams in the series follow the same logic as in the first three diagrams.

The answer is 3.

9.

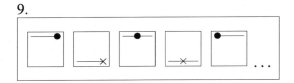 

This series contains squares with lines in them that alternate position between the top and the bottom of the square. In addition, a black circle and an X appear on the line in alternating diagrams. The last diagram contains a black circle, so the missing diagram will have to be a line with an X. The X and the black circle move along the line from one end to the other in three steps. This means that the next diagram in the series should consist of a square with a line across the bottom and an X at the left side of the line.

The answer is 2.

10.

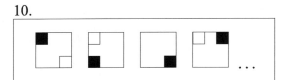 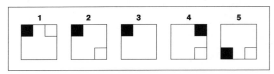

This series contains black and white squares within a larger square. The black square moves in an anti-clockwise direction. The white square alternates between the bottom right-hand corner and the top left-hand corner continuously. The next diagram should contain a white square in the bottom right-hand corner, and a black square in the top left-hand corner.

The answer is 2.

11.

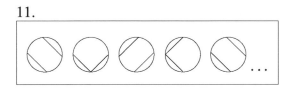 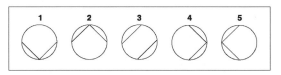

This series consists of two types of diagrams. The first is a circle with two parallel lines inside it, and the second is a circle with two lines that form a 90 degrees angle. These two types of diagrams alternate. This means that the next diagram in the series should be a circle with two lines in it, forming a 90 degrees angle. In addition, the two lines forming the 90 degrees angle move in a clockwise direction (90 degrees each time).

The answer is 2.

12.

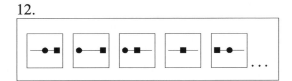 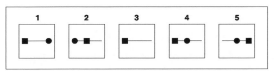

In this series, the black circle and square are moving across the line. Both the square and the circle alternate, making one move every second diagram. The square moves from the right, to the centre and then to the left, and the circle moves from the centre to the left, back to the centre and then to the right. The next diagram in the series should have a square on the left and a circle on the right.

The answer is 1.

13.

  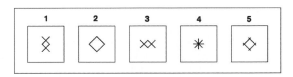

In this series the 1st, 3rd and 5th object consist of a square that has 4 lines moving towards each other creating eventually an X. In the 2nd and 4th square the lines are moving towards each other as well, expected to form a diamond in the 6th (missing) object.

The answer is 2.

14.

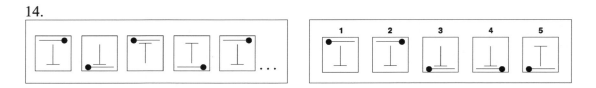

Notice that the first and last items are identical. This means that the next item should be identical to the second item in the series.

The answer is 3.

15.

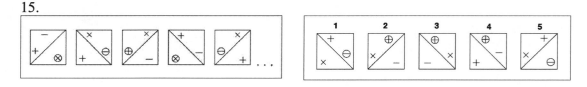

There are three rules in this series:

1. The diagonal line in the large square alternates from one diagram to the next. In one diagram it slants to the right, and in the next diagram it slants to the left. The next diagram in the series should contain a diagonal line that slants to the left. This eliminates options 2 and 5.

2. Inside each square there are three symbols: '+', '-' and 'x'. Two symbols always appear in the top section of the square and the third always appears in the bottom section of the square. Each diagram has a different symbol in the bottom section, in the following order: 'x', '+' and '-'. This means that in the next diagram, the minus sign should appear on its own. This eliminates options 1 and 4.

3. In each diagram, one of the symbols is circled in the following order: 'x', '-' and '+'. In the next diagram, the plus sign should have a circle around it.

The answer is 3.

16.

   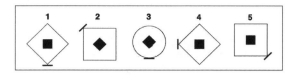

This series consists of three geometric shapes – a circle, a diamond and a square. Each of the shapes appears twice in a row. Within each of these shapes a smaller black geometric shape appears – a diamond, a circle and a square and these to, appear twice in a row. We can already determine that the missing object should be a square with a black square in it – only option 5 (so we do not need to work out the movement of the small line on the outside as well in order to determine the answer).

<u>The answer is 5.</u>

17.

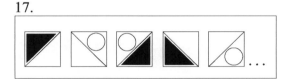   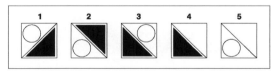

There are three rules in this series:

1. Three different triangles (an empty triangle, a black triangle and a triangle with a circle) alternate, and each type appears twice in a row. The next diagram in the series should include both a black triangle and a white triangle with a circle in it. This eliminates options 4 and 5.

2. The diagonal line in the square switches position. In one diagram it slants to the right, and in the next it slants to the left. In the next diagram, the line should slant to the left. This eliminates option 1.

3. Each type of triangle appears twice in a row, and its position in the second diagram is a mirror image of the triangle in the preceding diagram. This means that in the missing diagram, the circle should be in the bottom left-hand corner of the square.

<u>The answer is 2.</u>

18.

   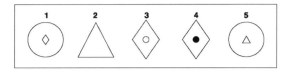

There are three rules in this series:

1. The large shapes appear in the following order: circle, triangle and diamond. Therefore, the missing diagram should be a diamond. This eliminates options 1, 2 and 5.
2. The colour of the inner shapes alternates from black to white, meaning that the next colour should be white.
3. The inner shape also appears in a specific order: triangle, diamond and circle. The missing diagram should have a circle inside the larger shape.

<u>The answer is 3.</u>

19.

   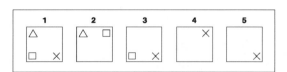

This series includes two mini-series. The first pattern has an X in it, and the second has a square and a triangle. The two patterns alternate within the series. This means that the next diagram should consist of a square with an X in it. This eliminates options 1, 2 and 3. The X moves between the top right-hand corner and the bottom left-hand corner. This means that in the next diagram, it should be in the top right-hand corner.

<u>The answer is 4.</u>

20.

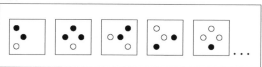   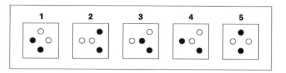

Imagine white and black circles moving one step to the right in each square. This means that circle(s) enter the square from the left and leave from the right. For example, the black circle in the centre of the first square, moves onto the right-hand side in the second square and disappears in the third square. Following this logic, the white circle on the right of the fifth square should disappear in the missing diagram. The black and white circles should move to the right-hand side and the white circle on the left should move to the centre of the square.

The answer is 4.

21.

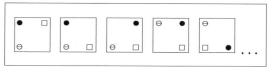   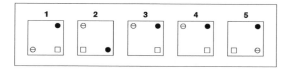

Each diagram has three shapes: a black circle, a square and a white circle with a line across it. The black circle changes position every second diagram. In the first two diagrams, it's in the top left-hand corner. Then it moves clockwise to the top right-hand corner. Finally, in the fifth diagram, it's in the bottom right-hand corner. The black circle should remain in the same place in the missing diagram, since it moves every other diagram. Before we continue to analyse the positions of the remaining two shapes, we can see by process of elimination that the only option with the black circle in the bottom right-hand corner is option 2.

The answer is 2.

22.

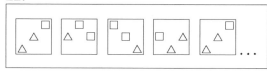   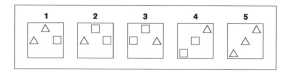

Imagine that the objects in the first square move one step to the left and a new object enters from the right. In the missing diagram, the triangle on the bottom left-hand side of the 5th diagram should move out and the triangle and the square behind it should move one step to the left. An additional shape (unknown) should enter from the right.

The answer is 2.

23.

 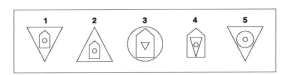

There are two rules in this series:
1. There are three large shapes: a house, a circle and a triangle, and each appear twice in a row. We can conclude that the missing diagram should include a large triangle with its tip facing down. This eliminates options 2, 3, and 4.
2. There are three shapes that appear in the middle of the larger shapes: a triangle, a circle and a house. This means that the missing diagram should include a house. At this point the answer can already be determined, so there is no need to figure out the pattern of the smallest shapes.

The answer is 1.

24.

 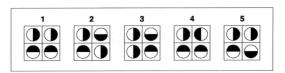

Each diagram consists of four squares, each with a circle inside. Only one of the circles rotates anti-clockwise in each diagram. The order of the rotating circles is also anti-clockwise. This means that the next circle to rotate is the one in the top right-hand corner. This eliminates options 2 and 3. The rest of the circles in the diagram should remain in the same position as in the fifth diagram.

The answer is 1.

25.

This is a combined series that consists of two patterns: the first has three triangles organised diagonally (1st, 3rd and 5th diagrams) and the second has three triangles that are organised in a different pattern (2nd and 4th diagram). The two patterns alternate from one diagram to the next. Following this logic, we know that the missing diagram will be of the second type. In this type, the two triangles on the sides remain constant and the triangle in the centre moves up and down. The next move will be downwards.

The answer is 3.

26.

 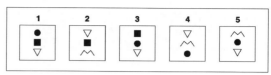

This series consists of an 'M', a triangle, a circle and a square. The rules are:

1. The triangle moves up and down in every diagram. In the missing diagram, the triangle should be at the bottom. This eliminates options 2 and 4.

2. The 'M' appears twice in a row in the same position, and then disappears and reappears one diagram later in a different position. Because it has already appeared twice, it shouldn't be in the missing diagram. This eliminates option 5.

3. The square and circle appear twice in a row, but in different positions. Then they disappear. The square should still be in the missing diagram, but not in the same position. This means that it should be in the centre, which leaves the circle at the top.

The answer is 1.

27.

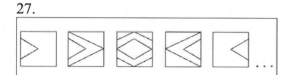 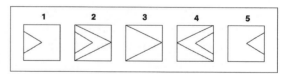

Imagine a series of shapes moving from left to right through a square window. Each object reveals an additional part of the shape whilst another part which has moved across the window disappears. Following this logic the next shape to appear in the window should either be blank or a tip emerging from the left – which is the only available option.

The answer is 1.

28.

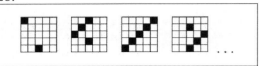 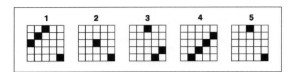

In this series a black square located at the bottom of the central column moves upward one place in the column each time. A diagonal moves across the square from the top left hand corner towards the bottom right hand corner. In the first object only a small part (a black square) from that diagonal can be seen. A larger part of that diagonal is revealed in the next object and so on. We can deduct that the black square in the central column will reach the top spot in the missing object and that the diagonal will reach the bottom right hand corner leaving only one visible black square at the bottom right hand corner.

The answer is 5.

29.

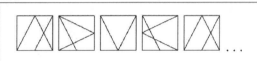 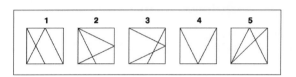

The series consists of squares each with a triangle and an additional line in it. The triangle points up in the first object and then moves between facets in clockwise direction. This means that in the missing object it should be pointing to the right. The additional line leans to the right in the first object and to the left in the following object and so on alternating between sides. In the missing object it should be pointing to the left.

The answer is 2.

30.

 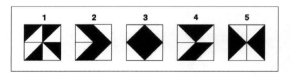

The series is made up of squares each divided into 4 smaller squares that have black triangles in them. Two triangles in two squares move between objects and the remaining two remain as is. Between the 1st and 2nd object the two top triangles move. In the transition between the 2nd and 3rd object the two triangles in the two squares on the left move and so on and so forth in counter clock wise direction. Between the 5th and missing object the triangles in the top squares should move.

The answer is 4.

Test 4 Diagrammatic Reasoning IQ

The Diagrammatic Reasoning IQ Test is one of the most important and most commonly used IQ tests. It assesses patterns of perception, logical thinking and cognitive ability. The test also assesses attention to detail, memory and spatial reasoning skills.

Since this is considered to be a classic IQ test, it is often administered to job applicants <u>regardless</u> of their field of expertise or profession.

Instructions

For each question, select the **<u>one</u>** answer that completes the matrix.

The level of difficulty increases gradually as the questions progress. If you think that there are two logical answers to a question, choose the simplest answer.

Wrong answers do not influence your results, so try to answer all of the questions.

Remember

You have 32 minutes to answer 34 questions.

Good luck!

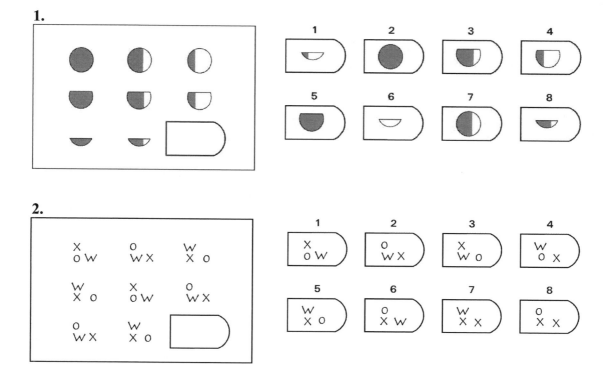

3.

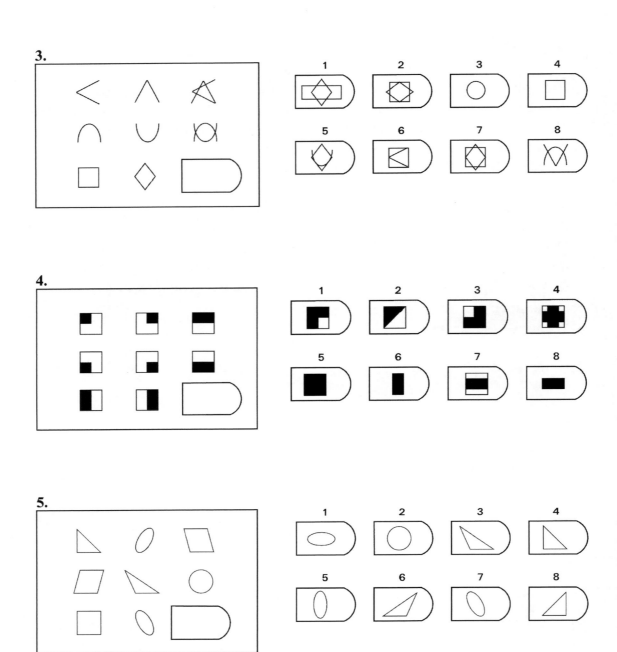

4.

5.

6.

7.

8.

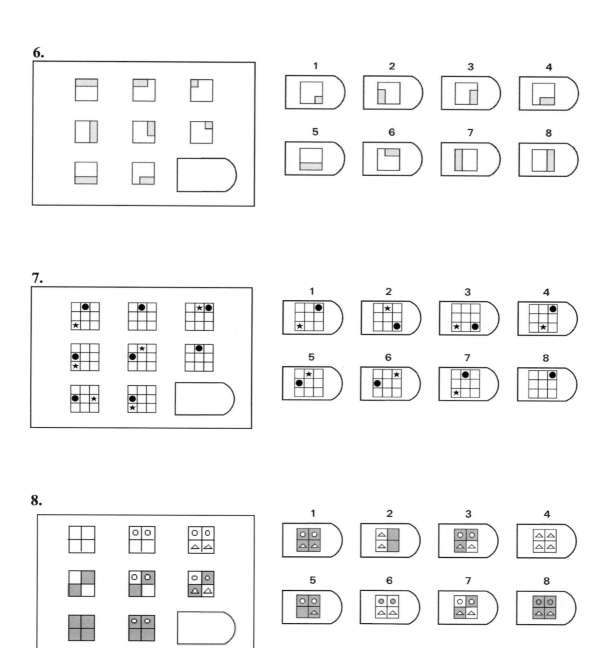

9.

10.

11.

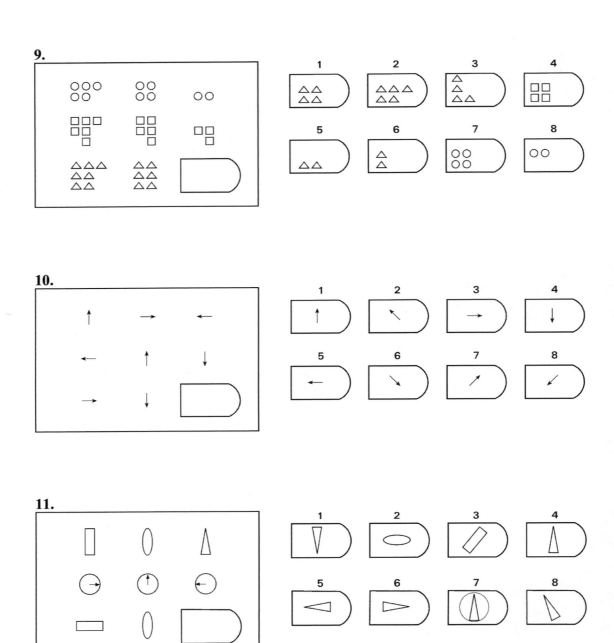

12.

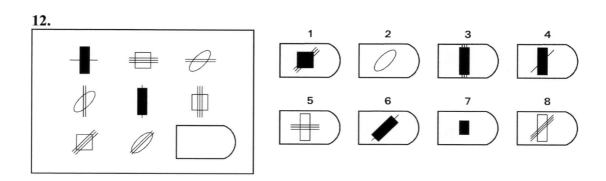

13.

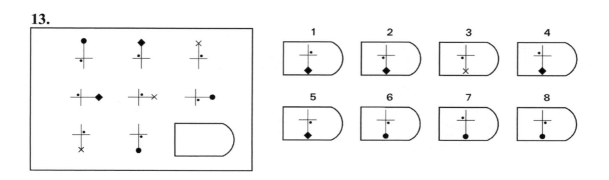

14.

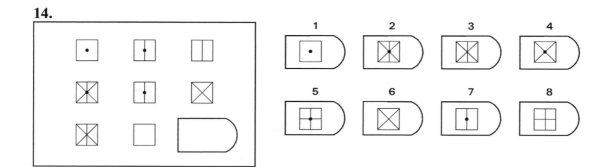

15.

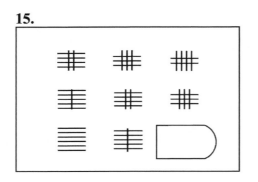

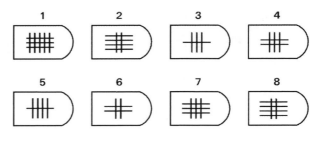

16.

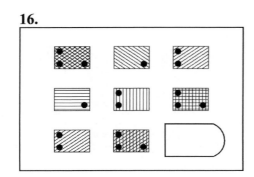

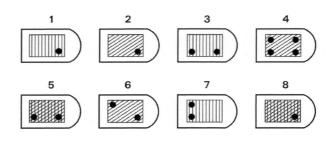

17.

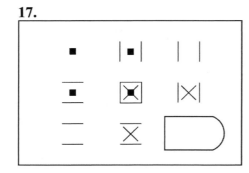

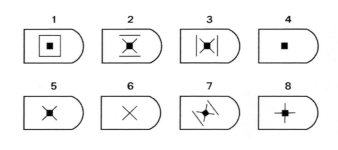

18.

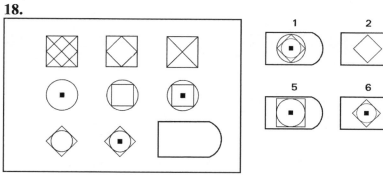

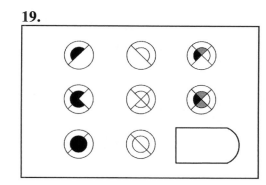

19.

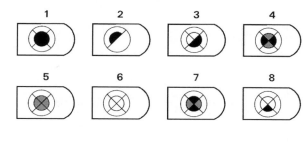

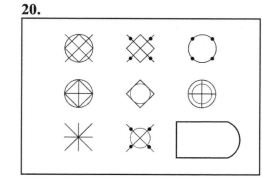

20.

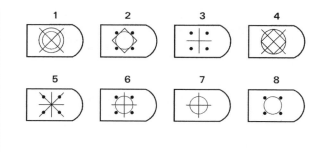

21.

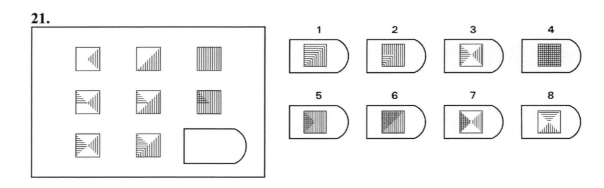

22.

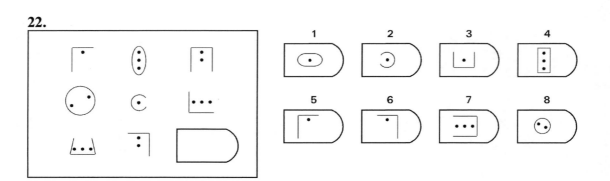

23.

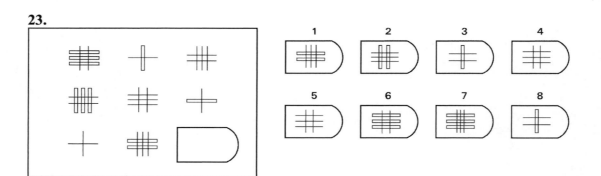

24.

25.

26.

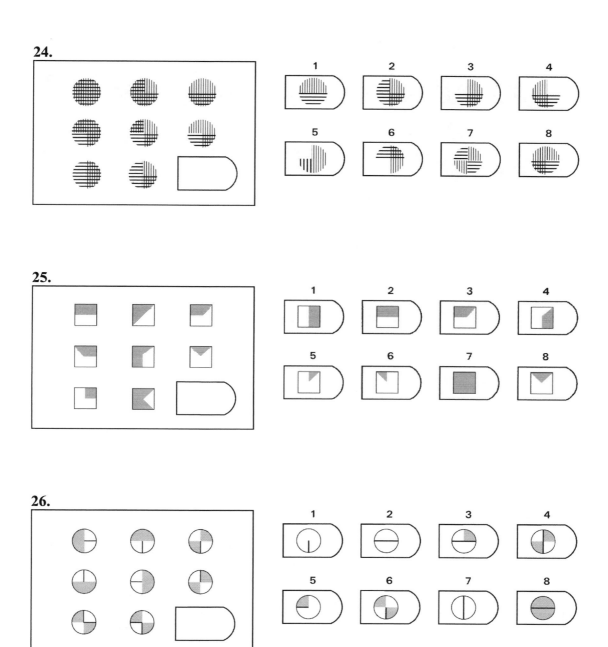

27.

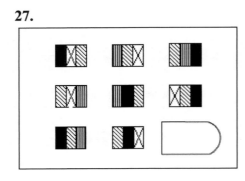

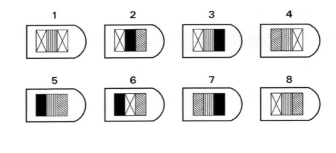

28.

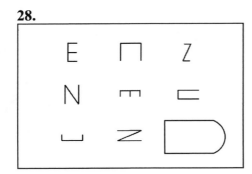

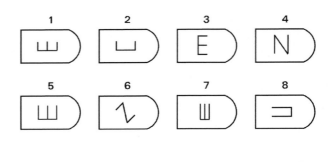

29.

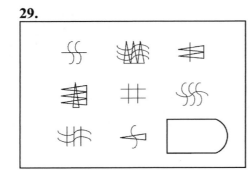

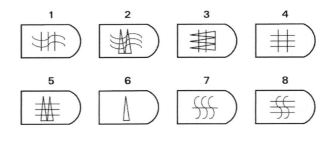

30.

31.

32.

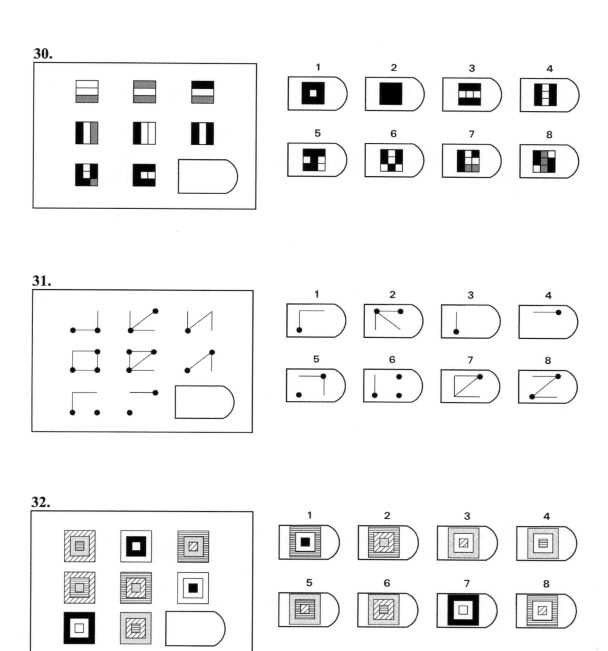

33.

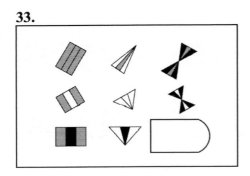

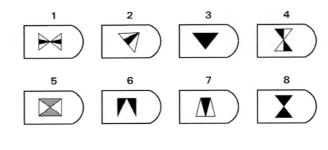

34.

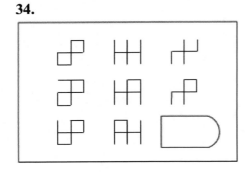

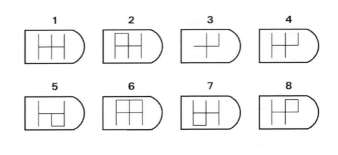

Test 4 General Tips:

- Always try to look for logical patterns horizontally, vertically and diagonally. There may be patterns in more than one direction, but finding one may be enough to solve the problem.
- Even if the correct choice stands out, make sure you scan all the response options. Even if the question seems very straightforward, there may be hidden pitfalls. There are sometimes tiny differences between the response options that can be easily overlooked.
- In many of the questions, the emerging pattern may be the union of two figures in a column or row, creating a third.
- In some questions, the emerging pattern may be the intersection of two figures in a column or row, creating a third.

Test 4 Answers:

1.

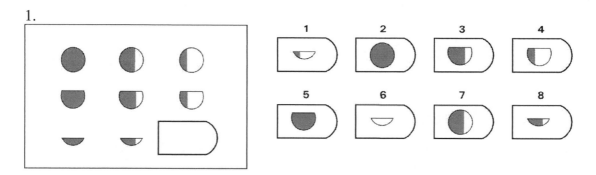

Each row contains a series of similar shapes that vary in their shaded patterns. The farther a shape is to the right, the less shaded it is. Therefore, the missing item should be similar in shape to the other two shapes in the same row, and similar in shading to the two shapes in the column above.

<u>The answer is 1</u>.

2.

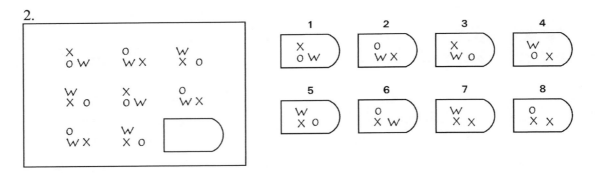

The letters in each row rotate clockwise and anti-clockwise in each column. In addition, the shapes in each diagonal line are constant.

The answer is 1.

3.

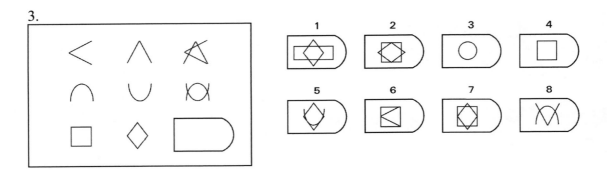

The figures at the right end of each row are a combination of the other two shapes. The missing figure should be a combination of the square and the diamond.

The answer is 7.

4.

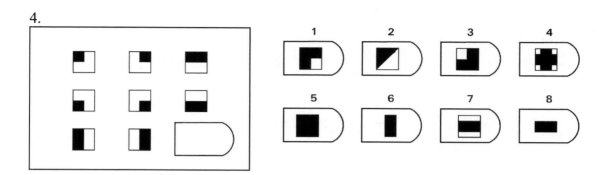

The figures at the right end of each row are a combination of the first and second figures

<u>The answer is 5.</u>

5.

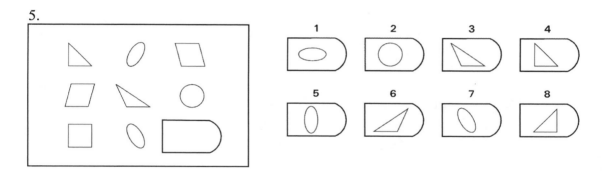

Each row consists of a triangle, a circle and a square. Each object appears once in a regular symmetrical position, once tilting to the right and once tilting to the left. The missing shape is a triangle, and since the other two triangles are in a regular symmetrical position and leaning to the left, the missing triangle should be leaning to the right.

<u>The answer is 6.</u>

6.

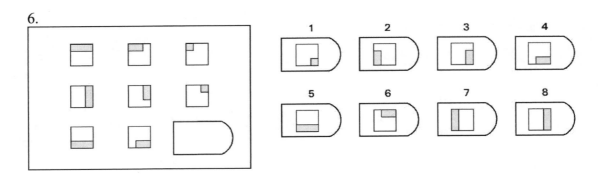

In order to solve this problem, we can look at the figures from either a horizontal or a vertical direction. From the horizontal direction, the shaded part of the square decreases as the figures move to the right. From the vertical direction, the shaded part of the figure moves 90 degrees clockwise as it progresses downwards.

The answer is 1.

7.

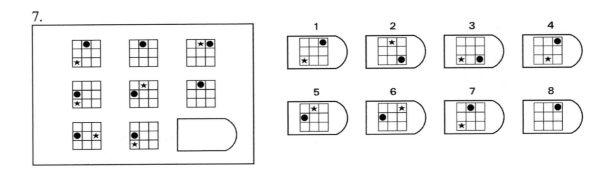

In the first and second figures from the left in each row, the black dot is in the same position. In the third figure, it moves clockwise. In the first row it moves one position, in the second row it moves two positions and in the third row it should move three positions to the top right-hand corner of the grid. The star in each row moves three positions clockwise between the first and second figure from the left, and then in the third figure, remains in the same position as in the second figure. So in the missing figure, the star should be in the bottom left hand corner.

Note: In some figures the star appears to be missing, but it is actually hiding behind the black dot.

The answer is 1.

8.

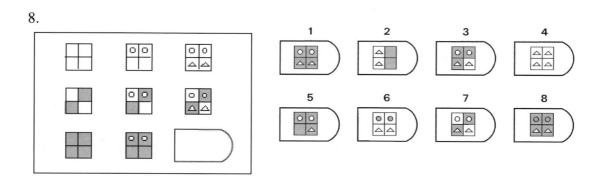

Each row has the same grid shade and each column includes the same number of elements (i.e., white circles and white triangles). The missing shape should be shaded completely grey and have white circles and triangles.

Note: Options 1 and 8 are very similar, but in option 8 the circles are also shaded. This makes it an incorrect option.

The answer is 1.

9.

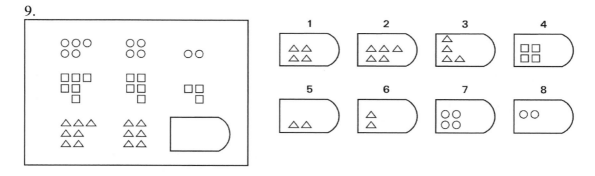

Each row has sets of a specific shape. The number of shapes in each set increases in each column starting from the top. For example, the top spot in the first column has five circles in it, the middle spot has six squares and the bottom spot has seven triangles.

Following this logic, the missing section should have four triangles. This means that only options 1 and 3 are possible. In order to determine the correct answer, we must now concentrate on the rows. In each row, the number of shapes decreases from left to right. In the second position, the right side of each set disappears and in the third position (far right) the top line disappears. So option 1, where the four triangles do not include the top row, has to be the right answer.

The answer is 1.

10.

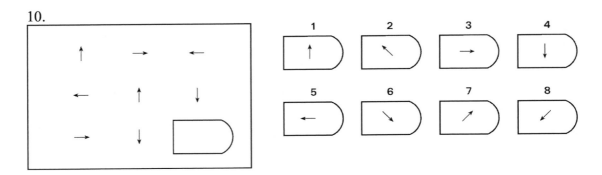

There are two ways to solve this problem. In each row, from left to right, the arrow moves 90 degrees clockwise between the first and second positions and 180 degrees clockwise between the second and third positions. This means that the missing arrow should point upwards, 180 degrees clockwise from the arrow in the middle position in the bottom row. Another and perhaps quicker way to solve this problem is by following the pattern that has the two arrows in the middle and right positions of each row always pointing in opposite directions. Here we can also conclude that the missing arrow in the bottom row should be pointing upwards.

The answer is 1.

11.

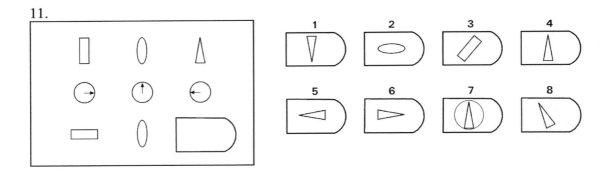

Each column has two similar figures in the top and bottom positions. Each column also has a figure in the middle, which is always a circle with an arrow pointing in a certain direction. We can conclude that the missing figure is a triangle. All of the figures in the top row are vertical. In the bottom row, each figure is pointing in the direction of the arrow located above it in each column. Therefore, the missing figure is a triangle and it should be pointing to the left

The answer is 5.

12.

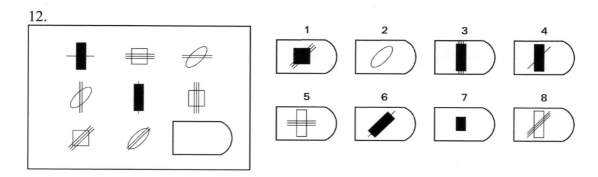

The grid above has three basic shapes – an ellipsoid, a square and a black rectangle. Each of the shapes appears three times, once in each row or column. We can therefore conclude that the missing shape is a black rectangle. Each shape has a constant number of lines crossing through it (rectangle – 1, ellipsoid – 2, square – 3). Therefore, we can also conclude that the missing rectangle will have only one line crossing through it. In each row, the lines are slanted in a certain direction. In the top row the lines are horizontal, in the middle row they're vertical and in the bottom row they're slanted diagonally. The missing shape should be a black rectangle, with a single diagonal line crossing through it.

The answer is 4.

13.

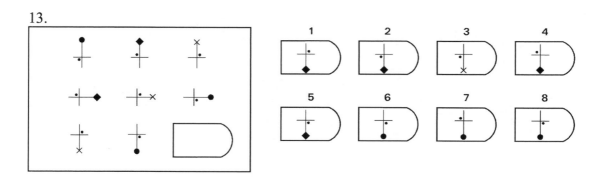

Each row has three figures: one with an X, one with a circle and one with a diamond. In the bottom row, the figure with the diamond is missing. In addition, all of the shapes in each row are pointing in the same direction. This means that the diamond in the missing figure should be located at the bottom of the figure. Finally, in each figure there is a dot. In each row, the dot moves clockwise. In the missing figure, the dot should be in the bottom left hand corner.

The answer is 2.

14.

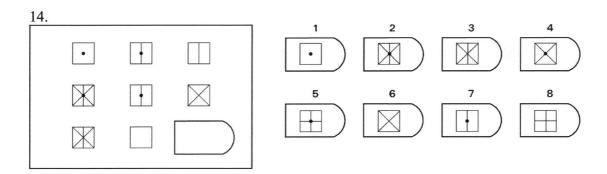

This problem can be solved by looking at either the rows or the columns, using the same logic. In the columns, each figure at the bottom is the union of the two figures above it, without all of the identical parts. For example, in the top left figure there is a dot in the centre. The figure below has also a dot in the centre, as well as three lines crossing it. Since both figures include a dot, the dot is eliminated from the bottom figure. In the second column, the top and centre figures are identical, so the bottom figure is blank. The figures in the third column have lines cutting across them, but in different directions. Therefore, the missing figure should be a simple union of the two figures.

The answer is 3.

15.

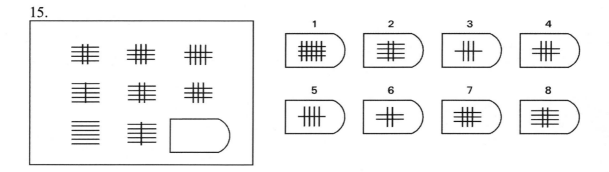

In this problem, we see vertical and horizontal lines. Looking from top to bottom, the rule is that a horizontal line is added and a vertical line is eliminated. Therefore, the missing figure should include four horizontal lines and two vertical lines.

The answer is 8.

16.

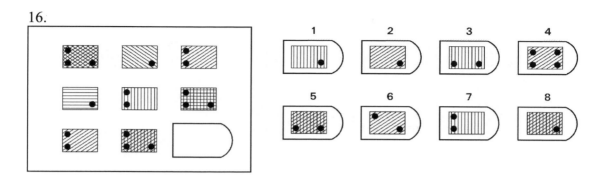

There are two ways to solve this problem:

1. Each row consists of three figures, and two of them unite to become the third. For example, in the first row, the middle figure and the figure on the far right combine to create the first figure. The first and second figures in the second row combine to create the third. Therefore, we can deduce that the first and the third (missing figure) will create the middle figure. Only option 1 combined with the bottom left figure can create the middle bottom figure.

2. Another way to solve this problem is to note that all of the figures in each row have both a different number of black circles and a different background pattern. This means that the missing figure in the bottom row should only have one black circle (options 1, 2 or 8). Since option 2 has the same background pattern as the first figure and option 8 has the same background pattern as the middle figure, option 1 is the only valid solution

<u>The answer is 1.</u>

17.

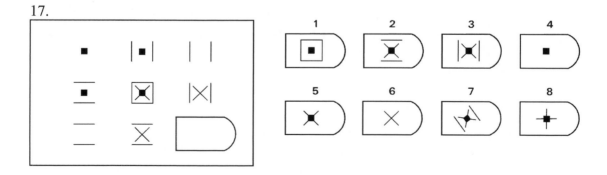

In each column, the top and bottom figures combine to create the middle figure. In the right column, the top figure has two parallel lines. The bottom (missing) figure should be an X, so that combined with the top figure they create the middle figure.

<u>The answer is 6.</u>

18.

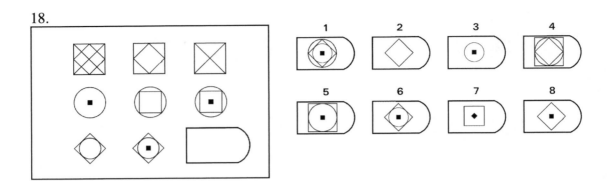

The first rule that stands out is that in each row, the outermost shapes in each figure remain constant: the square in the 1st row, the circle in the 2nd row and the diamond in the 3rd row. This means that the missing item should be a diamond, eliminating all options aside from 8, 6 and 2.

To determine the second rule, look at the rows. Notice that two shapes always combine to create the third. This means that the missing figure should have a black dot in the centre only, so that when combined with the figure on the left it creates the middle figure.

The answer is 8.

19.

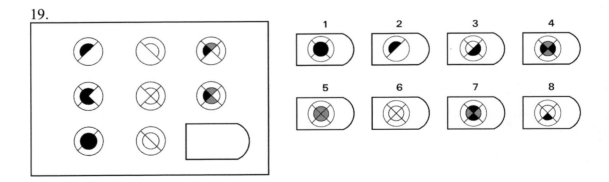

In each row, the left and middle figures combine to create the third. However, in areas where the black and white inner circles intersect, the colour of these common areas turns grey. So if we combine the two figures in the bottom row, the inner circles intersect. This results in a completely grey inner circle.

The answer is 5.

20.

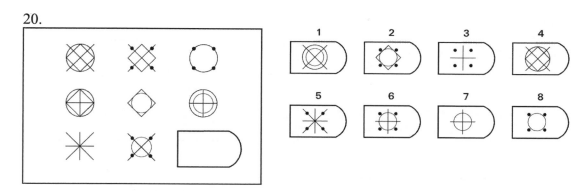

In each row, the figure on the left is a combination of the other two figures without the intersecting elements. For example, in the first row, the figure on the left combines the elements of the other two figures without the black dots. The black dots are eliminated because they are in both the figure in the middle and the figure on the right.

Using the same logic, the missing figure combined with the figure in the middle of the bottom row should produce the figure on the left. The X in the middle figure appears in the first figure, so we can assume that it isn't in the missing figure. However, the circle and the dots in the second figure are missing in the first figure, which means that they should be in the missing figure. The missing figure should include the circle, four dots and the plus sign that appears in the first figure (and not in the second).

<u>The answer is 6.</u>

21.

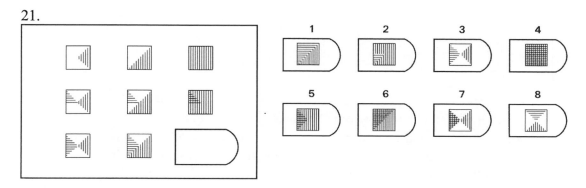

To solve this problem, we first have to determine the pattern in the grids: rows and columns. In each column, there is a consistent shape that repeats itself in all of the figures. There is a consistent shape in each row as well, except for the first. In the third column to the right, the filled-in lined square appears in each figure. This means that it should also appear in the missing figure. In the bottom row, the lined triangle pointing to the right appears in all of the figures. The missing figure should therefore be a combination of the two.

<u>The answer is 5.</u>

22.

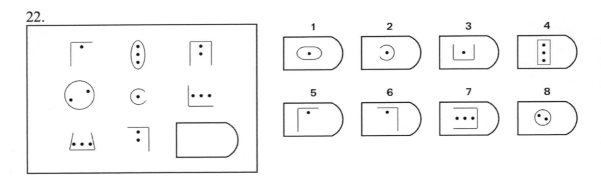

Each row consists of three figures, each with a different shape: an 'L' shape, a '∩' shape with three sides and a closed, rounded circle or ellipsoid. In addition, the figures in each row all have a different number of dots in them. One figure has one dot, another has two dots and the third has three dots. The bottom row is missing the closed, rounded figure, and it should have a single dot.

The answer is 1.

23.

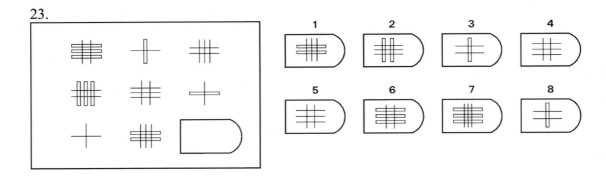

To determine the first rule, notice that in each row, one figure is made up of thin, vertical and horizontal lines and the other two figures are made up of a combination of thick and thin lines. In one figure the thick lines run horizontally and the thin lines run vertically, and in the other figure they alternate.

To determine the second rule, notice that in each row one figure is made up of a single horizontal and vertical line, while the two other figures include two vertical lines and three horizontal lines, and vice versa. In the bottom row, we see the figure which has only thin lines, and it consists of only two lines. Therefore, we know that the missing figure should be made up of a combination of thick and thin lines and that it should include three horizontal thin lines and two thick vertical lines (the opposite of the second figure).

The answer is 2.

24.

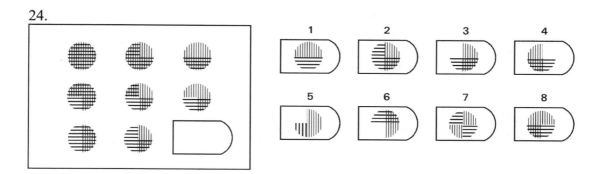

Notice that in the first (left) column, the figure at the top is made up of horizontal and vertical lines forming a complete circular grid. In the middle figure in the same column, the vertical lines are eliminated in the bottom left quarter. In the figure on the bottom left, the upper left quarter of vertical lines are eliminated. Exactly the same logic follows in the other two columns. If we concentrate on the column on the right, in the second figure the bottom left quarter of vertical lines are eliminated. This means that in the third and missing figure, the upper left quarter of vertical lines should be eliminated, creating a circle that is 3/4 filled.

The answer is 3.

25.

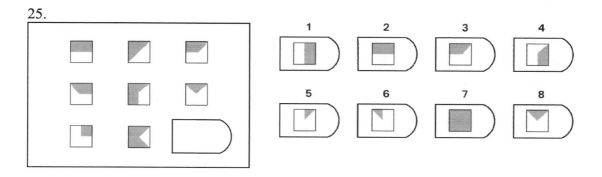

This problem only has one rule. In the rows, the shaded areas that the left and middle figures share combine to create the third figure. The only shaded area that the left and middle figures in the bottom row share is the one illustrated in option 5.

The answer is 5.

26.

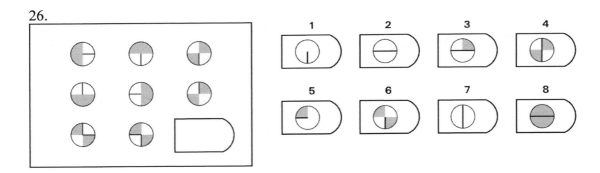

To solve this problem, look at the patterns in both the columns and the rows. Initially concentrate only on the shaded elements.

Rule 1:

In each row, the figure on the right is a combination of the other two shaded figures, without the intersecting elements. For example, the figure in the first row on the left has a shaded left hemisphere, whereas the second figure has a shaded upper hemisphere. The intersecting portion of the two figures is the top left quarter of the circle. So in the figure on the right, the top left quarter of the circle is not shaded. Looking at the bottom row, the shaded areas in both figures are identical. This means that these areas in the missing figure shouldn't be shaded at all (i.e., a white circle).

Rule 2:

Now concentrate on the black lines in each figure. In each column, the lines in the figure on the bottom are a combination of the lines in the other two figures. So in the column on the right, the two black lines in the figures, when combined, should create a straight line (diameter) from top to bottom.

The result of the two combinations (columns and rows) should create a white circle with a vertical line (diameter) across.

The answer is 7.

27.

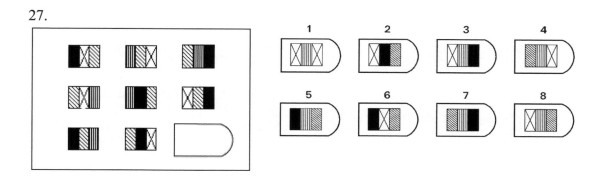

The figures in this grid are each made up of three rectangular parts. In each row, each rectangle appears in two figures (e.g., the black rectangle appears in the first and third figures in the first row). The exception is the rectangle with the diagonal lined pattern, which appears in each figure in a different position each time. This means that in the missing figure, the rectangle with the diagonal lined pattern should be on the right side of the figure. Because the black rectangle already appears in the other two figures, it shouldn't appear in the missing figure. The only option that includes a rectangle with a diagonal lined pattern on the right and that doesn't include a black rectangle is option 8.

The answer is 8.

28.

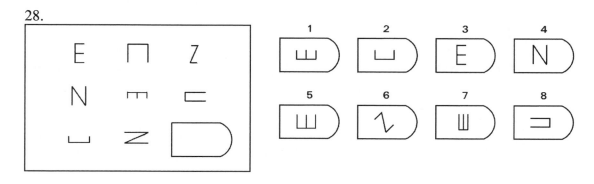

This grid has three types of shapes: E, Z, and ⊓.
Rule 1:
Each column has all three shapes. Therefore, the missing shape should be an E.
Rule 2:
Each figure appears once in its natural form, once as very narrow and once as wide. The E should therefore be narrow.
Rule 3:
Each figure faces a different direction each time: down, up or sideways (to the right). Therefore the missing shape should be facing up.

The answer is 7.

29.

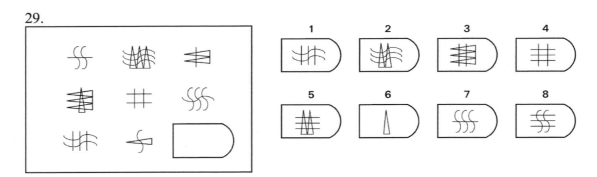

There are three types of shapes that make up the figures in the grid: (1) wavy lines, (2) straight lines and (3) cones. Rather than looking at a row or a column, observe the entire grid. Each of the shapes appears in a vertical or horizontal position either once, twice or three times. Yet each shape can only appear once in these formats. For example, two wavy lines (top left hand corner) in a vertical position will only appear once in the entire grid. Therefore, the missing figure should consist of two vertical cones and three horizontal straight lines. These do not appear in any of the other figures in the grid.

The answer is 5.

30.

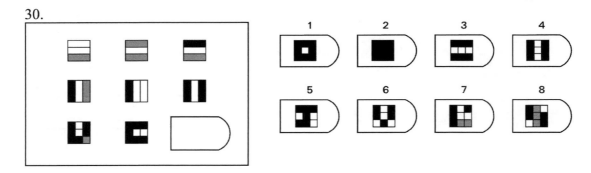

This problem can be solved by looking at either the rows or the columns. For example, in each row, the left and middle figures combine to create the figure on the right-hand side, according to the following rules:

Rule 1:

Any two identical elements located in the same positions in the left and middle figures will remain the same. For instance, in the first row, the grey lines at the bottom and the white lines in the centre of the first two figures are identical. They remain the same in the third figure.

Rule 2:

If the elements of the first two figures from the left are different, they will change to black in the third figure.

Based on these rules, the missing figure should be entirely black, apart from its white centre.

The answer is 1.

31.

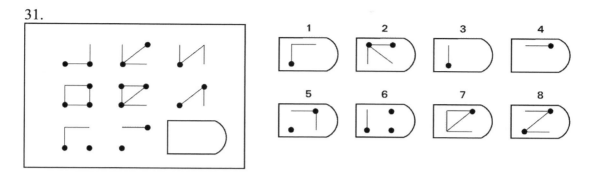

In each row, the dots that intersect in the first two figures from the left appear in the third figure, and those that don't intersect disappear. In addition, the lines that intersect in the first two figures from the left disappear in the third figure and those that don't intersect appear.

The only dot that intersects in the two bottom row figures is the one on the bottom left (the rest will disappear) and the only line that does not intersect is the vertical line on the left (the rest will disappear).

<u>The answer is 3.</u>

32.

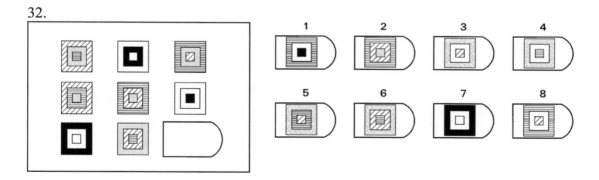

Each figure is made up of three squares.
Rule 1:
In each row, one figure has black and white squares.
Rule 2:
In each row, two figures have grey shaded squares that are the same size.
Rule 3:
In each row, two figures have horizontal and diagonal lined squares that alternate in size. There is a black and white figure in the bottom row, so this option can already be eliminated. The missing figure should have a large grey shaded square (like the second figure), a medium sized horizontal-lined square and a small diagonal-lined square.

<u>The answer is 5.</u>

33.

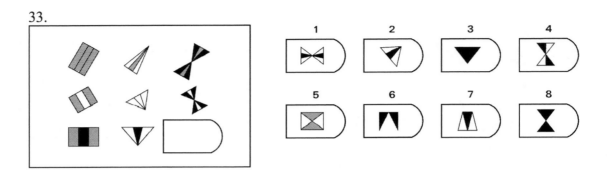

Rule 1:

Each column has a series of comparable figures.

Rule 2:

In each column, the top figure is tilted to the right, the middle figure is tilted to the left and the bottom figure is centred.

Rule 3:

The top two figures in each column combine to create the third. The sections that have the same patterns remain as is, while the sections that have different patterns turn black in the bottom figure. The missing figure should be entirely black.

The answer is 8.

34.

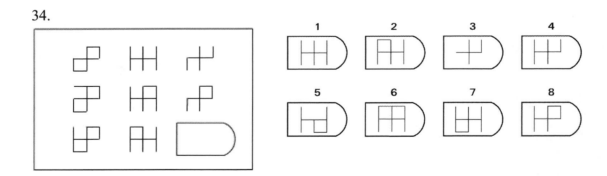

In each row, the figure on the right represents the lines the other two figures have in common. Option 4 represents the lines the two figures in the bottom row have in common.

The answer is 4.

Test 5 Diagrammatic Reasoning

This test assesses your ability to infer rules from a flow chart and apply them to a new situation. There are few versions of this test, and they differ slightly in graphic format. On some tests the rules are represented by numbers, and on others they are represented by icons or graphics. Diagrammatic reasoning tests are commonly used to assess IT and engineering professionals. This test requires high level analytical skills and the ability to work through complex problems.

Instructions
This test includes a number of diagrams. In each diagram, combinations of letters can be modified by different rules or commands. These commands are represented by numbers. Each number symbolises one rule, and it may appear more than once in a diagram. However, the meanings of the numbers may vary from one diagram to the next.

Your task is to follow the paths indicated by the arrows and determine the effect each command has on the letter combinations. Then apply the commands to the corresponding problem.

Example:

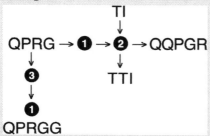

Options:

JLO → ❸ → ?

A. JLOO

B. JJLO

C. JJOL

D. LOO

Solution:
The aim is to understand rule ❸. To do so, first determine the rule for ❷ and ❶. First, look at the - **TI** → ❷ → **TTI** – section. Since **TI** becomes **TTI** when applying rule ❷, this means that rule ❷ says to double the first letter. Since **QPRG** becomes **QQPGR** when applying rules ❶ and ❷, and we know that rule ❷ says to double the first letter, we can conclude that rule ❶ says to swap the last two letters. **QPRG** becomes **QPRGG** when applying both rules ❸ and ❶. We already know that ❶ says to swap the last two letters. We can therefore conclude that ❸ says to double the last letter (rule ❶ doesn't change the result, because the last letter is doubled first and then swapped). Since rule ❸ says to double the last letter, **JLO** becomes **JLOO**.   The correct answer is A.

Remember
Work as quickly and as accurately as you possibly can.

The test consists of 12 problems, and you have 8 minutes to solve as many as you can.

Good Luck!

1.

JKLMN → ❶ → ❷ → KLMN
↓
STU → ❸ → ST
↓
❷
↓
JKML

1.1 RMTA → ❶ → ?
    A. RMT
    B. MTA
    C. RMAT
    D. MAT

1.3 RMTA → ? → RT
    A. ❸❷❶
    B. ❸❷❸
    C. ❸❸
    D. ❷❶❸

1.2 RMTA → ❷ → ❸ → ?
    A. RMA
    B. RMT
    C. MAT
    D. RTM

1.4 ? → ❸ → ❷ → BIN
    A. BNIG
    B. BING
    C. GBNI
    D. BNI

2.

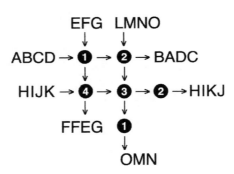

EFG LMNO
↓   ↓
ABCD → ❶ → ❷ → BADC
↓   ↓
HIJK → ❹ → ❸ → ❷ → HIKJ
↓   ↓
FFEG ❶
↓
OMN

2.1 HOME → ❷ → ?
    A. OHME
    B. HOEM
    C. OME
    D. HHOME

2.3 HOME → ? → OOHEM
    A. ❶❹❷
    B. ❹❶❷
    C. ❶❸❷
    D. ❶❷❸

2.2 HOME → ❶ → ❷ → ❸ → ?
    A. HOE
    B. OEM
    C. OHME
    D. HEM

2.4 ? → ❹ → ❸ → ❷ → HOME
    A. OHME
    B. OHEM
    C. HOEM
    D. HHOEM

3.

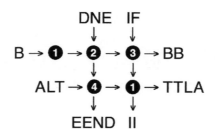

3.1 ERP → ❸ → ❷ → ?
  A. RPP
  B. RRP
  C. ERR
  D. EER

3.3 ? → ❷ → ❹ → ❷ → SSHIFTT
  A. TFIHS
  B. FIHSS
  C. TIFIH
  D. TFIHSS

3.2 SHIFT → ? → HIFT
  A. ❹❸❷
  B. ❹❸❹
  C. ❸❹❶
  D. ❹❶❹

3.4 REPE → ❷ → ? → ❸ → REP
  A. = ❶
  B. = ❷
  C. = ❸
  D. = ❹

Test 5 Answers

1.
1.1

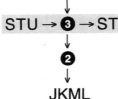   **Rule ❸** says to drop the last letter.

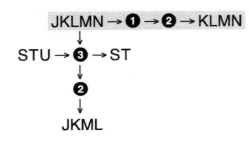   Since **Rule ❸** says to drop the last letter, **Rule ❷** must say to swap the last two letters

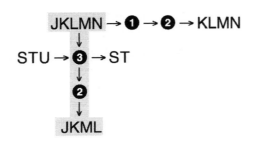   Since **Rule ❷** says to swap the last two letters, **Rule ❶** must say to drop the first letter.

<u>The answer is - RMTA →❶→ MTA (option B).</u>

1.2; 1.3; 1.4

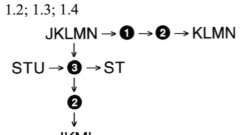   In problem 1.1 we have determined the following rules:
❶ - drop the first letter
❷ - swap the last two letters
❸ - drop the last letter
Using these rules, we can now solve problems 1.2, 1.3 and 1.4 because they're based on the same diagram.

1.2

$$\underline{\text{The answer is} - \text{RMTA} \rightarrow ❷ \rightarrow \text{RMAT} \rightarrow ❸ \rightarrow \text{RMA} \ \ (\text{option A}).}$$

1.3

$$\underline{\text{The answer is} - \text{RMTA} \rightarrow ❸ \rightarrow \text{RMT} \rightarrow ❷ \rightarrow \text{RTM} \rightarrow ❸ \rightarrow \text{RT} \ \ (\text{option B}).}$$

1.4

$? \rightarrow ❸ \rightarrow ❷ \rightarrow$ BIN

In this problem, we have to work our way backwards:

We know that **Rule ❷** says to swap the last two letters – BIN → BNI. Since we are working our way backwards, **Rule ❸** says to add a letter to the end rather than to drop a letter. Looking at the possible options, notice that options A, C, and D all include the letters BNI, in that order. However, only option A includes a combination of four letters with an additional letter at the end – BNIG (rather than at the beginning, as in option C). Therefore G is the only possible letter that can be added to the end.

$$\underline{\text{The answer is BNIG (option A).}}$$

2.

2.1

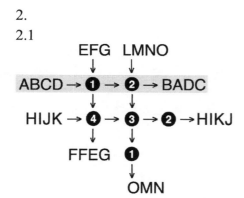

The transition from ABCD → BADC involves swapping letters twice. In one of the steps the first two letters are swapped, and in the other step the last two letters are swapped. We have to determine which step relates to which **Rule** (❶ and ❷).

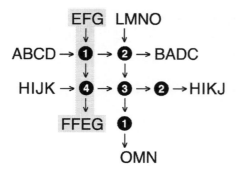

To make the transition from EFG → FFEG, we have to swap letters from EF-FE and then double the first letter. We already know that **Rule ❶** says to swap letters, but we don't know if it's the first two letters or the last two letters. We can now deduce that **Rule ❶** says to swap the first two letters. We also know now that **Rule ❹** says to double the first letter. Looking back to step 1, we can now deduce that **Rule ❷** says to swap the last two letters,

$$\underline{\text{The answer is} - \text{HOME} \rightarrow ❷ \rightarrow \text{HOEM} \ \ (\text{option B}).}$$

2.2

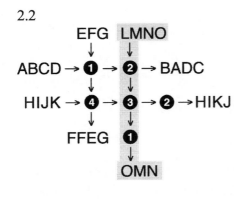

In question 2.1, we identified the following rules:

❶ - swap the first two letters

❷ - swap the last two letters

❹ - double the first letter

The transition from LMNO → OMN involves **Rules ❶, ❷** and **❸**. Since **❶** and **❷** say to swap letters, **❸** must say to drop a letter. Based on the diagram, we can deduce that **❸** says to drop the first letter.

The answer is - HOME → **❶** →OHME → **❷** → OHEM → **❸** → HEM (option D).

2.3

In questions 2.1 and 2.2 we identified the following **Rules**:

❶ - swap the first two letters

❷ - swap the last two letters

❸ - drop the first letter

❹ - double the first letter

Using these rules we can now solve problem 2.3, which is based on the same diagram.

The answer is - HOME→**❶**→OHME→**❹** →OOHME→ **❷** → OOHEM (option A).

2.4

? → **❹** → **❸** → **❷** → HOME

In this problem, we have to work our way backwards:

Rule **❷** says to swap the last two letters, so HOME → **❷** → HOEM.

We know that rules **❸** and **❹** say to drop the first letter and then double it, respectively. This means that the rules cancel each other out.

The answer is - HOEM (option C).

3
3.1

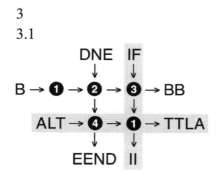

We can deduce that the transition from ALT → TTLA involves reversing the letter order and doubling the first letter. We can also deduce that the transition from IF → II involves doubling the first letter and dropping the last letter. Since both transitions involve **Rule ❶**, we can determine the following **Rules**:

❶ - double the first letter
❸ - drop the last letter
❹ - reverse the letter order

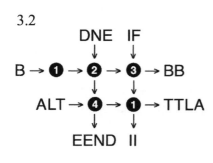

Since we know that the transition from DNE → EEND involves reversing the letter order (❹), we can conclude that rule ❷ says to double the last letter.

The answer is - ERP → ❸ → ER→ ❷ → ERR (option C).

3.2

DNE IF
  ↓   ↓
B → ❶ → ❷ → ❸ → BB
       ↓   ↓
ALT → ❹ → ❶ → TTLA
       ↓   ↓
EEND II

In question 3.1, we identified the following **Rules**:

❶ - double the first letter
❷ - double the last letter
❸ - drop the last letter
❹ - reverse the letter order

Using these rules, we can now solve problem 3.2.

The answer is - SHIFT → ❹ → TFIHS → ❸ → TFIH → ❹ → HIFT (option B).

3.3

? → ❷ → ❹ → ❷ → SSHIFTT

To solve this problem, we'll work our way backwards. Based on the previous problems, we know the function/result of each rule.

Since rule ❷ says to double the last letter, working our way backwards, the last letter is dropped (SSHIFTT → SSHIFT).

Since rule ❹ says to reverse the letter order, this works both ways (SSHIFT → TFIHSS)

Finally, rule ❷ says to double the last letter, so the last letter is dropped in reverse order (TFIHSS → TFIHS).

<u>The answer is - TFIHS (option A).</u>

3.4

REPE → ❷ → ? → ❸ → REP

In question 3.1 we identified the following rules:

❶ - double the first letter

❷ - double the last letter

❸ - drop the last letter

❹ - reverse the letter order

Using these rules, we can now solve problem 3.4.

We have to work our way through from both ends to solve the problem. First, rule ❷ says to double the last letter, so REPE → REPEE.

Starting from the end, ❸ says to drop the last letter, but in reverse this actually means a letter is added (it doesn't matter which one).

So we now know that: REPE → ❷ → REPEE → ? → REPE → ❸ → REP

The transition from REPEE to REPE involves dropping the last letter. We know that rule ❸ says just this.

<u>The answer is (option C).</u>

Test 6 Diagramming

This test assesses your ability to follow a logical sequence and a set of complex instructions. It also assesses your ability to handle multiple commands that may be dependent upon one another. These skills are required in most IT jobs. They are also sought after in fields that require an understanding of software development, such as programming and software engineering.

Instructions:

Each problem on this test includes 3-4 symbols in the left-hand column. Next to each symbol there is a command. The rule for each command is provided below. For each problem, work your way from top to bottom, changing the symbols as you go along. Then select an answer from the list of response options.

Command Key:

- ♫ replace symbol above
- ➲ rotate symbol 90 degrees clockwise
- ℭ rotate symbol 90 degrees anti-clockwise
- ⊙ reverse shade of symbol
- ⊗ omit symbol

Remember

Work as quickly and as accurately as you possibly can.

The test consists of 8 problems and you have 4 minutes to solve as many as you can.

Good Luck!

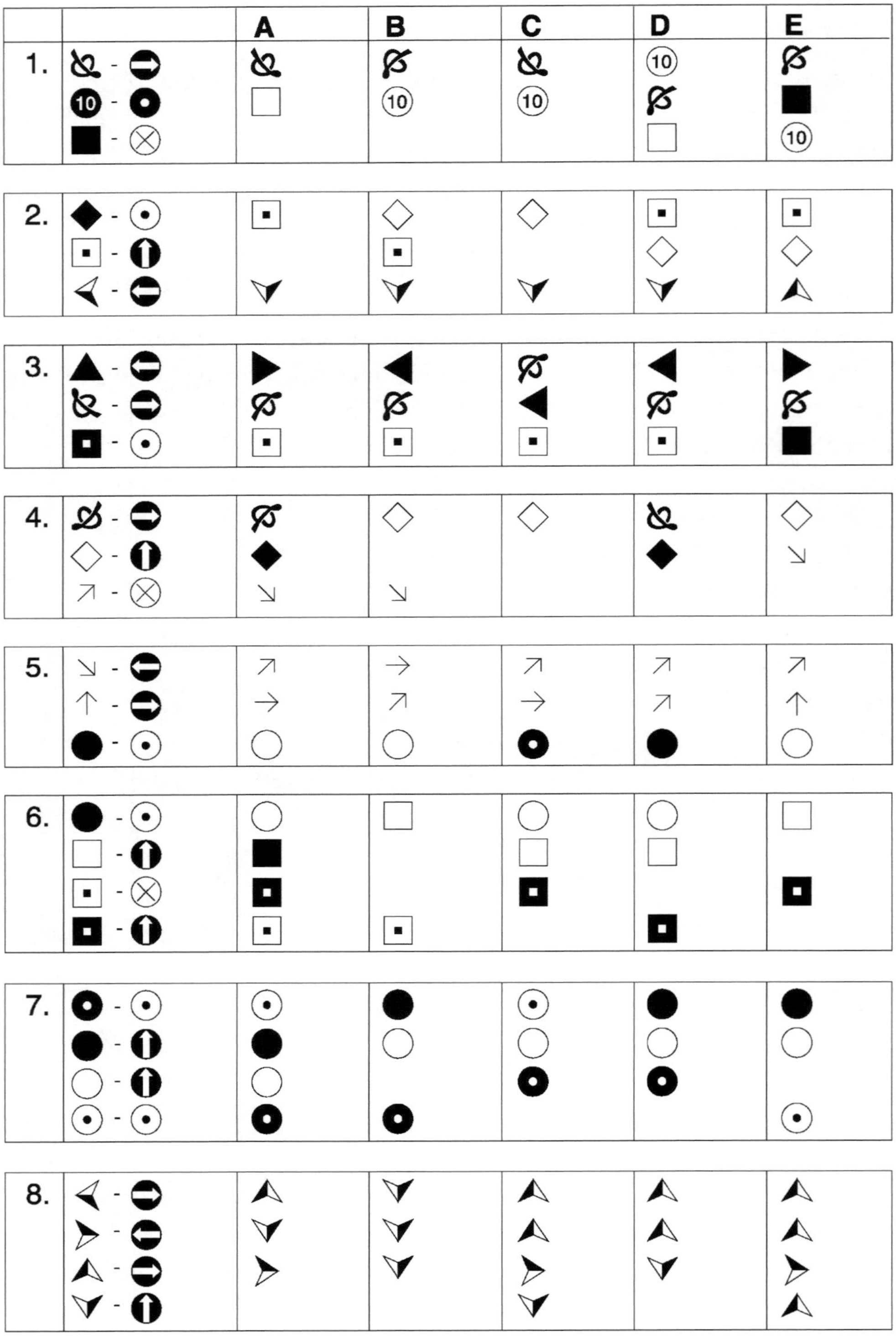
A
B
C
D
E
1.
10
2.
3.
4.
5.
6.
7.
8.

Test 6 General Tips:

- Search for the 𝝔 command (the command that replaces symbols). This way you won't waste precious time applying commands to a symbol that may be replaced further down.
- Omit (⊗) symbols only <u>after</u> you have replaced (𝝔) symbols first (see 'tip' above). **Note**: Do this only after you have identified the replacement symbol (𝝔), to avoid omitting a symbol that is replaced further down.
- Eliminate any inapplicable or incorrect options that stand out.

Command Key:
- 𝝔 replace symbol above
- ⮑ rotate symbol 90 degrees clockwise
- ⮐ rotate symbol 90 degrees anti-clockwise
- ⊙ reverse shade of symbol
- ⊗ omit symbol

Test 6 Answers:

		A	B	C	D	E
1.	☊ - ➲ ⑩ - ⊙ ■ - ⊗	☊ ☐	⌀ ⑩	☊ ⑩	⑩ ⌀	⌀ ■ ⑩

This question does not have the replacement command (𝝔), so the next step is to check for omission commands (⊗). The bottom symbol should be omitted. This means that options D and E can be eliminated immediately. The top symbol has to be rotated 90 degrees clockwise. Only the symbol in option B has been rotated, so there is no need to continue checking the remaining command.

<u>The answer is B.</u>

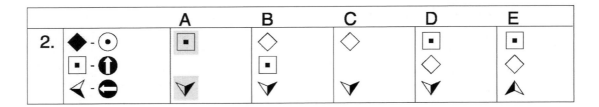

Notice the replacement command next to the middle symbol. This means that the top symbol is replaced and a blank spot should remain in the middle. Only options A and C have blank spots (eliminating options B, D and E). In addition, only in option A is the top symbol replaced by the middle symbol (■). Therefore, option A has to be the correct answer and there is no need to continue checking the remaining command.

The answer is A.

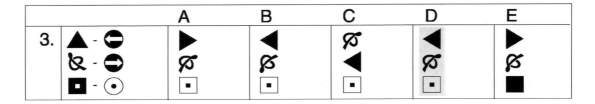

A quick scan shows that there are no replacement or omission commands. Therefore, we must work our way from top to bottom. The first command says to rotate the symbol 90 degrees anti-clockwise, so the triangle should be pointing to the left (eliminating options A, C and E). The second symbol in the middle is to be rotated 90 degrees clockwise. Of the remaining two options (B and D), the symbol only rotates in the correct direction in option D. For additional confirmation, a quick look at the bottom symbol confirms that it has reversed shading as required.

The answer is D.

		A	B	C	D	E
4.	⌀ - ➡ ◇ - ⬆ ↗ - ⊗	⌀ ◆ ↘	◇ ↘	◇ 	⅋ ◆ 	◇ ↘

A quick scan shows that there is both a replacement command and an omission command. This means that the white diamond in the centre replaces the top symbol, and the position in the middle remains blank. The omission command omits the ↗ symbol. We can determine at this stage that the only suitable option remaining is option C.

The answer is C.

		A	B	C	D	E
5.	↘ - ⬅ ↑ - ➡ ● - ⊙	↗ → ◯	→ ↗ ◯	↗ → ◉	↗ ↗ ●	↗ ↑ ◯

A quick scan shows that there are no replacement or omission commands, therefore we must work our way from top to bottom. This problem is slightly more difficult than the previous ones, since there are two similar symbols that are pointing in different directions. The top symbol is pointing southeast, and it should rotate anti-clockwise 90 degrees to the northeast. This only eliminates option B. The middle symbol is pointing north (up), and it should rotate 90 degrees clockwise so that it's pointing to the east (right). We can now eliminate options D and E. The bottom symbol has to be reverse-shaded from black to white, which leaves option A as the only possible correct answer.

The answer is A.

		A	B	C	D	E
6.	● - ⊙	○	□	○	○	▢
	□ - ⬆	■		□	□	
	▪ - ⊗	▪		◼		◼
	◼ - ⬆	▪	▪		◼	

This column contains four symbols and has two replacements commands, next to the second and fourth symbols. The second symbol (□) replaces the top symbol and the fourth symbol (◼) replaces the third symbol. This means that the second and fourth positions should be empty. A quick scan shows that the only option where the second and fourth positions are empty is option E. Therefore we can already determine that E must be the correct answer, and there is no need to proceed to the other commands.

The answer is E.

		A	B	C	D	E
7.	◉ - ⊙	⊙	●	⊙	●	●
	● - ⬆	●	◉	○	○	○
	○ - ⬆	○		◉	◉	
	⊙ - ⊙	◉	◉			⊙

This column includes two replacements commands, next to the second and third symbols. This means that the second symbol should replace the top symbol and the third symbol should replace the second symbol, leaving an empty spot in the third position. At this stage, options A, C and D can already be eliminated. The remaining command, next to the bottom symbol, is reverse-shaded (⊙ → ◉).

The answer is B.

		A	B	C	D	E
8.	◄ - ➡ ➤ - ⬅ ▲ - ➡ ▼ - ⬆	▲ ▼ ➤	▼ ▼ ▼	▲ ▲ ➤ ▼	▲ ▲ ▼	▲ ▲ ➤ ▲

This problem is slightly more difficult, because there are four similar shapes. There is one replacement command next to the bottom symbol, which replaces the third symbol from the top and leaves a blank space in the last position (eliminating options C and E). The first symbol at the top should rotate 90 degrees clockwise, pointing up. Only options A and D remain valid at this stage. The second symbol from the top rotates 90 degrees anti-clockwise, so it should point upwards as well. We can now eliminate option A.

<u>The answer is D.</u>

Test 7 Diagrammatic Thinking

This test assesses your ability to follow a logical sequence and apply consistent checks as you progress. It is mainly aimed at job applicants that are looking for technological positions, but some recruiters may use the test to evaluate anyone with a programming, engineering or technical background. There are a number of versions of the test on the market. We will provide you with practice of the most comprehensive version, so keep in mind that you may come across other similar tests that are simpler (e.g., that don't use development and comparison figures).

Instructions
Each problem on this test consists of a diagram, with two figures displayed on the left hand side: a **development** figure and a **comparison** figure. Your task is to follow the development figure from the beginning through the diagram, to change its characteristics as required by the circle-shaped **process** boxes and to follow the directions as required by the square-shaped **test** boxes. When you reach the end of the diagram identify the finished development figure from the complete list of figures provided, and indicate your answer.

Look at the two types of boxes below.

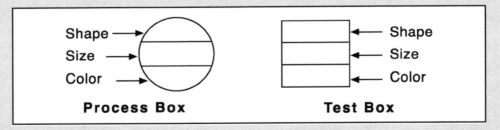

Every box in the diagram is divided into three layers. The top layer relates to the shape of the development figure (triangle or diamond), the middle layer relates to the size (large or small) and the bottom layer relates to the colour (red or green).
When you see a process box, you have to change the development figure according to the instructions in the box. Wherever a cross appears in a level, you have to change that particular aspect of the figure. For example, if there is a cross in the middle level, you have to change the size of the development figure. If there is no cross, then this particular aspect of the development figure remains unchanged.

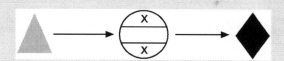

In this example, both the shape and the colour of the development figure
have been changed (indicated by an X). The colour has changed from grey to black and
the shape has changed from a triangle to a diamond. The size remains unchanged.

When you see a test box, you have to compare the development figure with the
comparison figure. If they match in all of the aspects that are indicated by a question
mark, then you should follow the direction provided by the letter "Y" for YES. If the
development figure differs from the comparison figure in any of the required aspects, as
indicated by question marks, you should follow the direction indicated by "N" for NO.

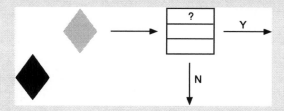

In this example, the shape of the development figure, indicated by the question mark in
the top layer of the square test box, is the same as the comparison figure. Therefore the
correct path to follow is the "Y" path.

Remember

Work as quickly and accurately as you can.

You have 5 minutes to complete the 8 problems on this test.

Good Luck!

1.

Which shape is at the end of the process in the following diagram?

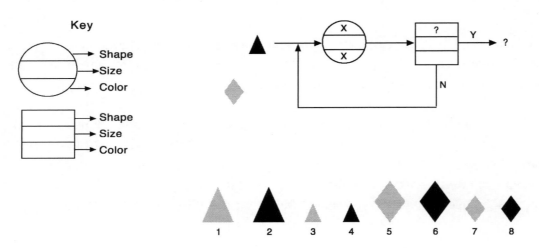

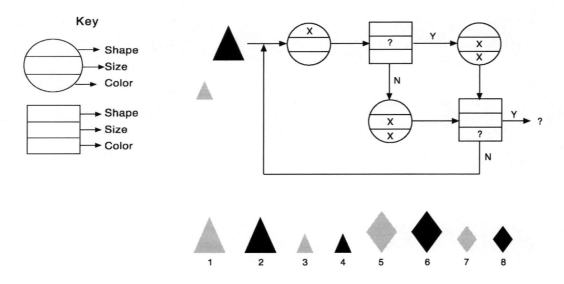

2.

Which shape is at the end of the process in the following diagram?

3.

Which shape is at the end of the process in the following diagram?

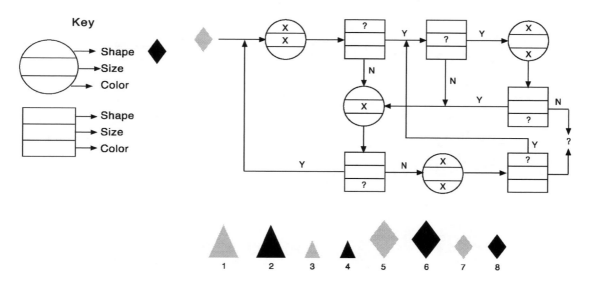

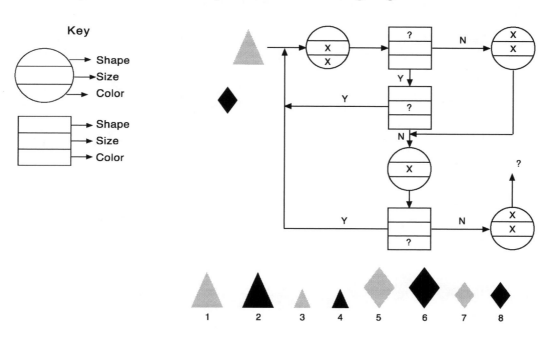

4.

Which shape is at the end of the process in the following diagram?

5.

Which shape is at the end of the process in the following diagram?

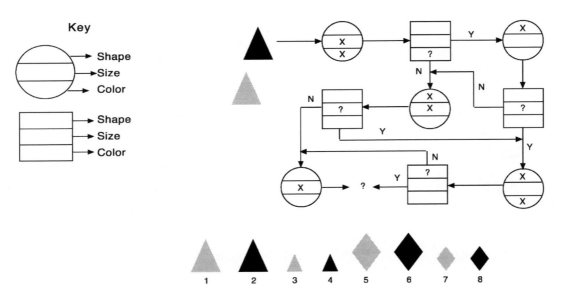

6.

Which shape is at the end of the process in the following diagram?

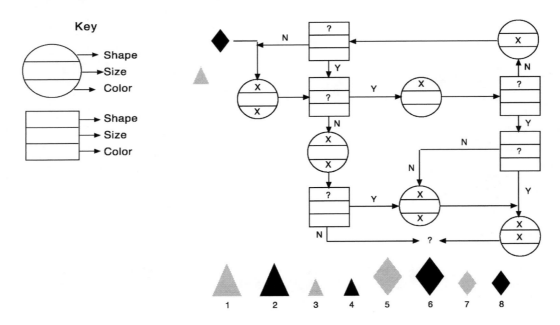

7.

Which shape is at the end of the process in the following diagram?

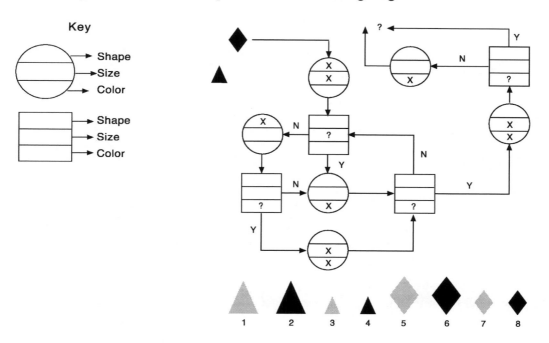

8.

Which shape is at the end of the process in the following diagram?

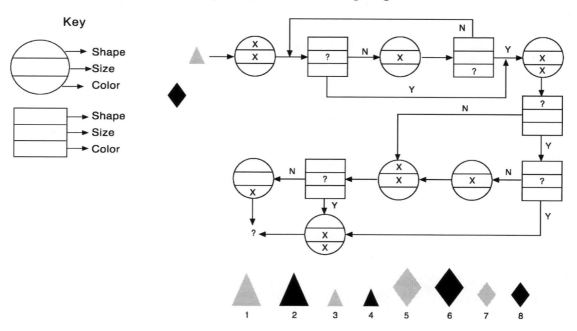

Test 7 Answers:

1.

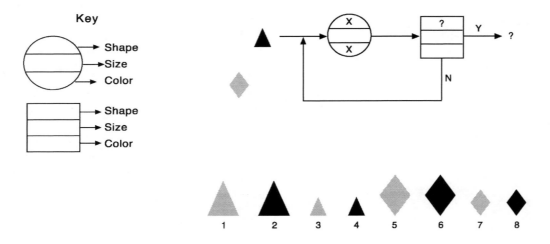

- The small black triangle (development figure) is supposed to go through the top part of the process box (circle), after which it will become a diamond.
- It also goes through the bottom part of the process box (circle), and changes colour from black to grey.
- This will result in a small, grey diamond that matches the shape of the comparison figure.
- Therefore we follow the 'Y' route to the end. The process ends with a small grey diamond (option number 7).

The answer is 7.

2.

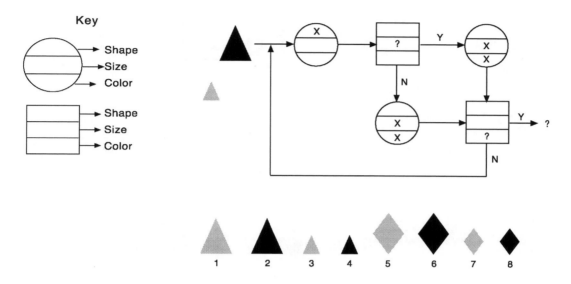

- The large black triangle goes through the top part of the process box, and changes into a large black diamond.
- In the test box, a question mark indicates that we must compare the size of the two figures. The size of the development figure differs from the comparison figure (large diamond vs. small triangle), therefore the process continues through the 'N' route.
- The large black diamond changes its size and colour by transforming into a small grey diamond which is the same colour as the comparison figure (comparison of colours is required in the next test box).
- Therefore we follow the 'Y' route to the end. The process ends with a small grey diamond (option number 7).

<u>The answer is 7.</u>

3.

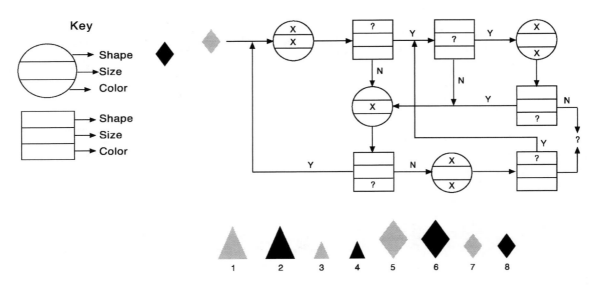

- The small grey diamond becomes a large grey triangle.
- The shape differs from that of the comparison figure (small black diamond), so we continue along the 'N' route and the size of the figure changes. We now have a small grey triangle.
- The colour of the triangle differs from that of the comparison figure, so we follow the 'N' route.
- The colour and shape of the figure changes, and we now have a small black diamond.
- The shape of the diamond is similar to that of the comparison figure, so we follow the 'Y' route to the next test box.
- The size of the diamond is similar to that of the comparison figure, so we follow the 'Y' route and the shape and colour of the figure changes. We now have a small grey triangle.
- The colour of the triangle differs from that of the comparison figure, so we follow the 'N' route to the finishing point. The process ends with a small grey triangle (option number 3).

The answer is 3.

4.

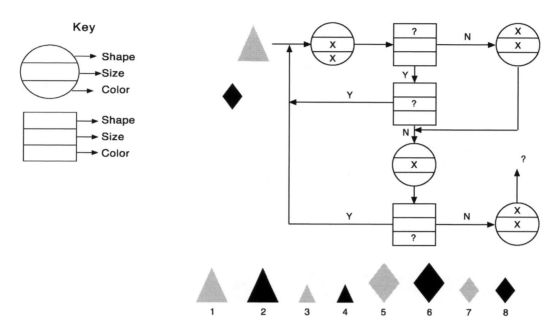

- In the first process box, the size and colour of the large grey triangle changes and the figure becomes a small black triangle.
- The following test box requires comparison of shapes. The shape of the triangle is different from that of the comparison figure (small black diamond), therefore we continue along the 'N' route.
- The shape and size of the figure change and the result is a large black diamond. We continue to the next process box, and the size changes once more. We now have a small black diamond.
- The colour of the diamond is similar to that of the comparison figure (black) so we continue along the 'Y' route to the first process box again. The size and colour of the figure changes, and we now have a large grey diamond.
- The shape of the diamond is similar to that of the comparison figure, so we follow the 'Y' route.
- The size of the diamond is different from that of the comparison figure, so we follow the 'N' route and the size of the diamond changes to small.
- The colour of the diamond is different from that of the comparison figure, so we follow the 'N' route and the shape and size changes. We now have a large grey triangle. The process ends with a large grey triangle. (option number 1).

The answer is 1.

5.

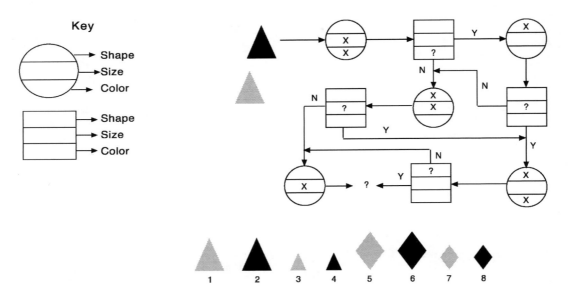

- The large black triangle changes size and colour in the first process box, and becomes a small grey triangle.
- The test box tells us to compare colours. The colour of the triangle is similar to that of the comparison figure (grey), so we follow the 'Y' route and the shape of the triangle changes. We now have a small grey diamond.
- The size of the diamond is different from that of the comparison figure, so we follow the 'N' route and the shape and size change, as required in the next process box. We now have a large grey triangle.
- The size of the triangle is similar to that of the comparison figure, so we follow the 'Y' route and the shape and colour changes. We now have a large black diamond.
- The shape of the diamond is different from that of the comparison figure, so we continue along the 'N' route and the size changes. We now have a small black diamond. The process ends with a small black diamond. (option number 8).

The answer is 8.

6.

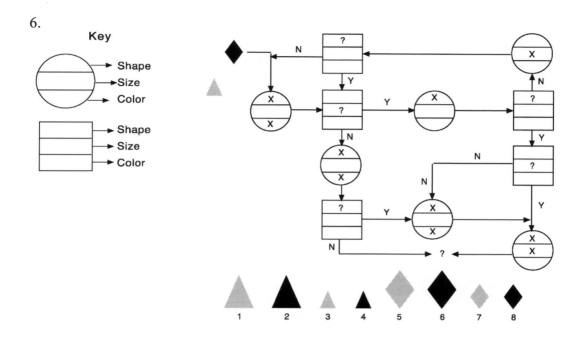

- The small black diamond changes shape and colour in the first process box, becoming a small grey triangle.
- The test box tells us to compare the size of the figures. The size of the triangle is similar to that of the comparison figure (small) so we continue along the 'Y' route.
- The shape of the triangle changes, and we now have a small grey diamond. The shape is different from that of the comparison figure, so we follow the 'N' route and the size changes. We now have a large grey diamond.
- The shape of the diamond is different from that of the comparison figure, so we follow the 'N' route and change the shape and colour. We now have a large black triangle.
- The size of the triangle is different from that of the comparison figure, so we follow the 'N' route and change the shape and colour. Once again we have a large grey diamond.
- The shape of the diamond is different from that of the comparison figure, so we follow the 'N' route to the end. The process ends with a large grey diamond (option number 5).

The answer is 5.

7.

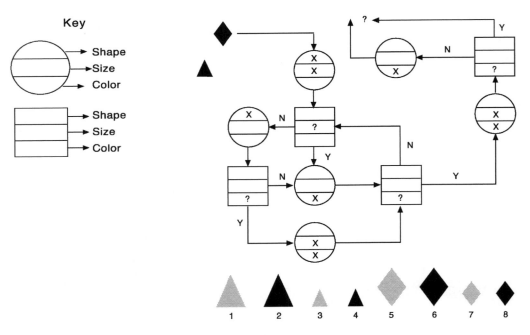

- The small black diamond changes shape and size in the first process box, and we have a large black triangle.
- We are asked to compare the size of the comparison and development figures in the next test box, and in fact they are different.
- We follow the 'N' route and change the shape so that we now have a large black diamond.
- The colour of the diamond is similar to that of the comparison figure, so we follow the 'Y' route.
- We change the size and colour so that we now have a small grey diamond. We continue to the next test box. The colour of the diamond is different from that of the comparison figure, so we follow the 'N' route.
- The size is similar to that of the comparison figure (next test box), so we follow the 'Y' route.
- The colour changes, and we now have a small black diamond.
- The colour of the diamond is similar to that of the comparison figure, so we follow the 'Y' route and the size and colour change. We now have a large grey diamond.
- The colour of the diamond is different from that of the comparison figure, so we follow the 'N' route and the colour changes (last process box). We now have a large black diamond. The process ends with a large black diamond (option number 6).

The answer is 6.

8.

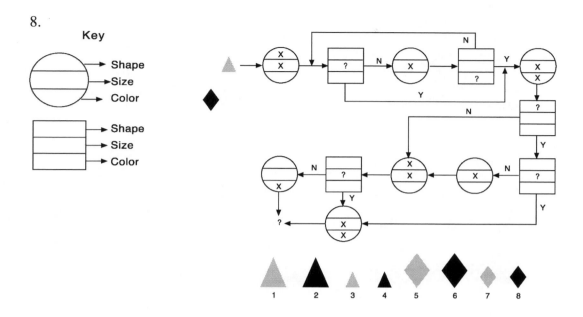

- The small grey triangle changes shape and size in the first process box, becoming a large grey diamond.
- In the first test box, we are asked to compare the size with that of the comparison figure (small black diamond). The sizes of the figures are different, so we follow the 'N' route.
- The size changes, and we now have a small grey diamond.
- In the next test box, we are asked to compare colours. The development figure has a different colour from that of the comparison figure, so we follow the 'N' route.
- The development figure is similar in size to the comparison figure, so we follow the 'Y' route.
- The next process box changes the size and colour of the development figure, so that we now have a large black diamond.
- It is similar in shape to the comparison figure, so we follow the 'Y' route.
- The development figure (large black diamond) is different in size from the comparison figure, so we follow the 'N' route.
- The next process box changes the size of the figure, so that we now have a small black diamond.
- The next process box changes the shape and size of the diamond, so that we now have a large black triangle.
- The triangle is different in size from the comparison figure, so we take the 'N' route. The colour of the triangle changes in the last process box, and we now have a large grey triangle. The process ends with a large grey triangle (option number 1).

The answer is 1.

2

NUMERICAL TESTS

Numerical tests are the largest category of aptitude tests. The use of numbers in various forms, from basic arithmetic to complex mathematical models, is needed in almost every position. Bankers, accountants and computer programmers are expected to have advanced level numerical skills, managers that are responsible for budgets have to be comfortable reading profit and loss spreadsheets, and shopkeepers should be comfortable doing basic arithmetic.

Different positions require different mathematical skills, hence the considerable variation in test types and levels of difficulty. However, keep in mind that for most positions you're likely to be given at least one or two numerical tests.

The use of calculators is permitted in some cases, but as a general rule these tests aim to assess your ability to reach a solution quickly and effectively. Therefore, even questions that may seem complex at face value should have a relatively simple solution that doesn't require a calculator or any other aid. If you're confident with basic arithmetic, using proportions, percentages and rough estimates, you should do well. When you have trouble finding the solution to the problem at a first glance, look at the possible answers provided. You may be able to get to the correct answer by eliminating options.

Candidates generally fear numerical tests, and this fear is not entirely justified. Remember that numerical abilities can be improved dramatically, just like verbal abilities, if you do enough practice. If it's been a while since you've used your numerical skills, then now is the time to shape up and practice.

Important:
Numerical tests are often a source of concern for job applicants. But with proper preparation, as this book provides, you're very likely to find the real tests rather easy. Common sense, a few tricks and some practice will improve your performance.

Test 8 Numerical Estimation

An estimation test examines your ability to quickly and accurately provide numerical estimates. This test may be administered for managerial, administrative and clerical positions. When approaching the questions, you are expected to figure out the correct answer without doing an exact calculation. This test has a tight time frame, and you probably won't be able to complete it within the given time limit. Try to answer as many questions as possible.

Instructions:
Please select one correct answer for each question.
You are required to estimate the correct answer without using a calculator and select the option that is closest to the correct answer.
Remember
You have 2 minutes to complete the test.
Work as fast as you can!

Good Luck!

		A.	B.	C.	D.
1.	16 x 19 ≈	330	570	690	198
2.	6.5 x 2.1 ≈	1.6	69	13.5	7.9
3.	6,524 - 3,891 ≈	3,200	4,700	2,717	1,900
4.	13 x 7.6 ≈	93.4	120	85.3	71
5.	194.6 ÷ 6 ≈	81	22	32.4	107
6.	0.6 x 9.1 ≈	9.7	3.91	4.7	5.5

		A.	B.	C.	D.
7.	71.4 + 109.3 ≈	161.4	190	181	250
8.	16.7 - 5.96 ≈	8.1	10.2	7.9	12
9.	8,946 ÷ 279 ≈	32	61	6.7	4.5
10.	How much is 8% of 116?	3.9	61	9.28	11.2

Test 8 General Tips:

- In general, when estimating, it's wise to 'round off' numbers. When there's a decimal, always try to round up or down to the nearest round number.

Example 1:   The number 28.8 should be rounded up to 29 or 30.

- When solving estimation problems, try to eliminate impossible answers. So besides concentrating on the question, always have a look at the options. You may be able to eliminate a few of them.

Example 2:   29.7 ÷ 2.9 =
If we round up the numbers, 30÷3 = 10. The correct solution should be slightly higher than 10. This means that any option that's smaller or significantly higher than 10 can be ruled out.

- When solving multiplication problems, try to see if the options are multiples of the numbers in question.

Example 3:   372 x 5 =
The correct answer has to end with a 5 or a 0, since these are both multiples of 5.

Test 8 Answers:

		A.	B.	C.	D.
1.	16 x 19 ≈	330	570	690	198

The number 19 can be rounded up to 20. 16x2 = 32. This means that 16x20 = 320. The closest number is 330.

The correct answer is A.

		A.	B.	C.	D.
2.	6.5 x 2.1 ≈	1.6	69	13.5	7.9

The number 6.5 can be rounded up to 7, and 2.1 can be rounded down to 2, therefore 7x2 = 14. The closest number is 13.5.

The correct answer is C.

		A.	B.	C.	D.
3.	6,524 - 3,891 ≈	3,200	4,700	2,717	1,900

The number 6,524 can be rounded down to 6,500, and 3,891 can be rounded up to 4,000. 6,500-4,000 = 2,500. The closest number to 2,500 is 2,717.

The correct answer is C.

		A.	B.	C.	D.
4.	13 x 7.6 ≈	93.4	120	85.3	71

The number 7.6 can be rounded up to 8, and 13x8 = 104. The number 104 is closest to 93.4 (option A), but it is also relatively close to 120 (option B). However, since we rounded 7.6 <u>up</u> to 8, we know that the real solution (13x7.6) is <u>smaller</u> than 104. Therefore, we can answer confidently that 93.4 is closest to the correct answer.

The correct answer is A.

		A.	B.	C.	D.
5.	194.6 ÷ 6 ≈	81	22	32.4	107

The number 194.6 can be rounded up to 200, and 200÷6 = 33. The number 32.4 is, by far, the closest number.

The correct answer is C.

	A.	B.	C.	D.
6. 0.6 x 9.1 ≈	9.7	3.91	4.7	5.5

The number 9.1 can be rounded down to 9. The four options are relatively close, therefore we need to be particularly careful. First round 9.1 down to 9, and calculate that 0.6x9 = 5.4. We can also reach this answer by calculating that 6x9 = 54 and adding a decimal point to reach 5.4. If we were to round 0.6 down to 0.5, then 0.5x9 = 4.5 and we would have selected the wrong option (C – 4.7). Always look at all the options first, and if they are relatively close then be extra careful when rounding up or down.

<u>The correct answer is D.</u>

	A.	B.	C.	D.
7. 71.4 + 109.3 ≈	161.4	190	181	250

The number 71.4 can be rounded down to 70, and the number 109.3 can be rounded up to 110. Then calculate that 70+110 = 180. The number 180 is closest to 181.

<u>The correct answer is C.</u>

	A.	B.	C.	D.
8. 16.7 - 5.96 ≈	8.1	10.2	7.9	12

The options in this question are relatively close to one another, so we have to be careful when rounding them. The number 16.7 should be rounded down to 16.5, and the number 5.96 should be rounded up to 6. Then calculate that 16.5-6 = 10.5. The number 10.5 is closest to 10.2.

<u>The correct answer is B.</u>

	A.	B.	C.	D.
9. 8,946 ÷ 279 ≈	32	61	6.7	4.5

8,946 is a large number and can be rounded up to 9,000. The number 279 can be rounded up to 300. Then calculate that 9,000÷300 = 30. The closest number to 30 is 32.

<u>The correct answer is A.</u>

	A.	B.	C.	D.
10. How much is 8% of 116?	3.9	61	9.28	11.2

We know that 10% of 116 is 11.6. This already indicates that the two feasible options are C (9.28) and D (11.2). However, since the question asks how much is 8% rather than 10%, the solution has to be the lower option.

<u>The correct answer is C.</u>

Test 9 Numerical Reasoning

This test is the first in a series of mathematical problem solving tests. A number of other numerical and critical reasoning tests exist that are at the same level or higher. This test is usually administered for technical, computer and managerial positions.

Instructions
On this test, there are five possible answers for each question.
- Choose **one** answer for each question.
You may use a pen and paper for calculations.
Remember
You have 4 minutes to complete the test.

Good Luck!

1. A normal visit to a specialist physician costs $68. Private health insurance that covers specialist treatment costs $350 per annum. How many visits to a specialist physician will justify buying private health insurance?
    A. 5   D. 8
    B. 6   E. 9
    C. 7   F. 10

2. It takes 8,000 medium size oranges to make 500 litres of orange juice. How many oranges does it take to make 1,279 litres of orange juice?
    A. 79.9   D. 12,509.6
    B. 3,127.4   E. 18,947
    C. 6,254.8   F. 20,464

3. There are 756,000 boxes in the warehouse. Next month, a new shipment will arrive and the quantity will increase to 847,000 boxes. By what percentage will the new shipment increase the quantity of stock?
    A. 5.44%   D. 12.03%
    B. 6.71%   E. 89.25%
    C. 8.92%

4. A registered mechanic has done 255 engine overhaul treatments that took him a total of 1,912.5 hours to complete. He's applied for a new contract that requires 17 overhaul treatments. How many hours should the work take him?

A. 2.6

B. 7.5

C. 127.5

D. 181

E. 227.5

5. A high quality 100ml perfume is made of a mixture of 12ml perfume essence and 88ml water. What is the ratio of perfume to water?

A. 1:7

B. 3:22

C. 1:8

D. 3:12

E. 1:9

6.

Vegetable Produce Per Annum			
Vegetable	2002	2003	2004
Eggplant	8.2 tonnes	8.5 tonnes	8.3 tonnes
Potato	16.7 tonnes	16.8 tonnes	16.7 tonnes
Onion	4.7 tonnes	4.9 tonnes	4.7 tonnes
Sweet Potato	3.7 tonnes	3.9 tonnes	4.5 tonnes

How many times did the vegetable produce experience growth between the years 2002 to 2004 (inclusive)?

A. 3

B. 4

C. 5

D. 6

E. 7

7. Each branch on a banana tree has an average of 31kg of fruit. Every branch has seven bunches of bananas, each with six bananas. What's the average weight of a single banana?

A. 53gr

B. 627kg

C. 738gr

D. 821kg

E. 1,250gr

8. A tray of 18 boxes with 200 grams worth of instant coffee packets makes 6,000 cups of coffee. How many 200 gram boxes are required to make 4,000 cups?

A. 15

B. 12

C. 10

D. 150

E. 120

Test 9 Answers:

1. $68x5 (visits) = $340, which is still less than the $350 that the health insurance costs. Therefore, from the 6th visit onward the insurance is worthwhile.

    The answer is B.

2. There are two ways of solving this problem.
    The first is by doing the actual calculation:
    8,000 (oranges) ÷ 500 (litres of juice) = 16 oranges per litre
    1,279 (litres) × 16 = 20,464.
    The second is using estimation, which may be quicker:
    1,279 litres is roughly 2.5 times the initial amount of 500 litres. Therefore, the amount of oranges required to produce 1.279 litres is 2.5 times the initial number of oranges = 8,000x2.5 = 20,000.

    The answer is F.

3. There are two ways of solving this problem.
    The first is by doing the actual calculation:
    (847,000x100) ÷ 756,000 = 112.03.
    112.03-100 = 12.03.
    The new stock has increased by 12.03%. (Keep in mind that you can't use a calculator!)
    The second, and recommended way of solving this problem is by using estimation and eliminating options.
    The number of boxes has increased by approximately 100,000 - from 756,000 to 847,000. And 10% of 756,000 is 75,600. To do this calculation, all you have to do is divide by a 100 or drop a zero. We can therefore conclude that the increase in stock is slightly bigger than 10% (100,000>75,600). The only options that are higher than 10% are options D and E, but option E is considerably higher (89.25%). Therefore, option D is the only possibility.

    The answer is D.

4. We can solve this problem by doing the actual calculation:
    $1{,}912.5 \div 255 = 7.5$ (hrs per treatment). $7.5 \times 17 = 127.5$
    And we can also estimate and eliminate:
    The number 1,912.5 can be rounded up to 2,000, and 255 can be rounded down to 250. We can then calculate that $2000 \div 250 = 8$. It takes roughly 8 hours to do a single overhaul treatment, and $8 \times 17 = 136$.
    The only option that is close is option C – 127.5.

    The answer is C.

5. The ratio of perfume essence to water is 12:88. We can make the ratio smaller by dividing them both by 4 so that it is presented 3:22. Another possibility is to scan the answering options and determine which option is equivalent to 12:88.

    The answer is B.

6. Count the number of times the market has grown from one year to the next. The eggplant market grew once between 2002-2003, the potato market grew once between 2002-2003, the onion market grew once between 2002-2003 and finally the sweet potato market grew twice: between 2002-2003 and between 2003-2004. In total, the vegetable produce has experienced growth 5 times.

    The answer is C.

7. Each branch contains 42 bananas ($6 \times 7 = 42$). So a single banana weighs
    $31 \div 42 = 0.738$ kg $= 738$ grams.
    We can avoid doing the calculation by eliminating. It's clear that $31 \div 42$ is less than one, and so a single banana weighs less than 1kg $= 1{,}000$ grams. The only options that are less than 1,000 grams (1kg) are A and C. Option A is too small (53 grams) and therefore, the only available option is C (738 gram). Note that some of the answers options are given in grams and others in kilograms.

    The answer is C.

8. The number 4,000 is 2/3 of 6,000. If 18 boxes are required to produce 6,000 cups of coffee, then 2/3 of this amount are required to produce 4,000 cups. $18 \times 2/3 = 12$.

    The answer is B.

Test 10 Numerical Critical Reasoning

Numerical critical reasoning tests assess an applicant's ability to evaluate and interpret numerical data. You will be asked to use and manipulate data provided in graphs, charts and tables in order to answer the questions that follow.

In most cases, each data set (e.g., graph, table) is followed by 4-5 questions. Some tests have only one data set, and all subsequent questions (approximately ten) pertain to this set.

These tests are usually administered to candidates applying for managerial, supervisory, sales and professional positions.

In some cases, you will be permitted to use a calculator. You will always be provided with pen and paper for calculations.

Instructions

On this test, you'll find graphs and tables containing data. You will be asked to answer questions related to each data set.

Remember

The test consists of 20 questions and has a time limit of 25 minutes.

Each question has only one correct answer.

Please make sure you have a calculator, a pen and some paper.

Work as quickly and as accurately as you can.

Good Luck!

1.

Job Prospects for University Graduates				
	1990		2000	
Type of University	Unemployed	Employed	Unemployed	Employed
Private	155	1,475	125	1,350
State	125	1,610	150	1,250

1.1 How many more people were employed in 1990 compared with 2000?

    A. 75   D. 100

    B. 360   E. 135

    C. 485

1.2 What proportion of the unemployed graduates for 2000 studied in private universities?

    A. 0.45   D. 0.17

    B. 0.54   E. 0.30

    C. 0.20

1.3 What percentage of students was unemployed in1990?

    A. 10.5   D. 8.3

    B. 0.8   E. 9.6

    C. 7.8

1.4 Which group of graduates had the highest unemployment rate?

    A. 1990, private, unemployed   D. 2000, state, unemployed

    B. 1990, state, unemployed   E. Cannot Say

    C. 2000, private, unemployed

1.5 What was the difference between the highest and lowest unemployment rate amongst the group of graduates?

    A. 10.5%   D. 4.2%

    B. 7.8%   E. 3.5%

    C. 9.3%

2.

Internet Service Providers (ISP) Satisfactory Survey					
Overall*	ISP 1	ISP 2	ISP 3	ISP 4	ISP 5
50 and below	256	226	89	25	112
50-65	398	387	586	892	254
65-85	1,056	854	687	452	785
85 and above	458	470	75	124	389

* Score (1-100)

2.1   Which ISP scored 50 and below the least number of times?
  A.   ISP1   D.   ISP4
  B.   ISP2   E.   ISP5
  C.   ISP3

2.2   How many scores of 65-85 did ISP1 and ISP3 receive between them?
  A.   1,743   D.   687
  B.   2,597   E.   1,056
  C.   369

2.3   What proportion of scores were 50 and below for ISP5?
  A.   13.75%   D.   20%
  B.   11.2%   E.   7.2%
  C.   9.8%

2.4   Which ISP had the lowest percentage of 85 and above scores?
  A.   ISP1   D.   ISP4
  B.   ISP2   E.   ISP5
  C.   ISP3

2.5   Which ISP reached the highest overall score with regard to customer satisfaction?
  A.   ISP1   D.   ISP4
  B.   ISP2   E.   ISP5
  C.   ISP3

3.

Food Preference Survey (percentages			
Food	Gender		
	Males	Females	Males & Females
Steak	25	8	18
Salad	6	25	13
Ice cream	15	16	15
Chocolate	12	19	16
Hamburger	18	4	12
Soup	8	10	9
Pasta	10	11	10
Cheese	6	7	7

3.1   If 12,000 people participated in this survey, how many of them liked soup?
- A.   960
- B.   1,080
- C.   1,200
- D.   1,360
- E.   1,420

3.2   Which food do males and females prefer the most distinctively?
- A.   Salad
- B.   Hamburger
- C.   Steak
- D.   Cheese
- E.   Chocolate

3.3   What percentage of survey participants indicated food other than soup and cheese as their favourite?
- A.   83%
- B.   84%
- C.   86%
- D.   87%
- E.   Cannot Say

3.4   Of the options below, which food item do men most commonly eat?
- A.   Chocolate
- B.   Hamburger
- C.   Ice Cream
- D.   Steak
- E.   Cannot Say

3.5   If the sample consists of 12,000 males and females, and we can assume that the number of females who prefer pasta is 649, then how many males participated in the survey?
- A.   2,400
- B.   1,200
- C.   5,900
- D.   6,100
- E.   Cannot Say

4.

	Currency Exchange Rates						
	Brazilian Real	Canadian Dollar	Euro	British Pound	Japanese Yen	Swiss Franc	U.S. Dollar
USD ($)	2.28	1.14	0.83	0.56	118.5	1.29	--------
Euro (€)	2.74	1.37	------	0.6	142.4	1.55	1.20
Yen (¥)	0.019	0.009	0.007	0.005	--------	0.011	0.008

4.1 Estimate the value of 1,000 British pounds to a Euro.

A. 6€   D. 66€
B. 60€   E. 660€
C. 600€

4.2 Using the USD exchange rate as the convertible currency, seven Swiss Francs are worth how many Brazilian Real?

A. 5.43 Real   D. 12.38 Real
B. 1.29 Real   E. None of the above
C. 15.96 Real

4.3 How many Brazilian Real can you buy for 5,000 Canadian Dollars, using the USD exchange rate?

A. 11,400   D. 5,000
B. 1,500   E. 2,500
C. 10,000

4.4 What is the value of 500 British pounds in Brazilian Real, using the Yen exchange rate?

A. 1,900   D. 1,000,000
B. 19,000   E. None of the above
C. 100,000

4.5 A rumour about an upcoming recession in Japan has reduced the value of the Yen 7% compared with the Euro. How many Euros can you now buy for 500 Yen?

A. 3.5   D. 3.76
B. 3.26   E. None of the above
C. 3.15

Test 10 Answers:

1.
1.1
How many more people were employed in 1990 compared with 2000?
- The number of employed in 2000 = Private + State = 1,250+1,350 = 2,600.
- The number of employed in 1990 = Private + State = 1,475+1,610 = 3,085
  The difference in the number of employed in 1990 and 2000 = 3,085-2,600 = 485.

The answer is C.

1.2
What proportion of the unemployed graduates for 2000 studied in private universities?
- The total number of unemployed graduates in 2000 = 125+150 = 275.
  The proportion of unemployed who studied in private universities = 125/275 = 0.45.

The answer is A.

1.3
What percentage of students was unemployed in1990?
- The total number of students in 1990 = 155+125+1,475+1,610 = 3,365.
- The total number of unemployed in 1990 = 155+125 = 280.
- The percentage of students unemployed in 1990 = (280÷3,365) x100 = 8.3%.

The answer is D.

1.4
Which group of graduates had the highest unemployment rate?
- The unemployment rate for each category is measured by calculating the proportion of unemployed students from the total number of students in each category.
- The greater the proportion, the higher the unemployment rate.
- The proportion of unemployed students from state universities in 2000 is the highest = 150/1,400 = 0.107 = 10.7%.

The answer is D.

1.5

What was the difference between the highest and lowest unemployment rate amongst the group of graduates?

- The unemployment rate for each group of graduates = (number of unemployed ÷ total number of students)x100 =
- Unemployment rate 1990 for private university graduates = $(155 \div (155+1,475)) \times 100 = 9.5\%$.
- Unemployment rate 1990 for state university graduates = $(125 \div (125+1,610)) \times 100 = 7.2\%$.
- Unemployment rate 2000 for private university graduates = $(125 \div (125+1,350)) \times 100 = 8.5\%$.
- Unemployment rate 2000 for state university graduates = $(150 \div (150+1250)) \times 100 = 10.7\%$
- The difference between the highest unemployment rate (2000 state university) and the lowest unemployment rate (1990 state university) = 10.7-7.2 = 3.5%

The answer is E.

2.

2.1

Which ISP scored 50 and below the least number of times?

ISP4 received only 25 scores of 50 and below, which is the lowest in comparison to all of the other ISP's.

The answer is D.

2.2

How many scores of 65-85 did ISP1 and ISP3 receive between them?

- ISP1 received 1,056 scores of 65-85 and ISP3 received 687 scores of 65-85.
- Between them they received = 1,056+687 = 1,743.

The answer is A.

2.3

What proportion of scores were 50 and below for ISP5?

The proportion of scores that were 50 and below for ISP5 =

(The number of scores that were 50 and below for ISP5 ÷ total number of scores for ISP5) x100 = (112÷1,540) x100 = 7.2%.

The answer is E.

2.4

Which ISP had the lowest percentage of 85 and above scores?

- First we have to calculate the percentage of 85 and above scores for each category: (The number of scores that were 85 and above for each ISP ÷ total number of scores for each ISP) x100.
- ISP1: (458÷2,168) x100 = 21.1%
- ISP2: (470÷1,937) x100 = 24.3%
- ISP3: (75÷1,437) x100 = 5.2%
- ISP4: (124÷1,493) x100 = 8.3%
- ISP5: (389÷1,540) x100 = 25.3%

ISP3 had the lowest percentage of 85 and above scores with 5.2%.

The answer is C.

2.5

Which ISP reached the highest overall score with regard to customer satisfaction?

- In order to determine which ISP received the highest overall score, we have to calculate the percentage for each score category and then calculate the average score.
- Since each category has a range of scores, for the sake of simplicity we will give each category a number. We'll assign the lowest category, 50 and below, the number 1, and we'll assign the highest category, 85 and above, the number 4. The higher the number, the better the score.

Category	Score
50 and below	1
50-65	2
65-85	3
85 and above	4

- Average score per ISP = ((number of '1' scores x score) + (number of '2' scores x score) + (number of '3' scores x score) + (number of '4' scores x score)) / total number of scores
- Average score ISP1 = ((256x1) + (398x2) + (1,056x3) + (458x4)) /2,168 = 2.7.
- Average score ISP2 = ((226x1) + (387x2) + (854x3) + (470x4)) /1,937 = 2.81.
- Average score ISP3 = ((89x1) + (586x2) + (687x3) + (75x4)) /1,437 = 2.52.
- Average score ISP4 = ((25x1) + (892x2) + (452x3) + (124x4)) /1,493 = 2.45.
- Average score ISP5 = ((112x1) + (254x2) + (785x3) + (389x4)) /1,540 = 2.94.

ISP5 has the highest overall score of 2.94

The answer is E.

3.

3.1

If 12,000 people participated in this survey, how many of them liked soup?

9% of the survey respondents (male and female) liked soup. Out of 12,000 people this is (12,000×0.09) = 1,080 people.

The answer is B.

3.2

Which food do males and females prefer the most distinctively?

- Calculate the differences between genders for the categories that stand out.
- Salad is 19% (25-6), steak is 17% (25-8) and hamburger is 14% (18-4).
- The correct answer is salad at 19%.

The answer is A.

3.3

What percentage of survey participants indicated food other than soup and cheese as their favourite?

- For males and females together, soup has 9% and cheese has 7% = 16% of participants say cheese and soup are their favourite foods.
- 100% of survey participants minus 16% who preferred soup and cheese = 84% that preferred other foods.

The answer is B.

3.4

Of the options below, which food item do men most commonly eat?

The information is about food preference, not about frequency of consumption (e.g., We know that males prefer steaks but we don't know how often they actually eat them). The correct answer is *cannot say*.

The answer is E.

3.5

If the sample consists of 12,000 males and females, and we can assume that the number of females who prefer pasta is 649, then how many males participated in the survey?

- The number of females who prefer pasta is 649, making up 11% of females. This means that the number of females participating in the sample = (100x649)÷11 = 5,900 females.
- 12,000-5,900 = 6,100 males participated in the survey.

The answer is D.

4.

4.1

Estimate the value of 1,000 British pounds to a Euro.

One British pound is worth 0.6 Euro. Therefore, 1,000 British Pounds x 0.6 = 600 Euros.

The answer is C.

4.2

Using the USD exchange rate as the convertible currency, seven Swiss Francs are worth how many Brazilian Real?

- One USD is worth 1.29 Swiss Francs, therefore 7 Swiss Francs are worth 5.43 USD (7÷1.29).
- One USD is worth 2.28 Real. Therefore, 5.43 USD (which are worth 7 Swiss Francs) = 5.43 USDx2.28 Real = 12.38 Real

The answer is D.

4.3

How many Brazilian Real can you buy for 5,000 Canadian Dollars, using the USD exchange rate?

- 5,000 (Canadian Dollars) ÷1.14 (USD: CAD exchange rate) = 4,386 USD
- 4,386 (USD) x2.28 (USD: BRL exchange rate) = 10,000 Brazilian Real

The answer is C.

4.4

What is the value of 500 British pounds in Brazilian Real, using the Yen exchange rate?

- 500 (British pounds) ÷0.005 (JPY: GBP exchange rate) = 100,000 Yen.
- 100,000 (Yen) x0.019 (JPY: BRL exchange rate) = 1,900 Brazilian Real.

The answer is A.

4.5

A rumour about an upcoming recession in Japan has reduced the value of the Yen 7% compared with the Euro. How many Euros can you now buy for 500 Yen?

- 500 Japanese Yen before the reduction were worth = 500x0.007 = 3.5 Euro.
- After a reduction of 7%: (100%-7% = 93% = 0.93) they are now worth 3.5x0.93 = 3.26 Euro

The answer is B.

Test 11 Advanced Numerical Critical Reasoning

Advanced numerical critical reasoning tests (also known as numerical evaluation tests or interpreting numerical data tests) assess a candidate's ability to evaluate and interpret numerical data. They are similar to numerical critical reasoning tests, except that they're on a higher level. You will be asked to use and manipulate data provided in graphs, charts and figures in order to answer the questions that follow. In most cases, graphs and tables are followed by 4-5 questions. Some tests have only one data set and approximately ten questions.

These tests are usually administered to candidates applying for managerial, supervisory, sales and professional positions, and for jobs that require workers to make decisions and inferences based on numerical data.

In some cases, you will be permitted to use a calculator. You will always be provided with pen and paper for calculations.

Instructions

On this test, you'll find graphs and tables containing data. You will be asked to answer questions related to each data set.

Remember

The test consists of 35 questions and has a time limit of 35 minutes.

Each question has only one correct answer.

Please make sure you have a calculator, a pen and some paper.

Work as quickly and as accurately as you can.

Good Luck!

1.   **Silverbrick International Lager Breweries Ltd 2005**

Brewery	Operational Costs*	Marketing & Development*	Monthly Output**	Total Output as % of 2004	Revenues*
Uxbridge, UK	3.6	12	12,000	120%	25
Malmo, Sweden	0.3	2.2	1,200	90%	3
Torino, Italy	2.8	3.5	8,000	70%	14
Ottawa, Canada	0.28	8	1,000	80%	3
Canberra, Australia	0.3	7	4,500	110%	8
1 litre is sold for 1.5 euros.					

* Millions Euros   ** Thousands litres

1.1 Which brewery produced the least in 2004?
- A. Uxbridge, UK
- B. Malmo, Sweden
- C. Torino, Italy
- D. Ottawa, Canada
- E. Canberra, Australia

1.2 If production for the brewery in Ottawa, Canada were expected to increase by 40% in 2006, by how many thousands of litres would its monthly output differ in 2006 compared with the output in 2004?
- A. 80 less
- B. 150 less
- C. the same
- D. 80 more
- E. 100 more
- F. 140 more
- G. 150 more
- H. 160 more
- I. 200 more
- J. Cannot Say

1.3 If the Monthly Output for the Torino brewery represented approximately 60% of the total output (with the remainder being water), how many thousands of litres of water were produced every month?
- A. 1,333
- B. 13,333
- C. 8,000
- D. 133
- E. 533
- F. 5,333
- G. 5,666
- H. 53
- I. 13
- J. Cannot Say

1.4 Which of these breweries has the highest ratio of operational costs to revenues?
- A. Uxbridge, UK
- B. Malmo, Sweden
- C. Torino, Italy
- D. Ottawa, Canada
- E. Canberra, Australia

1.5 If a 25% increase in marketing and development costs will lead to a 35% increase in revenues, what will the ratio of marketing and development costs to revenues be in Canberra, Australia following the rise?
- A. 0.081
- B. 0.085
- C. 0.81
- D. 1.23
- E. Cannot Say

2.

London – Sydney Daily Flights

To Heathrow	To Gatwick	From Heathrow	From Gatwick
4:45	04:00	06:00	10:00
9:15	09:30	12:00	12:30
13:45	15:00	Until	15:00
Until	Until	24:00	Until
22:45	20:30		22:30
Schedule in GMT. Sydney is GMT + 10			
Flight time 26 hours			

2.1 How many flights are there from Sydney to London daily?

A. 4   D. 9
B. 5   E. 11
C. 7

2.2 What is the first available flight to Sydney from London after 5:00 pm?

A. 17:15   F. 19:00
B. 17:30   G. 20:00
C. 17:45   H. 22:30
D. 18:00   I. 24:00
E. 18:30   J. Cannot Say

2.3 What time will it be in Sydney, Australia when the first morning flight from London arrives?

A. 6 am   F. 6 pm
B. 8 am   G. 6 pm + 1 day
C. 6 am +1 day   H. 8 pm + 1 day
D. 2 pm + 1 day   I. 12 pm
E. 8 am + 1 day   J. Cannot Say

2.4 How many flights are due to arrive in London between 15:00-17:30 GMT?

A. 1   D. 4
B. 2   E. 5
C. 3

2.5 Which flight would you have to catch from London in order to reach Sydney on the same day?

A. 4:00 from Gatwick   D. 9:15 from Heathrow
B. 4:45 from Heathrow   E. No Flight
C. 9:30 from Gatwick

3.

Popular Sports 2005 - Number of Viewers (thousands)							
Australia		**UK**		**Netherlands**		**Greece**	
Rugby	3,000	Football	17,000	Football	2,865	Basketball	3,265
Cricket	2,750	Rugby	7,325	Skating	1,200	Football	1,568
Tennis	1,875	Cricket	6,585	Horse Riding	650	Surfing	650
Surfing	1,325	Tennis	4,685	Basketball	325	Sailing	485
Football	1,100	Badminton	325	Sailing	212	Tennis	235
Sailing	775	Sailing	150	Tennis	75	Swimming	62
Total Population	**17,000**		**60,000**		**16,000**		**10,500**

3.1   What proportion of the Dutch population watches Dutch football?

A.   0.179%
B.   1.79%
C.   5.58%
D.   11.79%
E.   17.9%
F.   0.558%
G.   55.8%
H.   17.0%
I.   18.0%
J.   Cannot Say

3.2   How many more Australian viewers watched sailing competitions compared with Greek viewers?

A.   290
B.   2,900
C.   29,000
D.   290,000
E.   2,900,000
F.   1,260
G.   12,600
H.   126,000
I.   1,260,000
J.   Cannot Say

3.3   What is the approximate ratio of British football viewers to Australian football viewers?

A.   15.5 : 1
B.   6.4 : 1
C.   16: 1
D.   6 : 1
E.   Cannot Say

3.4   What proportion of the people in all four nations are tennis viewers?

A.   56%
B.   5.6%
C.   0.56%
D.   0.056%
E.   0.65%
F.   6.6%
G.   66%
H.   8.5%
I.   0.85%
J.   Cannot Say

3.5   How much smaller is the proportion of Dutch horse riding viewers compared with Greek surfing viewers?

A.   By 4.06%
B.   By 6.19%
C.   By 2.13%
D.   By 0.0213%
E.   No Difference

4.

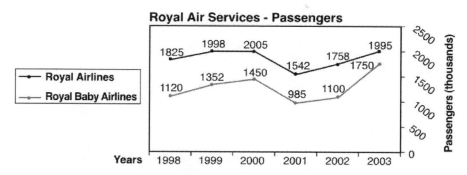

Royal Air Services - Passengers

Royal Airlines
Royal Baby Airlines

1825   1998   2005   1758   1995
1120   1352   1450   1542   1750
                        985   1100

Passengers (thousands)
2500 2000 1500 1000 500 0

Years   1998   1999   2000   2001   2002   2003

4.1 Approximately what proportion of Royal Air Services passengers flew Royal Baby Airlines in 2001?

A.	15%	F.	40%
B.	20%	G.	45%
C.	25%	H.	50%
D.	30%	I.	55%
E.	35%	J.	Cannot Say

4.2 If an average ticket with Royal Airlines cost £195 in 2001, and prices increased by an average of 12% in 2002, what were the approximate revenues of Royal Airlines from ticket sales in 2002?

A.	£3,850,000	D.	£380,000,000
B.	£385,000,000	E.	Cannot Say
C.	£3,800,000		

4.3 Over which two-year period did Royal Airlines have the greatest number of passengers?

A.	1998-1999	D.	2001-2002
B.	1999-2000	E.	2002-2003
C.	2000-2001		

4.4 Approximately what proportion of overall ticket sales did Royal Baby Airlines account for in 2003?

A.	25%	D.	40%
B.	30%	E.	45%
C.	35%		

4.5 In 2006, Royal Airlines and Royal Baby Airlines are each expected to sell 10% more than the number of tickets sold by Royal Airlines in 2000. The average Royal Baby Airlines ticket price is £75, and the average Royal Airlines ticket price is £232. What are the expected revenues from ticket sales in 2006 for Royal Air Services?

A.	677 thousand	D.	6.77 million
B.	677 million	E.	558 million
C.	677 hundred		

5.

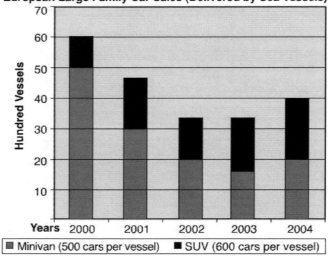

European Large Family Car Sales (Delivered by Sea Vessels)

Minivan (500 cars per vessel) ■ *SUV (600 cars per vessel)*

5.1 What was the total number of large family cars sold in 2004?

A.	40 thousand	E.	2 million
B.	400 thousand	F.	2.2 million
C.	1 million	G.	2.4 million
D.	1.2 million	H.	Cannot Say

5.2 How many hundreds of SUV vessels were sold in 2002?

A.	15	E.	35
B.	20	F.	40
C.	25	G.	45
D.	30	H.	Cannot Say

5.3 How many more vessels of minivans were sold between the years 2000-2004, compared with SUVs?

A.	1,500	D.	5,500
B.	3,500	E.	6,500
C.	5,000	F.	13,000

5.4 Sea delivery per car (either SUV or minivan) costs $25. What were the sea delivery costs for large family cars in 2002?

A.	$19 million	D.	$47.5 million
B.	$42.5 million	E.	Cannot Say
C.	$45.5 million		

5.5 What was the ratio of minivans to SUVs sold in 2000?

A.	1 : 3	D.	2 : 5
B.	25 : 6	E.	None of the above
C.	6 : 25		

6.

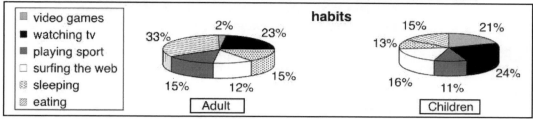

Are we so different?
Survey Results on Children & Adults Preferred Leisure Activities

Numbers of Survey Partcipants

Adults: 7,600   Children: 2,400

6.1 Roughly estimate how many of the total survey respondents surf the Internet.
    A.   360   D.   1,300
    B.   760   E.   Cannot Say
    C.   1,100

6.2 Which leisure activity has the highest ratio of children to adults?
    A.   Video games   D.   Internet
    B.   TV   E.   Sleeping
    C.   Sports   F.   Eating

6.3 What is the overall percentage of children in this survey?
    A.   20.5%   D.   26%
    B.   22%   E.   31.5%
    C.   24%

6.4 Of all survey respondents, what is the approximate percentage who enjoys watching TV and playing sports?
    A.   31%   E.   39%
    B.   33%   F.   41%
    C.   35%   G.   43%
    D.   37%   H.   None of the above

6.5 Recent studies indicate that the number of adults who enjoy playing video games is growing by 20% every year, while the number of children who play video games isn't expected to change. How long will it take for the number of adults who play video games to exceed the number of children in the survey sample?
    A.   2 years   E.   6 years
    B.   3 years   F.   7 years
    C.   4 years   G.   8 years
    D.   5 years   H.   9 years

7.

2005 Results of the 'Daily Magic' Newspaper Global Delivery

	Successfully Delivered Newspapers Per Courier Per Day*	Percentage of Newspapers Lost During Delivery	Number of Couriers Working Annually
London	12,504	5%	758
Sydney	7,704	11%	321
Paris	8,007	13%	569
New York	15,600	6%	358
Milan	3,069	8%	259

* excluding those that were lost

7.1 How much does it cost to deliver a newspaper successfully in Sydney (excluding lost papers)?

A. $1.2
B. $1.4
C. $1.6
D. $1.8

E. $2.0
F. $2.2
G. $2.4
H. Cannot Say

7.2 What is the ratio of successfully delivered newspapers to lost newspapers in London?

A. 1:5
B. 1:19
C. 20:1

D. 1:20
E. 19:1
F. Cannot Say

7.3 Estimate how many couriers from Sydney would have been needed to deliver the same number of newspapers as in London.

A. 512 Couriers
B. 513 Couriers
C. 517 Couriers

D. 521 Couriers
E. 523 Couriers
F. Cannot Say

7.4 Estimate how many newspapers were lost during delivery in New York.

A. 930
B. 1,000
C. 1,200

D. 900
E. 1,500
F. Cannot Say

7.5 What would Sydney's lost rate have to be to match the number of successful deliveries in Paris (excluding lost papers)?

A. 5%
B. 7.5%
C. 10%

D. 12.5%
E. 15%
F. They will never match.

Test 11 Answers:

1.
1.1
Which brewery produced the least in 2004?
- In order to determine which brewery produced the least in 2004, we need to use the 2005 monthly output and the total output as a percentage for 2004.
- Monthly output for 2004 = (monthly output 2005x100%) /total output as a percentage for 2004.
- Monthly output for 2004x12 = yearly output for 2004.
- Ottawa, Canada - (1,000Kx100) /80 = 1,250K per month in 2004.
- 1,250Kx12 = 15,000K litres in 2004.
- TIP: In this question, Ottawa, Canada's low output stands out. Therefore, you can make an educated guess by looking at the data without having to do the actual calculation.

The answer is D.

1.2
If production for the brewery in Ottawa, Canada were expected to increase by 40% in 2006, by how many thousands of litres would its monthly output differ in 2006 compared with the output in 2004?
- We need to determine how many litres the Canadian brewery is expected to produce monthly in 2006 = (monthly output for 2005 x expected increase in %) /100% = monthly output for 2006.
- (1,000Kx140) /100 = 1,400K litres per month in 2006.
- We need to calculate how many litres the Canadian brewery produced monthly in 2004 = monthly output for 2004 = (monthly output 2005x100) /total output as a percentage for 2004.
- (1,000Kx100%) /80% = 1,250K per month in 2004.
- Monthly output for 2006 - monthly output for 2004 = 1,400K-1,250K = 150K litres more beer was produced per month in 2006 compared with 2004.

The answer is G.

1.3
If the monthly output for the Torino brewery represented approximately 60% of the total output (with the remainder being water), how many thousands of litres of water were produced every month?
- We first have to determine how many thousands of litres of beer and water were produced. We know the amount of beer produced (8,000 litres), which represents 60% of the total output.
- (Monthly output Torino beer x 100) /60 = monthly output of beer and water = (8,000x100) /60 = 13,333 litres.

- Subtract <u>the amount of beer produced</u> from <u>the total amount of water and beer produced</u> to determine the amount of water produced.
- Monthly output of water and beer - monthly output of beer = monthly output of water = 13,333-8,000 = 5,333 litres of water.

The answer is F.

1.4
Which of these breweries has the highest ratio of operational costs to revenues?
- The ratio is calculated in the following manner: operational costs / revenues = ratio.
- Torino, Italy = 2.8/14 = 0.2 is the highest ratio.

The answer is C.

1.5
If a 25% increase in marketing and development costs will lead to a 35% increase in revenues, what will the ratio of marketing and development costs to revenues be in Canberra, Australia following the rise?
- Calculate the 25% increase in marketing and development costs: marketing and development costs x 1.25 = 7x1.25 = 8.75.
- Calculate the 35% increase in revenues: revenues x 1.35 = 8x1.35 = 10.8
- Calculate the new ratio for marketing and development costs to revenues = 8.75/10.8 = 0.81.

The answer is C.

2.
2.1
How many flights are there from Sydney to London daily?
- There are five daily flights (4:45, 9:15, 13:45, 18:15, 22:45) from Sydney to Heathrow and four daily flights (04:00, 09:30, 15:00, 20:30) from Sydney to Gatwick.
- The total number of flights from Sydney to London is 9.

The answer is D.

2.2
What is the first available flight to Sydney from London after 5:00 pm?

- Flights to Sydney leave from Heathrow at 06:00, 12:00 and every 6 hours until 24:00. Therefore, there is an additional flight at 18:00.
- Flights to Sydney from Gatwick leave at 10:00, 12:30, 15:00 and at intervals of 2.30 hours until 22:30. Therefore, the first flight after 15:00 is at 17:30.
- The first available flight after 17:00 is the 17:30 (5:30 pm) flight from Gatwick.

The answer is B.

2.3

What time will it be in Sydney, Australia when the first morning flight from London arrives?

- The first flight to leave London in the morning is the 6:00 am from Heathrow. The flight duration is 26 hours, which means the flight arrives at 8:00 am GMT the following day.
- Since Sydney time is GMT + 10, local time will be 6 pm + 1 day.

The answer is G.

2.4

How many flights are due to arrive in London between 15:00-17:30 GMT?

- Flight duration is 26 hours. The schedule shown is in GMT, therefore the 13:45 to Heathrow is due to arrive at 15:45 the following day and the15:00 to Gatwick is due to arrive at 17:00 the following day.
- There are a total of 2 flights.

The answer is B.

2.5

Which flight would you have to catch from London in order to reach Sydney on the same day?

Since the flight duration is more than 24 hours, there is no possibility of reaching Australia the same day.

The answer is E.

3.

3.1

What proportion of the Dutch population watches Dutch football?

- The number of Dutch football viewers is 2.865 million (2,865 thousand). The population of The Netherlands is 16 million (16,000 thousand).
- The proportion of the Dutch population that watches Dutch football = $(2,865,000 \div 16,000,000) \times 100 = 17.9\%$

The answer is E.

3.2

How many more Australian viewers watched sailing competitions compared with Greek viewers?

- The number of Australian sailing viewers is 775,000.
- The number of Greek sailing viewers is 485,000.
- The difference between the two = 775,000-485,000 = 290,000.

- TIP: The number of viewers in both countries is in the same range (hundreds of thousands – 6 digits). Therefore, the difference between the two should be in the same range. We can eliminate all options that have more or less than six digits, apart from D and H. All we have to do is estimate the difference between 775 and 485.

The answer is D.

3.3

What is the approximate ratio of British football viewers to Australian football viewers?
- The number of British football viewers is 17,000,000.
- The number of Australian football viewers is 1,100,000.
- The approximate ratio of British to Australian football viewers is 17,000,000/1,100,000 = 15.45. The ratio is 15.45:1.
- TIP: Just by looking at the figures 17 million and 1.1 million, we already know that the ratio has to be slightly lower than 17:1. This means that we can eliminate options B, D and E.

The answer is A.

3.4

What proportion of the people in all four nations are tennis viewers?
- The combined population of all four nations is:
  17,000,000+60,000,000+16,000,000+10,500,000 = 103,500,000.
- The number of tennis viewers in all four nations is:
  1,875,000+4,685,000+75,000+235,000 = 6,870,000.
- The proportion is: (6,870,000÷103,500,000) x100 = 6.6%.

The answer is F.

3.5

How much smaller is the proportion of Dutch horse riding viewers compared with Greek surfing viewers?
- The proportion of Dutch horse riding viewers = (the number of horse riding viewers ÷ Dutch population) x100 = (650,000÷16,000,000) x100 = 4.06%.
- The proportion of Greek surfing viewers = (the number of surfing viewers ÷ Greek population) x100 = (650,000÷10,500,000) x100 = 6.19%.
- The difference = 6.19-4.06 = 2.13%.

The answer is C.

4.
4.1

Approximately what proportion of Royal Air Services passengers flew Royal Baby Airlines in 2001?

- The total number of passengers travelling with Royal Air Services in 2001 was 1,542,000+985,000 = 2,527,000.
- The percentage of travellers flying with Royal Baby Airlines = (the number of passengers using Royal Baby Airlines ÷ amount of passengers using Royal Air Services) x100 = 985,000÷2,527,000 = 38.98% ≈ 40%

The answer is F.

4.2

If an average ticket with Royal Airlines cost £195 in 2001, and prices increased by an average of 12% in 2002, what were the approximate revenues of Royal Airlines from ticket sales in 2002?

- Calculate the average price of a ticket on Royal Airlines in 2002. In order to do this, add 12% to £195, the average ticket price in 2001.
- £195x1.12 = £218.4
- The number of tickets sold by Royal Airlines in 2002 was 1,758,000. This means that the total revenues from Royal Airlines ticket sales in 2002 = 1,758,000x218.4 = £383,947,200 ≈ £385,000,000.

The answer is B.

4.3

Over which two-year period did Royal Airlines have the greatest number of passengers? You can answer this question by looking at the graph, rather than adding up the number of passengers travelling each year. The graph shows us that the black line is highest in 1999-2000. Therefore, Royal Airlines had the greatest number of passengers during this two-year period.

The answer is B.

4.4

Approximately what proportion of overall ticket sales did Royal Baby Airlines account for in 2003?

- The number of tickets sold by Royal Baby Airlines in 2003 was 1,750,000.
- The overall number of tickets sold by Royal Air Services in 2003 = 1,750,000+1,995,000 = 3,745,000.
- The percentage of tickets sold by Royal Baby Airlines in 2003 was (1,750,000÷3,745,000) x100 = 46.73% ≈ 45%.

The answer is E.

4.5

In 2006, Royal Airlines and Royal Baby Airlines are each expected to sell 10% more than the number of tickets sold by Royal Airlines in 2000. The average Royal Baby Airlines ticket price is £75, and the average Royal Airlines ticket price is £232. What are the expected revenues from ticket sales in 2006 for Royal Air Services?

- In 2000, Royal Airlines sold 2,005,000 tickets.
- The number of tickets each airline is expected to sell in 2006 is 2,005,000x1.1 = 2,205,500.
- The combined revenues in 2006 from ticket sales is = (2,205,500x75) + (2,205,500x232) = 677,088,500 ≈ £677 million.

The answer is B.

5.
5.1
What was the total number of large family cars sold in 2004?
- There were 20×100 vessels of minivans sold = 2,000.
- The same number of SUVs were sold (2,000 vessels).
- 500 minivans fit into one vessel = 500×2,000 = 1,000,000 minivans sold
- 600 SUVs fit into one vessel = 600×2,000 = 1,200,000 SUVs sold
- A total of 2,200,000 large family cars were sold in 2004.

The answer is F.

5.2
How many hundreds of SUV vessels were sold in 2002?
- The black block represents SUV sales. In the 2002 column, the SUV section starts at the 20 benchmark and ends at 35.
- Therefore, 35-20 = 15 hundred vessels of SUVs were sold.

The answer is A.

5.3
How many more vessels of minivans were sold between the years 2000-2004, compared with SUVs?
- To make the calculation easier, we'll initially use the numbers in the graph without adding the hundreds.
- The total number of minivan vessels sold between 2000-2004 = 50+30+20+15+20 = 135 minivan vessels
- The total number of SUV vessels sold between 2000-2004 = (60-50) + (45-30) + (35-20) + (35-15) + (40-20) = 80.
- The difference between the number of minivan vessels sold and the number of SUV vessels sold = 135-80 = 55.
- If we add the hundreds that we initially ignored, 55x100 = 5,500.
- 5,500 more minivan vessels were sold compared with SUV vessels.

The answer is D.

5.4
Sea delivery per car (either SUV or minivan) costs $25. What were the sea delivery costs for large family cars in 2002?

- In 2002, there were 20×100 = 2,000 vessels of minivans × 500 minivans in each vessel = 1,000,000 minivans.
- There were also 15×100 = 1,500 vessels of SUVs × 600 SUVs in each vessel = 900,000 SUVs.
- 1,000,000+900,000 = 1,900,000 cars sold in total × $25 per car delivery = $47,500,000 in delivery costs.

The answer is D.

5.5

What was the ratio of minivans to SUVs sold in 2000?

- In 2000, there were 10×100 = 1,000 vessels containing × 600 SUVs = 600,000 SUVs
- In terms of minivans, there were 50×100 = 5,000 vessels containing × 500 minivans = 2,500,000 minivans.
- To calculate the ratio, divide the larger number by the smaller number = 2,500,000/600,000 = 4.16.
- The ratio of minivans to SUVs in 2000 = 4.16:1 (in round numbers, 25:6).

The answer is B.

6.

6.1

Roughly estimate how many of the total survey respondents surf the Internet.

- 12% of 7,600 adults surf the Internet. 10% of 7,600 is 760, therefore the number of adults that surf the Internet should be slightly higher (12%) ≈ 900.
- 16% of 2,400 children surf the Internet, 10% of 2,400 is 240, and an additional 5% is 120 = 240+120 = 360
- The number of children who surf the Internet is slightly higher than 360 (16%) ≈ 400.
- 900+400 = roughly 1,300.

The answer is D.

6.2

Which leisure activity has the highest ratio of children to adults?

- Only 2% of adults play video games compared with 21% of children.
- The ratio is approx 11:1 (21:2).
- None of the other categories compare.

The answer is A.

6.3

What is the overall percentage of children in this survey?

- There are a total of 10,000 survey participants: 7,600 adults+2,400 children.
- The percentage of children in the survey = (number of children in survey ÷ total number of participants in survey) x100 = (2,400÷10,000) x100 = 24%

- TIP: Since the number of participants in the survey is 10,000, this means that 2,400 children (the number of children participating in the survey) = 24%. You can reach this solution without doing the full calculation.

The answer is C.

6.4
Of all survey respondents, what is the approximate percentage who enjoys watching TV and playing sports?
- In the adult group, 23% watch TV and 15% play sports = 38%.
- 7,600x (38÷100) = 2,888 adults enjoy watching TV and playing sports.
- In the children's group, 24% watch TV and 11% play sports = 35%.
- 2,400x (35÷100) = 840 children enjoy watching TV and playing sports.
- The total number of survey participants who enjoy watching TV and playing sports = 840+2,888 = 3,728.
- From a total sample of 10,000, the percentage of people who enjoy watching TV and playing sports is approximately 37%.

The answer is D.

6.5
Recent studies indicate that the number of adults who enjoy playing video games is growing by 20% every year, while the number of children who play video games isn't expected to change. How long will it take for the number of adults who play video games to exceed the number of children in the survey sample?
- 21% of children play video games = 504 children
- 2% of adults play video games = 152 adults
- 20% of 152 = 152x (20÷100) = 30.4 additional adults will play video games after the first year, bringing the subtotal to182 adults.
- After the second year, an additional 20% of the 184 (approximately 37) will play video games, bringing the number of adults playing video games to 221.
- Using the same method, calculate that after 3 years, 265 adults will play video games, after 4 years 318, after 5 years 381, after 6 years 457 and after 7 years 548 adults will play video games. This number exceeds the number of children playing video games.
- After 7 years, there will be more adults than children playing video games.

The answer is F.

7.
7.1
How much does it cost to deliver a newspaper successfully in Sydney (excluding lost papers)?
There is no information about newspaper prices, therefore we can't figure out the answer based on the existing data.

The answer is H.

7.2

What is the ratio of successfully delivered newspapers to lost newspapers in London?

- Out of a total of 100% of newspapers that leave the factory, 5% are lost. This means that for every 100 newspapers, 95 papers are delivered and five newspapers are lost
- Dividing 95 by 5 = 19. The ratio of successfully delivered newspapers to lost newspapers in London is 19:1.

The answer is E.

7.3

Estimate how many couriers from Sydney would have been needed to deliver the same number of newspapers as in London.

- In Sydney, there are 321 couriers delivering 7,704 newspapers.
- $7,704 \div 321 = 24$ newspapers per courier.
- In London, 12,504 newspapers are delivered successfully.
- Dividing the 12,504 by 24 gives us the number of couriers required for this task = $12,504 \div 24 = 521$ couriers

The answer is D.

7.4

Estimate how many newspapers were lost during delivery in New York.

- 15,600 newspapers were successfully delivered in NY, excluding those that were lost.
- We know that 6% of the total number of newspapers in New York is lost.
- This means that 15,600 newspapers make up 94% of the total amount (100-6 = 94).
- So $(15,600 \times 6) / 94 = 995.74 \approx 1,000$ newspapers are lost in New York every day.

The answer is B.

7.5

What would Sydney's lost rate have to be to match the number of successful deliveries in Paris (excluding lost papers)?

- With a loss rate of 11%, the 7,704 newspapers that are successfully delivered in Sydney make up 89% of the total newspapers delivered (100%-11%).
- The total number of deliveries in Sydney (including lost papers) is $(7,704 \times 100) / 89 = 8,656$.
- In Paris, 8,007 newspapers are delivered successfully. Calculate the percentage we have to deduct from 8,656 to receive 8,007.
- (The total number of successfully delivered newspapers in Paris x 100) ÷ the total number of newspapers delivered in Sydney (including lost papers) = $(8,007 \times 100) / 8,656 = 92.5\%$ of Sydney's newspapers have to be delivered successfully to match Paris's successful delivery rate.
- The rate of lost papers is therefore 100-92.5 = 7.5% (in comparison with the current existing 11% lost paper rate).

The answer is B.

Test 12 Number Series

The number series test asks you to identify the missing number/s in a sequence. To do this, you have to figure out the logical rule behind the series of numbers.

This test assesses both your understanding of arithmetic and your logical skills. Practice will most definitely improve your results.

Number series tests are not as common as the other numerical tests we have discussed, but are still quite prevalent. Often, these tests are used to test professionals that require high-level numerical skills, such as IT staff, business analysts and bankers.

Instructions

Each question in the test consists of a series of numbers. In each series, there are one or more missing numbers. You must identify the logical rule behind each series and determine which number(s) complete the series.

There is only one correct answer to each question.

Remember

The test consists of 10 questions and has a time limit of 5 minutes.

Work as quickly and as accurately as you can.

Good Luck!

		A.	B.	C.	D.
1.	2, 10, 40, 120, 240, _____	480	240	360	720
2.	2, 4, 0, 6, -2, _____	8	2	12	-4
3.	0.25, 0.5, 2.5, 5, 7, _____	14	17	34	25
4.	364, 121, 40, 13, 4, _____	1	2	3	0
5.	7, 12, 2, 17, -3, _____	22	-14	13	25

		A.	B.	C.	D.
6.	1, 5, 4, 16, 14, 42, _____	39	18	41	9

		A.	B.	C.	D.
7.	3, 8, 15, 24, 35, _____	13	36	48	46

		A.	B.	C.	D.
8.	6/3, 5/4, 4/5, 3/6, 2/7, _____	1/2	1/3	3/9	1/8

		A.	B.	C.	D.
9.	1, 3, 6, 2, -1, _____	-1/3	2	-3	4

		A.	B.	C.	D.
10.	0, 1, _____, _____, 16, 25	3,9	5,8	4,9	2,4

Test 12 General Tips:

1. Examine the difference between adjacent numbers.
   a. In a simple series, the difference between two consecutive numbers is constant.
      Example: 27, 24, 21, 18, _____
      Rule: There is a difference of (-3) between each item.
      The missing number is 15.
   b. In a more complex series the differences between numbers may be dynamic rather than fixed, but there still is a clear logical rule.
      Example: 3, 4, 6, 9, 13, 18, _____
      Rule: Add 1 to the difference between two adjacent items. After the first number add 1, after the second number add 2 and after the third number add 3, etc. In this case, the missing number is 24.
      Result: The missing number is 24.

2. See whether there is a multiplication or division pattern between two adjacent numbers.
      Example: 64, 32, 16, 8, _____
      Rule: Divide each number by 2 to get the next number in the series.
      Result: The missing number is 4.

3. Check whether adjacent numbers in the series change based on a logical pattern.
    Example: 2, 4, 12, 48, _____
    Rule: Multiply the first number by 2, the second number by 3 and the third number by 4, etc.
    Result: The missing item is 240.

4. See if you can find a rule that involves using two or more basic arithmetic functions $(+, -, \div, x)$.
    a. In this series, the functions alternate in an orderly sequence.
        Example: 5, 7, 14, 16, 32, 34, _____
        Rule: Add 2, multiply by 2, add 2, multiply by 2, etc.
        Result: The missing item is 68.
        Important:
        In a series that involves two or more basic arithmetic functions, the differences between adjacent items effectively create their own series. We recommend that you try to identify each pattern separately.
    b. **Example:** 4, 6, 2, 8, 3, _____
        Rule: In this series, the differences themselves create a series: +2, ÷3, x4, -5 The numbers advance by intervals of 1 and the arithmetic functions change in an orderly sequence. The next arithmetic function in the series should be +6, and so the next item in the series is 9 (3+6 = 9).
        Result: The missing number is 9.

5. If you can't find a rule using basic arithmetic, then see if the numbers in the series have any special characteristics.
    a. **Example:** 3, 5, 7, 11, 13, _____
        Rule: This series is made up of prime numbers. A prime number is a number that can only be divided by itself and by 1. The next prime number in the series is 17.
        Result: The missing number is 17.

    b. **Example:** 4, 9, 16, 25, 36, _____
        Rule: The numbers in this series are all square roots (x^2). Each number is a multiplication of itself (2x2, 3x3, 4x4, 5x5 and 6x6). The next number in the series is 7x7 = 49.
        Result: The missing number is = 49.

5. c. **Example:**   2, 5, 7, 12, 19, 31, _____
        Rule: In this series, each number comes from an arithmetic function with the preceding number.
                        In this example, 2+5 = 7, 5+7 = 12, 7+12 = 19, etc.
        Result: The missing number is = 50.

6. If you can't find a relationship between the numbers, see whether there are two separate patterns in the series.

    Example: 3, 8, 6, 6, 9, 4, _____

    This series contains two separate series and two rules.

    The first series is made up of the 1st, 3rd and 5th numbers: 3, 6 and 9. In this series, 3 is added to each subsequent number.

    The second series is made up of the 2nd, 4th and 6th numbers: 8, 6 and 4. In this series, 2 is subtracted from each subsequent number.

    The 7th number in the series should belong to the first series, therefore 3 should be added to the last number in the series: 9+3 = 12.

    Result: The missing number is 12.

Test 12 Answers:

	A.	B.	C.	D.
1. 2, 10, 40, 120, 240, ____	480	240	360	720

In this series, the first number is multiplied by 5 to get the next number in the series. The second number is multiplied by 4, the third by 3, and so on in descending order. Therefore the last number in the series should be multiplied by 1, and the correct answer is 240.

The answer is B.

	A.	B.	C.	D.
2. 2, 4, 0, 6, -2, _____	8	2	12	-4

In this series, first, calculate the difference between adjacent items: +2, -4, +6, -8. The difference between each two integers in the series increases by two in absolute value and the arithmetic function alternates between addition and subtraction. Therefore, if we add the number +10 to the final item (-2), the result is 8.

The answer is A.

	A.	B.	C.	D.
3. 0.25, 0.5, 2.5, 5, 7, _____	14	17	34	25

The logical rule behind this series is an alternating arithmetic function – multiplication, and then addition. The first number is multiplied by 2 to get the second number. Then 2 is added to the second number to get the third number, and so on: x2, +2, x2, +2. Therefore the last integer in the series, 7, should be multiplied by 2÷7x2 = 14.

The answer is A.

	A.	B.	C.	D.
4. 364, 121, 40, 13, 4, _____	1	2	3	0

The numbers in this series become gradually smaller. It is reasonable to assume that this happens through division, subtraction or a combination of the two. In this series, the number 1 is subtracted from each number, and then the resulting number is divided by three to get the next number in the series.

For example, 364-1 = 363÷3 = 121. The last number in the series is 4-1 = 3÷3 = 1.

The answer is A.

	A.	B.	C.	D.
5. 7, 12, 2, 17, -3, _____	22	-14	13	25

You can figure out the pattern behind this series in two ways:

1. The arithmetic function alternates between addition and subtraction. The difference between the first two numbers is +5, followed by -10, +15, -20 and finally +25. So -3+25 = 22.

2. You can also see this series as two separate series in one:

    A. 7, 2, -3,

    B. 12, 17, _____

In the first series (1st, 3rd, and 5th numbers), there is a difference of -5 between each second number.

In the second series (2nd & 4th numbers), there is a difference of +5 between each second number. Therefore the 6th item in the series is 17+5 = 22.

The answer is A.

	A.	B.	C.	D.
6. 1, 5, 4, 16, 14, 42, _____	39	18	41	9

In this series, the logical rule isn't particularly obvious. .Therefore, we recommend trying to figure out which arithmetic function would lead to the next number in the series.

$1 \times 5 = 5$

$5 - 1 = 4$

$4 \times 4 = 16$

$16 - 2 = 14$

$14 \times 3 = 42$

The rule involves alternating between multiplication of descending numbers beginning with 5 and subtraction of ascending numbers beginning with 1. So x5, -1, x4, -2, x3, -3, Therefore: 42-3 = 39.

The answer is A.

	A.	B.	C.	D.
7. 3, 8, 15, 24, 35, _____	13	36	48	46

In this series, 5 is added to the first number in the series and then each subsequent number increases by the (difference +2): 7, 9, 11. Therefore 13 (11+2) should be added to the last number in the series (35) = 35+13 = 48.

The answer is C.

	A.	B.	C.	D.
8. 6/3, 5/4, 4/5, 3/6, 2/7, _____	1/2	1/3	3/9	1/8

In this series, the numerator and denominator in each fraction each have a separate rule. Each numerator decreases by -1 and each denominator increases by +1. This means that -1 should be subtracted from the numerator (2) in the last number in the series (2/7) and +1 should be added to the denominator (7). The result is 1/8

The answer is D.

204 ■ Chapter 2   Numerical Tests

	A.	B.	C.	D.
9. 1, 3, 6, 2, -1, _____	-1/3	2	-3	4

In this series, all basic arithmetic functions are used (+, -, x, ÷) and all of them involve the number 3. The order of the arithmetic functions are: x3, +3, ÷3, -3. Because the last action was subtraction, the next one should be multiplication: (-1) x3 = (-3).

The answer is C.

	A.	B.	C.	D.
10. 0, 1, _____, _____, 16, 25	3,9	5,8	4,9	2,4

This series is made up of consecutive numbers that are square roots - 0^2, 1^2, 2^2, 3^2, 4^2, and 5^2. The missing numbers in the series are $2^2 = 4$ and $3^2 = 9$.

The answer is C.

3

VERBAL TESTS

We all communicate on a daily basis, and are accustomed to reading and writing at various levels and in various situations. Yet you may be surprised how your confidence can wane when these verbal skills are actually put to the test. This is especially true nowadays, when most of us are accustomed to using word processors that automatically correct our spelling mistakes and provide us with synonyms. You may even be making the same spelling mistakes over and over again without ever realising it, since you're automatically being corrected. This means that you should be preparing for spelling and vocabulary tests.

When you read a text, you usually make certain inferences based on both the information presented in the text and on your prior knowledge of the subject matter. These assumptions lead to the mistakes that so many people make when sitting exams.

In this chapter we'll provide a few samples of reading comprehension as well as logic, vocabulary and grammar tests.

Test 13 Verbal Critical Reasoning

Reading comprehension tests evaluate your ability to accurately interpret the information presented in a text and come to conclusions. Often, the content of the reading passages are somewhat related to your profession or field.

Instructions:
This test consists of 10 reading passages. Each text is followed by several statements.
Read the passage and determine the correct answer:
- Choose **True** if the statement has to be true, according to the passage.
- Choose **False** if the statement has to be false, according to the passage.
- Choose **Cannot Say** if you cannot determine whether the statement is true or false without further information.

Remember
Your answers must be based only on the information provided in the text.
You have 20 minutes to read 10 passages and respond to 40 statements.

Good Luck!

1.
> The operation of mobile phones is becoming increasingly complex and users are now required to take a more 'computer-like' approach to effectively operate a phone. For example, new mobile phones often have high level features such as text messaging, audio-visual facilities, Internet and computer gaming. Some users are likely to find it increasingly difficult to operate these features, although there is a large and growing sector of young users who seem more naturally competent at using them.

A.   Mobile phone users generally take a computer-like approach when operating their phones.   True / False / Cannot say

B.   Internet use is becoming increasingly common in mobile phones.
True / False / Cannot say

C.   The younger sector is more competent at using the audio-visual facilities in mobile phones.   True / False / Cannot say

D.   The increasingly complex operation of mobile phones means there are few users who are naturally competent.   True / False / Cannot say

2.

> The production of organic food products supplied in food stores continues to increase considerably, with demand particularly high in Europe and North America. Health awareness and higher standards of living are both enhancing consumption and the market is likely to triple over the next decade. The organic food industry is facing the challenge of how it will cope with the forecasted future demand.

A. Organic food production is the fastest growing field in the food industry.

<u>True</u> / <u>False</u> / <u>Cannot say</u>

B. The main cause of enhanced organic food consumption is the higher general standard of living.   <u>True</u> / <u>False</u> / <u>Cannot say</u>

C. Consumers are now more conscious of the value of organic food than they were in the past.   <u>True</u> / <u>False</u> / <u>Cannot say</u>

D. The consumption of organic food has tripled over the past decade.

<u>True</u> / <u>False</u> / <u>Cannot say</u>

3.

> A dependable state of peace between two populaces sharing the same region does not imply that the average life expectancy of humans will remain constant. Epidemics, natural disasters and unstable weather, particularly in response to the 'greenhouse effect' and the subsequent cooling and warming of effected regions, generate oscillations in mean life expectancy and lead populations to increase or decrease their average age.

A. Natural disasters are the indisputable cause of life expectancy oscillations.

<u>True</u> / <u>False</u> / <u>Cannot say</u>

B. Average life expectancy decreases due to the cooling of some regions.

<u>True</u> / <u>False</u> / <u>Cannot say</u>

C. Epidemics are one of the causes of fluctuations in mean life expectancy.

<u>True</u> / <u>False</u> / <u>Cannot say</u>

D. Average life expectancy is predicted to rise in the future.

<u>True</u> / <u>False</u> / <u>Cannot say</u>

4.

> It is now widely acknowledged that the movement against racism in Western European societies is gaining momentum. Openness to diversity and multicultural societies resulting from mass immigration have both contributed to a reduction in discrimination suffered by minority groups. Unfortunately, racial discrimination remains prevalent. It can create anarchy and damage the delicate fabric of society, which can undermine a nation's resiliency.

A.   Mass immigration leading to multicultural societies has contributed to increased racism in Western Europe.   True / False / Cannot say

B.   Racial discrimination is less apparent in heavily populated societies.
                                                                          True / False / Cannot say

C.   Societies that do not fight against racism may suffer in the future.
                                                                          True / False / Cannot say

D.   Social chaos can compromise the fragile structure of society.
                                                                          True / False / Cannot say

5.

> Admired university lecturers with a good reputation amongst students tend to concentrate on core subjects and have a carefully planned and inflexible developmental trajectory, while their teaching methods and class requirements are continuously adapted to contemporary themes. Distinguished lecturers differentiate between invaluable resources and transient themes. They blend topical subjects into their long established course material but will never eliminate a focal topic due to low current relevance. Having both the experience to concentrate on the essence and the motivation to stimulate students is what makes these lecturers successful.

A.   A good lecturer should not differentiate between a students' developmental trajectory and the class requirements.   True / False / Cannot say

B.   The themes in a course may change due to current relevance.
                                                                          True / False / Cannot say

C.   Current affairs are generally not relevant to university level lectures.
                                                                          True / False / Cannot say

D.   Expansive lecturing experience is a strong motivator for successful lecturers.
                                                                          True / False / Cannot say

6.

> A calculated estimation by the World Welfare Organisation indicates that there will be a radical reduction in the female population of rural China by the next decade. This will result in to a 5% difference between the number of males and females, leading to a gap of millions. This means that for every thousand married couples there will be approximately fifty eligible males that will never find a female partner, and in some regions this may rise to 200. The Chinese government is currently attempting to amend this gender distortion by placing tougher penalties on women who get illegal abortions and by criminalising prenatal ultrasound examinations.

A. The female population of China's countryside is lower than the ideal 50:50 gender distribution. <u>True</u> / <u>False</u> / <u>Cannot say</u>

B. If successful, the new governmental regulations in China are likely to widen the gender distribution. <u>True</u> / <u>False</u> / <u>Cannot say</u>

C. Prenatal ultrasound examinations are one of the suspected causes of the gender gap in rural China. <u>True</u> / <u>False</u> / <u>Cannot say</u>

D. In some places in rural China, the gender gap may result in millions of unmarried men. <u>True</u> / <u>False</u> / <u>Cannot say</u>

7.

> Airline companies are increasingly searching for novel tactics to succeed and keep afloat in the competitive airline industry. Using code sharing and forming Frequent Flyer Club partnerships has allowed these companies to capitalise on projects that they couldn't do on their own. The potential gains of such initiatives are huge. Airlines reduce their overhead by sharing unpopular air routes, which lowers both the overall risk and the operating costs. The increased flexibility of airline operations means that less business is lost. This is because in the case of an unexpectedly low amount of business, they can share services with partners.

A. If airlines combine operations on unpopular routes, they will increase operating costs. <u>True</u> / <u>False</u> / <u>Cannot say</u>

B. A possible consequence of code sharing partnerships is a reduction of the overall risk on unpopular air routes. <u>True</u> / <u>False</u> / <u>Cannot say</u>

C. An inability to share services in response to unexpectedly low business can reduce the flexibility of airline operations. <u>True</u> / <u>False</u> / <u>Cannot say</u>

D. There are certain services that airlines should offer on their own, without forming a partnership. <u>True</u> / <u>False</u> / <u>Cannot say</u>

8.

> The year 2006 marked a substantial shift in the working conditions of international long-distance call centre staff. This was due to both newly developed telecommunications technology, and the change in working hours. This shift in hours has put more stress on the employees. The typical working hours of call centre workers have changed dramatically to match with trans-Atlantic time zones. Throughout the shift of a call centre employee, he/she has to function dynamically and answer calls enthusiastically during unconventional hours. These late working hours also lead to less human interaction in the call-centre.

A. International long-distance call centre employees have had to change their working hours.   True / False / Cannot say

B. Call centre staff now has a more strenuous workload.
                                                          True / False / Cannot say

C. Call centre employees have to answer incoming calls much more enthusiastically than in the past.   True / False / Cannot say

D. Working regular hours during the day can lead to more social interaction amongst staff.   True / False / Cannot say

9.

> Political transformations in Chile due to the new democratically elected Aylwin government, initially launched by the effective eradication of the Pinochet military regime in 1990, triggered economic growth. The new government vowed to promote economic growth in parallel to the introduction of new social policies. This provided the reason d'etre for the social and labour policies directed at the poorest communities, which would yield greater social equality. The establishment of Chilean democracy has been crucial in drawing overseas investors, and this in turn has boosted Chile's economic growth.

A. Prior to Aylwin's government, there was no economic growth in Chile.
                                                          True / False / Cannot say

B. The government of Chile assumed that economic growth would follow the establishment of new social policies.   True / False / Cannot say

C. Chilean economic growth culminated in the establishment of Chilean democracy.
                                                          True / False / Cannot say

D. Only the poorest communities in Chile suffered from social inequality.
                                                          True / False / Cannot say

10.

> Companies wishing to grow occasionally use the method of franchising, which means providing a new owner with a permit to use their business identity and to purchase products exclusively from the company. Most companies will, however, aim to minimise the use of this method and often prefer the expansion of the companies' own branches. Companies who have previously used franchising have learnt the essential need to monitor the business operations of the franchised branch. Difficulties arise when franchisees and companies disagree on business policies such as customer care service, delivery efficiency and the quality of human interaction. Inadequate attention to the monitoring of franchisees on the part of the companies is typically the cause of subsequent problems.

A.   Franchising is likely to become the most popular method of increasing business expansion.   True / <u>False</u> / <u>Cannot say</u>

B.   Franchisees may have different views than the 'mother' company on how to manage the franchised business.   <u>True</u> / False / <u>Cannot say</u>

C.   Service delivery efficiency has reduced companies' will to franchise.
                                                                   <u>True</u> / False / <u>Cannot say</u>

D.   Companies are now more aware of the need to monitor franchisees.
                                                                   <u>True</u> / False / <u>Cannot say</u>

Test 13 Answers:

1.

A.   <u>Statement</u>: Mobile phone users generally take a computer-like approach when operating their phones.

According to the text, "users are now required to take a more computer-like approach". However, the text doesn't mention that mobile phone users actually do take a computer-like approach. In actual fact, the text also argues that, "some users are likely to find it increasingly difficult to operate these features".

                                                     <u>The answer is cannot say.</u>

1.

B.   Statement: Internet use is becoming increasingly common in mobile phones.

According to the text, "new mobile phones often have high level features such as text messaging, audio-visual facilities, Internet and computer gaming". This means that the Internet features are becoming increasingly common.

<u>The answer is true.</u>

C.   Statement: The younger sector is more competent at using the audio-visual facilities in mobile phones.

According to the text, "there is a large and growing sector of young users who seem more naturally competent at using them (these features)".

<u>The answer is true.</u>

D.   Statement: The increasingly complex operation of mobile phone means there are few users who are naturally competent.

According to the text, "there is a large and growing sector of young users who seem more naturally competent at using them (these features)".

<u>The answer is false.</u>

2.

A.   Statement: Organic food production is the fastest growing field in the food industry.

According to the text, "The production of organic food products… continues to increase considerably" and "is likely to triple over the next decade". However, the text never mentions that it's the fastest growing field in the food industry.

<u>The answer is cannot say.</u>

B.   Statement: The main cause of enhanced organic food consumption is the higher general standard of living.

The text clearly states that, "Health awareness and higher standards of living are both enhancing consumption". Therefore a higher standard of living is only one of two main causes of enhanced organic food consumption.

<u>The answer is false.</u>

2.

C.   <u>Statement</u>: Consumers are now more conscious of the value of organic food than in the past.

According to the text, "Health awareness…(is) enhancing consumption". Therefore we can infer that consumers are now more conscious of the value of organic food than in the past.

<u>The answer is true.</u>

D.   <u>Statement</u>: The consumption of organic food has tripled over the past decade.

The text states that, "the (organic food) market is likely to triple over the next decade". There is no reference to the past.

<u>The answer is false.</u>

3.

A.   <u>Statement</u>: Natural disasters are the indisputable cause of life expectancy oscillations.

According to the text, epidemics, natural disasters and unstable weather are all responsible for oscillations in mean life expectancy. Therefore, this is not a unique attribute of natural disasters.

<u>The answer is false.</u>

B.   <u>Statement</u>: Average life expectancy decreases due to the cooling of regions

The text states that, "…the subsequent cooling and warming of affected regions, generate oscillations in mean life expectancy and lead populations to increase or decrease their average age". Therefore, we don't know the direction in which cooling impacts life expectancy.

<u>The answer is cannot say.</u>

C.   <u>Statement</u>: Epidemics are one of the causes of fluctuations in mean life expectancy.

According to the text, "Epidemics, natural disasters and unstable weather,…generate oscillations in mean life expectancy". Therefore, epidemics are one of three factors impacting life expectancy.

<u>The answer is true.</u>

3.

D.   Statement: Average life expectancy is predicted to rise in the future.

Even if intuitively this statement feels true, there is no evidence to substantiate it in the text.

The answer is cannot say.

4.

A.   Statement: Mass immigration leading to multicultural societies has contributed to increased racism in Western Europe.

The text clearly states that, "multicultural societies resulting from mass immigration have contributed to a reduction in discrimination suffered by minority groups.

The answer is false.

B.   Statement: Racial discrimination is less evident in heavily populated societies.

The text has no information about heavily populated societies.

The answer is cannot say.

C.   Statement: Societies that do not fight against racism may suffer in the future.

The text states that societies that don't fight racism may suffer from "anarchy" and damage to the "delicate fabric of society".

The answer is true.

D.   Statement: Social chaos can compromise the fragile structure of society.

Although this statement sounds intuitively correct, the text does not support it. According to the text, racial discrimination can both create anarchy (chaos) and damage the fabric/ fragile structure of society. Yet the text doesn't show a causal link between the two.

The answer is cannot say.

5.

A.   <u>Statement</u>: A good lecturer should not differentiate between the students' developmental trajectory and the class requirements.

This statement makes logical sense, but is not supported by the text. The text stipulates that a good lecturer should have "an inflexible developmental trajectory", and "class requirements (that) are continuously adapted to contemporary themes". That is, the text suggests that a good lecturer differentiates between the students' developmental trajectory and the class requirements.

<u>The answer is false.</u>

B.   <u>Statement</u>: The themes in a course may change due to current relevance.

The text stipulates that a good lecturer will "…never eliminate a focal topic due to low current relevance".

<u>The answer is false.</u>

C.   <u>Statement</u>: Current affairs are generally not relevant to university level lectures.

This statement is tricky. The text states that good lecturers "…blend topical subjects into their long-established course material but will never eliminate a focal topic due to low current relevance". The focal topics dictate the course syllabus, and therefore have precedence over current affairs. This doesn't mean, however, that current affairs are not valuable. One can assume that they are, since current themes are blended into the course material. They may not be as valuable as the focal topics, but we cannot describe them as irrelevant.

<u>The answer is false.</u>

D.   <u>Statement</u>: Expansive lecturing experience is a strong motivator for successful lecturers.

According to the text, motivation and experience both contribute to being a good lecturer. However, there is no information as to whether experience influences motivation. Moreover, the text talks about, "having the experience to concentrate on the essence" rather than having extensive lecturing experience.

<u>The answer is cannot say.</u>

6.

A.   Statement: The female population of China's countryside is lower than the ideal 50:50 gender distribution.

According to the text, there's a 5% difference between the number of males and females and a "radical reduction in the female population" in China's countryside. This means that there are less than 50% females.

The answer is true.

B.   Statement: If successful, the new governmental regulations in China are likely to widen the gender distribution.

According to the text, "The Chinese government is currently attempting to amend this gender distortion by placing tougher penalties on women who get illegal abortions and by criminalising prenatal ultrasound examinations". These actions are aimed at decreasing the gender gap, not enlarging it.

The answer is false.

C.   Statement: Prenatal ultrasound examinations are one of the suspected causes of the gender gap in rural China.

As one method of reducing the gender gap, the Chinese government has decided to outlaw prenatal ultrasound examinations. This means they suspect that the information provided by ultrasounds leads to the abortion of female foetuses.

The answer is true.

D.   Statement: In some places in rural China, the gender gap may result in millions of unmarried men.

The gender gap may possibly lead to millions of unmarried men in some regions, but no such information is provided in the text.

The answer is cannot say

7.

A.   Statement: If airlines combine operations on unpopular routes, they will increase operating costs.

According to the text, "Airlines reduce their overhead by sharing unpopular air routes, which lowers both the overall risk and the operating costs".

The answer is false.

7.

B.   Statement: A possible consequence of code sharing partnerships is a reduction of the overall risk on unpopular air routes.

According to the text, "The potential gains of such initiatives (such as code sharing) are huge. Airlines reduce their overhead by sharing unpopular air routes, which lowers both the overall risk and the operating costs".

The answer is true.

C.   Statement: An inability to share services in response to unexpectedly low business can reduce the flexibility of airline operations.

If, according to the text, the ability to share services with partners in response to unexpectedly low business increases flexibility, then it can be inferred that the reverse is also true.

The answer is true.

D.   Statement: There are certain services that airlines should offer on their own, without forming a partnership.

The passage discusses how two specific services, code sharing and frequent flyer memberships, are mutually beneficial when airlines work together. However, there is no information about particular services that airlines should offer on their own.

The answer is cannot say.

8.

A.   Statement: International long-distance call centre employees have had to change their working hours.

The text clearly states that the, "typical working hours of call centre workers have changed dramatically to match with trans-Atlantic time zones".

The answer is true.

B.   Statement: Call centre staff now has a more strenuous workload.

The text points to changes in technology and working hours. There is no information about changes in the staff workload.

The answer is cannot say.

8.

C.   Statement: Call centre employees have to answer incoming calls much more enthusiastically than in the past

The text stipulates that employees have to answer calls enthusiastically, but provides no information about past requirements.

The answer is cannot say.

D.   Statement: Working regular hours during the day can lead to more social interaction amongst staff.

The final sentence of the passage states that, "These late working hours also lead to less human interaction in the call-centre". It can be inferred that during regular daily hours there would be a greater social element to employee working life.

The answer is true.

9.

A.   Statement: Prior to Aylwin's government, there was no economic growth in Chile.

While it can be inferred that Aylwin's government did improve economic growth in Chile through the statement, "The establishment of Chilean democracy has ... boosted Chile's economic growth", there is no mention of the extent of economic growth beforehand.

The answer is cannot say.

B.   Statement: The government of Chile assumed that economic growth would follow the establishment of new social policies.

The text suggests that the new government had vowed, "to promote economic growth in parallel to the introduction of new social policies", rather than one after the other.

The answer is false.

C.   Statement: Chilean economic growth culminated in the establishment of Chilean democracy.

The text suggests that, "the establishment of Chilean democracy has been crucial in drawing overseas investors, and this in turn has boosted Chile's economic growth". However, the text does not state that economic growth peaked after the establishment of Chilean democracy.

The answer is false.

D.   <u>Statement</u>: Only the poorest communities in Chile suffered from social inequality.

The text does state that the poorest communities in Chile suffered from social inequality. However, it doesn't mention whether the poorest communities were the only ones to suffer.

<u>The answer is cannot say.</u>

10.

A.   Statement: Franchising is likely to become the most popular method of increasing business expansion.

The text states clearly that most companies will, "… aim to minimise the use of this method". Therefore, franchising is not likely to become the most popular method of increasing business expansion.

<u>The answer is false.</u>

B.   Statement: Franchisees may have different views than the 'mother' company on how to manage the franchised business.

The text clearly states that, "Difficulties arise when franchisees and companies disagree on business policies…".

<u>The answer is true.</u>

C.   Statement: Service delivery efficiency has reduced companies' will to franchise.

The text explains that service delivery efficiency is a cause for disagreement between franchisees and companies, but it doesn't mention whether this is why companies are reluctant to franchise.

<u>The answer is cannot say.</u>

D.   Statement: Companies are now more aware of the need to monitor franchisees.

According to the text, "Companies who have previously used franchising have learnt the essential need to monitor the business operations of the franchised branch". However, the text doesn't mention companies that have never franchised.

<u>The answer is cannot say.</u>

Test 14 Verbal Critical Reasoning – Business

The Verbal Critical Reasoning Test – Business is an important verbal test you are likely to encounter in commercial environments. The test demands a relatively high level of concentration as well as good reading comprehension skills. In some cases, the test will be strongly slanted towards business and will be affiliated with the type of position you are applying for. The next test provides an example of this type of test content.

Instructions:
This test consists of 5 reading passages. Each text is followed by several statements.
Read each passage and determine the correct answer:
- Choose **True** if the statement has to be true, according to the passage.
- Choose **False** if the statement has to be false, according to the passage.
- Choose **Cannot Say** if you cannot determine whether the statement is true or false without further information.

Remember
Your answers must be based only on the information provided in the text.
You have 10 minutes to work through 5 reading passages and 20 statements.

Good Luck!

1. Our newly written organisational charter emphasises our commitment to the creation of long-term value through the discovery, development and conversion of new business initiatives. This statement expresses our company's inherently dynamic nature. The charter aims to communicate our dynamism by highlighting our readiness to explore new initiatives, our skill in pushing these to fruition and our ability to capitalise profits. The charter aims to instil this spirit within every single employee.

A. The company's dynamism is communicated in three attributes.
                                          True / False / Cannot say

B. Employees internalise the values in the charter and adopt the spirit of the company.
                                          True / False / Cannot say

C. The dynamism that characterises the company is expected to influence the behaviour of every employee.   True / False / Cannot say

D. The organisation hasn't always been dynamic, and the charter aims to instil this spirit.   True / False / Cannot say

2.

> Employees working within organisations have a legislative obligation to monitor the content of e-mails sent to external bodies and to eliminate potentially sensitive internal information, regardless of the perceived importance of that information. To guarantee that employees fulfil their legislative obligation and to prevent a possible leak of exclusive information, employers have prepared mandatory contracts stipulating this responsibility. Contracts must be signed by all employees and additionally, a copyright section must be included in every external e-mail. The copyright statement emphasises the confidentiality of the information provided. If employees are careless in handling information circulated via e-mail, they may risk serious punitive measures.

A.   Providing that the information employees send via e-mail isn't important, the legislative obligation to monitor its content doesn't apply.   True / False / Cannot say

B.   Supervisors should monitor employees' e-mail accounts to minimise the leak of exclusive information.   True / False / Cannot say

C.   Salary cuts and permanent dismissals are possible punitive actions employers can take, and therefore may be used to punish employee inattention to the e-mail content regulation.   True / False / Cannot say

D.   The copyright section added to each external e-mail specifies that the content of the e-mail is owned by the organisation.   True / False / Cannot say

3.

> Dr Doolittle released a rather self-disclosing press release yesterday. The purpose of the release was to inform all animal owners that the RZI (Royal Zoo Institute) had approached him and asked to purchase his services exclusively. According to insiders, the RZP (Royal Zoo Pharmacy), a division of the RZI, has been supplying Dr Doolittle with animal products for the past five years with little return. This has led to a debt larger than the value of Dr Doolittle's practice. The RZI has told reporters that they do expect to collaborate with Dr Doolittle, but the extent of the partnership is not yet clear.

A.   Dr Doolittle is going to work exclusively for the RZI.   True / False / Cannot say

B.   The RZI and Dr Doolittle have worked together indirectly for several years.
                                                                 True / False / Cannot say

C.   The RZP has no interest in Dr Doolittle's practice.   True / False / Cannot say

D.   Dr Doolittle's debt is expected to influence his decision to give up his clinic and join the RZI.   True / False / Cannot say

4.

> The new health and safety regulations state that helmets should be worn and fastened and head torches should be operating at all times whilst working within the mine. The use of other safety devices are prioritised according to previous depth regulations and in accordance with the daily instructions provided by the mine's security engineer. On detonation days, without exception, maximal safety wear should be worn inside and outside the mine within a 500 meter external diameter.

A.   The new health and safety regulations are more demanding than the previous ones.

<u>True</u> / <u>False</u> / <u>Cannot say</u>

B.   Miners working on the upper surface of the mine, near the mine's entrance, are not ever expected to wear safety devices other than a helmet and a head torch.

<u>True</u> / <u>False</u> / <u>Cannot say</u>

C.   Maximal safety devices are generally worn outside the mine only in the event of an explosion.   <u>True</u> / <u>False</u> / <u>Cannot say</u>

D.   The mine's security engineer is the only person with the authority to decide which safety gear is worn by miners.   <u>True</u> / <u>False</u> / <u>Cannot say</u>

5.

> The merger between the Australian owned BLP and the British owned Billis has led to the formation of a world class leader in the natural resources sector. While financially weaker, Billis brought its diversified business portfolio and high profitability to the merger. BLP, being a top Australian organisation, brought substantial capital and a strong governmental lobby. Oil, copper, coal and uranium will remain the primary products of the newly merged company. Nevertheless, BLP Billis is looking to penetrate other markets such as gas, silver, titanium, minerals and diamonds.

A.   Billis provided the major financial support for the merger.

<u>True</u> / <u>False</u> / <u>Cannot say</u>

B.   BLP Billis wants to alter its business focus from oil, copper, coal and uranium to new markets like gas, silver, titanium, minerals and diamonds.

<u>True</u> / <u>False</u> / <u>Cannot say</u>

C.   Billis's position in the newly merged company was influenced by its diversified business portfolio rather than its governmental lobby.   <u>True</u> / <u>False</u> / <u>Cannot say</u>

D.   Shareholders should expect greater return on the value of their shares as a result of the merger.   <u>True</u> / <u>False</u> / <u>Cannot say</u>

Test 14 Answers:

1.

A.   <u>Statement</u>: The company's dynamism is communicated in three attributes.

Three aspects of dynamism are described in the text. These are the, "readiness to explore new initiatives, our skill in pushing these to fruition and our ability to capitalise profits".

<u>The answer is true.</u>

B.   <u>Statement</u>: Employees internalise the values in the charter and adopt the spirit of the company

According to the text, the charter, "aims to instil this spirit within every single employee". This doesn't mean, however, that this will actually occur.

<u>The answer is cannot say.</u>

C.   <u>Statement</u>: The dynamism that characterises the company is expected to influence the behaviour of every employee.

According to the text, "The charter aims to instil this spirit (dynamism)…". The expectation therefore does exist.

<u>The answer is true.</u>

D.   <u>Statement</u>: The organisation hasn't always been dynamic, and the charter aims to instil this spirit.

The text clearly mentions, "our company's **inherently** dynamic nature". This implies that the company has always been dynamic.

<u>The answer is false.</u>

2.

A.   <u>Statement</u>: Providing that the information employees send via e-mail isn't important, the legislative obligation to monitor its content doesn't apply.

The text clearly states that content is to be monitored, "regardless of the perceived importance of that information".

<u>The answer is false.</u>

B.   <u>Statement</u>: Supervisors should monitor employees' e-mail accounts to minimise the leak of exclusive information.

According to the text, "employees …. have (an) … obligation to monitor the content of e-mails…". The text never says that this is part of the employer's role.

<u>The answer is false.</u>

C.   <u>Statement</u>: Salary cuts and permanent dismissals are possible punitive actions employers can take, and therefore may be used to punish employee inattention to the e-mail content regulation.

This statement implies that salary cuts and permanent dismissals are considered serious punitive actions. The passage suggests that, "If employees are careless in handling information circulated via e-mail, they may risk serious punitive measures". There is a direct correlation between the statement and the information provided in the passage.

<u>The answer is true.</u>

D.   <u>Statement</u>: The copyright section added to each external e-mail specifies that the content of the e-mail is owned by the organisation.

According to the text, "Contracts must be signed by all employees and additionally, a copyright section must be included in every external e-mail". **Copyright** means that the information is owned by the organisation.

<u>The answer is true.</u>

3.

A.   <u>Statement</u>: Dr Doolittle is going to work exclusively for the RZI.

The text states that, "Dr Doolittle released a rather self-disclosing press release yesterday. The purpose of the release was to inform all animal owners that the RZI (Royal Zoo Institute) had approached him and asked to purchase his services exclusively". The text doesn't say, however, that he had agreed to work exclusively for the RZI.

<u>The answer is cannot say.</u>

B.   Statement: The RZI and Dr Doolittle have worked together indirectly for several years.

According to the text, "the RZP (Royal Zoo Pharmacy), a division of the RZI, has been supplying Dr Doolittle with animal products for the past five years …".

The answer is true.

C.   Statement: The RZP has no interest in Dr Doolittle's practice.

The text states that, "the RZP (Royal Zoo Pharmacy), a division of the RZI, has been supplying Dr Doolittle with animal products for the past five years with little return." Therefore the RZP is showing an interest in Dr Doolittle's practice.

The answer is false.

D.   Statement: Dr Doolittle's debt is expected to influence his decision to give up his clinic and join the RZI.

This statement is tricky, because the answer can only be inferred from the text. Dr Doolittle owes a substantial amount of money to the RZI, and they have approached him and asked that he provide services to them exclusively. In addition, the RZI told reporters that they expect to collaborate with Dr Doolittle. Further, Dr Doolittle has informed others that he has been approached by the RZI. He wouldn't be likely to do that if he hadn't already decided on the partnership.

The answer is true.

4.

A.   Statement: The new health and safety regulations are more demanding than the previous ones.

The passage doesn't provide us with any information about the previous health and safety regulations.

The answer is cannot say

B.   Statement: Miners working on the upper surface of the mine, near the mine's entrance, are not ever expected to wear safety devices other than a helmet and a head torch.

According to the text, "On detonation days, without exception, maximal safety wear should be worn inside and outside the mine within a 500 meter external diameter". Therefore the statement is not true.

The answer is false.

C. Statement: Maximal safety devices are generally worn outside the mine only in the event of an explosion.

According to the text, "On detonation days, without exception, maximal safety wear should be worn inside and outside the mine within a 500 meter external diameter".

The answer is true.

D. Statement: The mine's security engineer is the only person with the authority to decide which safety gear is worn by miners.

The text states that, "The use of other safety devices are prioritised according to previous depth regulations and in accordance with the daily instructions provided by the mine's security engineer". So the use of safety devices is determined both by past regulations and by the engineer".

The answer is false.

5.
A. Statement: Billis provided the major financial support for the merger.

According to the passage, Billis is financially weaker than BLP, and in fact BLP provided the financial capital for the merger.

The answer is false.

B. Statement: BLP Billis wants to alter its business focus from oil, copper, coal and uranium to new markets like gas, silver, titanium, minerals and diamonds.

According to the text, "Oil, copper, coal and uranium will remain the primary products of the newly merged company. Nevertheless, BLP Billis is looking to penetrate other markets such as gas, silver, titanium, minerals and diamonds". BLP Billis is therefore seeking to expand, rather than alter, their business focus.

The answer is false.

C. Statement: Billis's position in the newly merged company was influenced by its diversified business portfolio rather than its governmental lobby.

According to the text, Billis brought a "diversified business portfolio" to the merger and BLP brought a "substantial governmental lobby".

The answer is true.

D. Statement: Shareholders should expect greater return on the value of their shares as a result of the merger.

While the merger does sound promising to shareholders, the text provides no information about how it will influence them specifically.

The answer is cannot say.

Test 15 Verbal Evaluation

Verbal evaluation tests are very similar to verbal critical reasoning tests, yet they are usually at a slightly lower level. They are given to job applicants that are seeking jobs with low to medium seniority, such as junior managers, sales staff and office managers.

Below you will find a few examples of questions that are used on verbal evaluation tests.

Instructions:
Read the passage and determine the correct answer:
- Choose **True** if the statement has to be true, according to the passage.
- Choose **False** if the statement has to be false, according to the passage.
- Choose **Cannot Say** if you cannot determine whether the statement is true or false without further information.

Remember
Your answers must be based only on the information provided in the text.
You have 10 minutes to work through 5 reading passages and 20 statements.

Good Luck!

1.

> In the past, home heating systems used different sources of energy such as wood, electricity and kerosene. However, these are expensive compared to a more recently discovered energy source - solar energy, whose only resource is the sun. Solar energy is an alternative energy source, but it can only be used for heating with a small number of appliances. In addition, solar energy is difficult to use for heating purposes in the winter, when it's most needed. This is because the sun doesn't come out as often during the winter, making solar energy less available.

A. Solar energy is hardly available in the winter.   True / False / Cannot say

B. The use of solar energy is restricted to a few heating devices.
                                                          True / False / Cannot say

C. If electricity were a lot cheaper, we would have no need for solar energy.
                                                          True / False / Cannot say

D. There are other major resources that can be used to provide solar energy instead of the sun.   True / False / Cannot say

2.

> According to new legislation concerning the income tax law, tax payers may be taxed positively or negatively depending on their annual revenues. Contrary to previous arrangements where income tax was charged only if an individual had reached a certain revenue threshold, the new legislation suggests compensation in the form of a negative income tax for those who fail to reach a minimum annual income. 'Income' in this context includes most monetary sources, such as paid salary, rented personal property earning, interest, dividend earnings and passive income. The only exemption would be a transfer of funds between first degree family members including children younger than 18 years old.

A. Money that a wife puts in her husband's bank account is, according to the new legislation, considered income.   True / False / Cannot say

B. The vast majority of taxpayers will continue to be taxed positively.
                                            True / False / Cannot say

C. A very low annual salary without other substantial sources of income will probably lead to a negative income tax refund.   True / False / Cannot say

D. Paid salary, personal property rental earnings, interest, dividend earnings and passive income are the only types of income that can determine a person's eligibility for negative income tax compensation.   True / False / Cannot say

3.

> Even though the minimum age for obtaining a driving license has increased in recent years, a substantial increase in car sales during the same period has resulted in a staggering rise in fatal car accidents. As the latest figures show, fatal car accidents are especially prevalent amongst young drivers who have less than five years of driving experience. Last winter, 50 per cent of all fatal road accidents involved drivers with up to five years driving experience. An additional 15 per cent were drivers who had between six to eight years of experience. The interim figures of the current year show that the massive advertising campaign called "fighting accidents" has resulted in some improvement. However, the truth is that the number of younger drivers involved in fatal car accidents is still intolerably high.

A. The majority of fatal car accidents, according to last winter's figures, involved drivers with less than 9 years experience. <u>True</u> / <u>False</u> / <u>Cannot say</u>

B. The considerable increase in car sales is the reason behind the sharp increase in fatal car accidents. <u>True</u> / <u>False</u> / <u>Cannot say</u>

C. Family cars that are not typically driven by younger drivers are less likely to be involved in fatal road accidents. <u>True</u> / <u>False</u> / <u>Cannot say</u>

D. The advertising campaign called "fighting accidents" has failed to reduce the number of car accidents. <u>True</u> / <u>False</u> / <u>Cannot say</u>

4.
> Full blown depression is widely acknowledged to be a severe medical illness and is commonly treated with medication. After decades of research and numerous experiments, effective drugs have been developed. These, on average, have successfully treated over 60% of depressed patients with relatively minor side-effects. Individuals who suffer from typical depression often respond better to drug therapy than the minority who suffer from the 'reversed symptoms' of depression. Experimental research indicates that 12 weeks of drug therapy can significantly reduce a number of symptoms including loss of appetite, sadness, lack of energy, anxiety and feelings of guilt. People who are less likely to respond well to drug therapy have several other treatment options, including cognitive behavioural therapy (CBT) and in extreme cases, electroconvulsive therapy (ECT).

A. People who suffer from moderate depression respond better to drug therapy.
<u>True</u> / <u>False</u> / <u>Cannot say</u>

B. Research has shown that drug therapy is ineffective for more than half of depressed individuals. <u>True</u> / <u>False</u> / <u>Cannot say</u>

C. Individuals who suffer from 'reversed-symptom' depression are unlikely to respond well to drug therapy compared with those who suffer from typical depression.
<u>True</u> / <u>False</u> / <u>Cannot say</u>

D. Depressed patients who don't respond well to drug therapy will improve if they turn to other forms of therapy such as CBT and ECT. <u>True</u> / <u>False</u> / <u>Cannot say</u>

5.

> There are several possible reasons for companies to participate in professional trade fairs. They can be excellent sales platforms providing the company with exposure to relevant customers and distributors, because trade fairs are one of those rare occasions where customers actively seek out specific products. Trade fairs can also be an image building opportunity aimed at strengthening the company's profile within a particular sector. Companies can do this by showing novel products and a lucrative booth design. These fairs can also be a good way for companies to gauge their competition, because they can get vital information about other products and generally assess the direction the field is heading in. Trade fairs are extremely expensive, especially because in each field, there are a number of important international fairs that should be attended every year. This often creates a financial burden on the minor players in a field or industry. In many instances, the enormous costs don't seem to justify the direct impact on business. But as one senior manufacturer recently said, "if you're not there, you don't exist".

A. Company participation in professional trade fairs is important for three reasons.

True / False / Cannot say

B. The more lucrative the booth design, the greater the sales return.

True / False / Cannot say

C. Professional trade fairs do not boost sales or strengthen a company's profile.

True / False / Cannot say

D. The financial payback of participating in trade fairs usually justifies the cost.

True / False / Cannot say

Test 15 Answers:

1.

A.   Statement: Solar energy is hardly available in the winter.

The sun is not available much in the winter, which means that solar energy isn't really available in the winter.

The answer is true.

1.

B.   <u>Statement</u>: The use of solar energy is restricted to a few heating devices.

The text suggests that, "it can only be used for heating with a small number of appliances.

<u>The answer is true.</u>

C.   <u>Statement</u>: If electricity were a lot cheaper, we would have no need for solar energy.

The fact that electricity is expensive doesn't imply that if it were cheaper, we wouldn't need solar energy. There may be other reasons for using electricity.

<u>The answer is cannot say.</u>

D.   <u>Statement</u>: There are other major resources that can be used to provide solar energy instead of the sun.

According to the text, there is "… a more recently discovered energy source - solar energy, whose only resource is the sun". There are, therefore, no other major resources for solar energy.

<u>The answer is false.</u>

2.

A.   <u>Statement</u>: Money that a wife puts in her husband's bank account is, according to the new legislation, considered income.

Money that is transferred between first degree family members is not considered income, according to the text.

<u>The answer is false.</u>

B.   <u>Statement</u>: The vast majority of taxpayers will continue to be taxed positively.

The text explains that negative income tax will be paid to those who fail to reach a minimum annual income. But the text doesn't provide us with any information as to how many people fall into this category.

<u>The answer is cannot say.</u>

2.

C.   Statement: A very low annual salary without other substantial sources of income will probably lead to a negative income tax refund.

The text states that, "the new legislation suggests compensation in the form of a negative income tax for those who fail to reach a minimum annual income".

<u>The answer is true.</u>

D.   Statement: Paid salary, personal property rental earnings, interest, dividend earnings and passive income are the only types of income that can determine a person's eligibility for negative income tax compensation.

According to the passage, "Income" in this context includes most monetary sources, such as …".The use of 'such as' suggests that there are other sources of income.

<u>The answer is false.</u>

3.

A.   Statement: The majority of fatal car accidents, according to last winter's figures, involved drivers with less than 9 years experience.

The statistics provided in the text indicate that 50% of car accidents involve drivers with up to five years experience, and 15% of car accidents involve drivers with 6-8 years of driving experience. This means that 65% of car accidents involve drivers with less than 9 years of experience, which is the majority.

<u>The answer is true.</u>

B.   Statement: The considerable increase in car sales is the reason behind the sharp increase in fatal car accidents.

The text clearly states that, "a substantial increase in car sales during the same period has resulted in a staggering rise in fatal car accidents".

<u>The answer is true.</u>

3.

C.   Statement: Family cars that are not typically driven by younger drivers are less likely to be involved in fatal road accidents.

The text doesn't provide any information about the types of cars driven by younger drivers.

The answer is cannot say.

D.   Statement: The advertising campaign called "fighting accidents" has failed to reduce the number of car accidents.

According to the text, the advertising campaign "fighting accidents" resulted in some improvement. This means that to some degree, it succeeded in reducing the number of car accidents.

The answer is false.

4.

A.   Statement: People who suffer from moderate depression respond better to drug therapy.

The text doesn't refer to the intensity of the depression, only to the distinction between different types of depression (typical vs. reversed symptom).

The answer is cannot say.

B.   Statement: Research has shown that drug therapy is ineffective for more than half of depressed individuals.

The text explicitly states that drugs can be used to successfully treat over 60% of depressed patients. This means that drugs are effective in treating over half of depressed individuals.

The answer is false.

C.   Statement: Individuals who suffer from 'reversed-symptom' depression are unlikely to respond well to drug therapy compared with those who suffer from typical depression.

The text confirms that, "Individuals who suffer from typical depression often respond better to drug therapy than the minority who suffer from the 'reversed symptoms' of depression".

The answer is true.

4.

D.   Statement: Depressed patients who don't respond well to drug therapy will improve if they turn to other forms of therapy such as CBT and ECT.

The text states that there are other forms of therapy for those who don't respond to drug therapy, but it doesn't say whether these forms of treatment are effective.

<u>The answer is cannot say.</u>

5.

A.   Statement: Company participation in professional trade fairs is important for three reasons.

The text does mention three reasons. These include: (1) sales platform (2) image building (3) gauging competition.

<u>The answer is true.</u>

B.   Statement: The more lucrative the booth design, the greater the sales return.

Although intuitively the statement may sound logical, there is no supporting information in the text about the relationship between sales and booth design.

<u>The answer is cannot say.</u>

C.   Statement: Professional trade fairs do not boost sales or strengthen a company's profile.

The information in the passage doesn't suggest that there are guaranteed financial returns from trade fairs, but it does say that they can be excellent sales platforms and image building opportunities. Therefore, it would be wrong to argue that trade fairs do not boost sales or strengthen a company's profile.

<u>The answer is false.</u>

D.   Statement: The financial payback of participating in trade fairs usually justifies the cost.

The information in the text suggests otherwise. The text states that, "In many instances, the enormous costs don't seem to justify the direct impact on business". If in many instances participation in fairs doesn't justify the cost, then we can't say that the financial payback usually justifies the cost.

<u>The answer is cannot say.</u>

Test 16 Logic

Logic tests fall under the category of verbal tests. They assess your word comprehension skills, but primarily they assess your ability to reach logical conclusions based on written and/or verbal problems. This type of test is administered for a wide variety of positions across a number of different industries, although not as frequently as reading comprehension tests. The logic test may be problematic for applicants who aren't native speakers of the testing language.

Instructions
- Choose one correct answer for each question.

Remember
You have 10 minutes to complete the test (18 questions).

Good Luck!

1. There are four famous topical pictures in a museum: scenery, a kitchen, a park and oranges. The paintings were painted by Jones, Smith, Hardy and Lane. The scenery painting is hanging next to Smith's painting. The scenery painting also hangs between the park and Hardy's painting. Jones didn't paint the scenery or the oranges. Who painted the kitchen?
    A. Jones
    B. Smith
    C. Hardy
    D. None of the above

2. Henrietta is Emma's daughter and Grace's mom. What is Emma to Grace?
    A. her mother
    B. her daughter
    C. her grandmother
    D. her granddaughter

3. Dan is Joshua's son and Guy's brother. Margaret is Guy's mother and Judy's daughter. Which of the statements below are true?
    A.   Judy is Joshua's mother-in-law.
    B.   Margaret is Dan's mother.
    C.   Judy is Guy's grandmother.
    D.   All of the above.

4. John looked in the mirror and said, "the father of the person I see in the mirror is Simon's brother". Which of the statements below are true?
    A.   Simon is John's father.
    B.   John is Simon's son.
    C.   John is Simon's uncle.
    D.   Simon is John's uncle.

5. All Germans speak Italian. All Italian speakers ride bicycles. Which of the following statements must be true?
    A.   All Italians speak German.
    B.   All bicycle riders are German.
    C.   All Germans ride bicycles.
    D.   Some of the Italians riding bicycles are Germans.

6. All owls have night vision, and birds that have night vision aren't black. Which of the following statements must be true?
    A.   Black ravens don't have night vision.
    B.   All owls are not black.
    C.   Birds that are black lack night vision.
    D.   All of the above

7. All psychologists are scientists. All nice people are psychologists. Which of the following statements must be true?
    A.   All psychologists are nice.
    B.   All scientists are psychologists.
    C.   All nice people are scientists.
    D.   Some nice people aren't scientists.

8. If there are no dancers that aren't slim and no singers that aren't dancers, then which statements are always true?
    A. There is not one slim person that isn't a dancer.
    B. All singers are slim.
    C. Anybody slim is also a singer.
    D. None of the above.

9. All materials are degradable. Some materials are solid. Which of the statements below are true?
    A. All solids are degradable.
    B. Some solids are degradable.
    C. All solids are materials.
    D. All degradable products are materials.

10. If there are universal objects that are invisible and all universal objects are in space, then which of the statements below are true?
    A. All objects that are visible are in space.
    B. All objects in space are universal objects.
    C. There are some universal objects in space that are invisible.
    D. None of the above.

11. If a person cannot testify on his/her own behalf and that person is appearing in court, then what is true?
    A. A person can appear in court as long as he/she does not testify on his/her own behalf.
    B. Anyone who appears in court cannot testify on his/her own behalf.
    C. Anyone testifying on his/her own behalf appears in court.
    D. Anyone appearing in court testifies on his/her own behalf.

12. Danny discovered the following facts while working on his geography assignment: 30% of Georgia's inhabitants are Native-American, 50% of Georgia's inhabitants work in the service industry, 20% work in agriculture and 60% drink Coke. Danny drew four conclusions. Which of the four conclusions must be true?
    A. Half of Georgia's coke-drinking inhabitants are Native-American.
    B. One-third of Georgia's coke-drinking inhabitants work in agriculture.
    C. In Georgia, there are more Native-American people working in the service industry than in the agricultural industry.
    D. Some of Georgia's service industry employees drink Coke.

13. This is data supplied by the cabbage growers union report for 2007: 80% of cabbages collected were heavy (over 0.5 kg), 10% of cabbages were green, 60% were red and 50% were big (having a diameter of over 10 cm). Which of the following statements must be false?
    A.   All red cabbages weren't big.
    B.   30% of red cabbages were big.
    C.   There were no cabbages that were both green and big.
    D.   Half of the cabbages were small.

14. All airplanes that don't stop in Spain fly to India. The first airplane didn't stop in Spain. Which of the following statements are true?
    A.   The first airplane didn't fly to India.
    B.   The first airplane flew to India.
    C.   All airplanes flying to India stop in Spain.
    D.   None of the above.

15. People who play instruments don't sing. All singers play instruments. Which of the following statements must be true?
    A.   All singers sing.
    B.   Singers don't sing.
    C.   Some singers don't sing.
    D.   None of the above.

16. Read the five statements below:
    1.   Jennifer runs faster than Robyn, but slower than Grace.
    2.   Emma is the slowest.
    3.   Grace and Harriet run at the same speed.
    4.   Harriet runs faster than Emma.
    5.   Robyn runs faster than Andrea.

    Which of the statements above are relevant to determine that Harriet runs faster than Andrea?
    A.   2, 3, 4
    B.   1, 3, 4
    C.   1, 2, 3
    D.   1, 3, 5

17. Short basketball players don't exist. There are short football players. Which statements are true?
    A.   There are football players that aren't basketball players.
    B.   All basketball players are football players.
    C.   A short person can't be a football player.
    D.   None of the above.

18. All birds with wings fly. There are black birds. Which statements are true?
    A.   Anything that isn't black isn't a bird.
    B.   Anything without wings isn't a bird.
    C.   All birds with wings are black.
    D.   None of the above.

Test 16 Answers:

General Tip:
As you work through a logic problem, sketch out the relationships between various elements in the question. This will help you reach the correct conclusion quickly.

1.   There are four famous topical pictures in a museum: scenery, a kitchen, a park and oranges. The paintings were painted by Jones, Smith, Hardy and Lane. The scenery painting is hanging next to Smith's painting. The scenery painting also hangs between the park and Hardy's painting. Jones didn't paint the scenery or the oranges. Who painted the kitchen?

      The scenery painting is hanging next to Smith's painting, and between Hardy's painting and the painting of the park. We can conclude, therefore, that Smith painted the park. Since Jones didn't paint the scenery painting, the oranges painting or the park painting (done by Smith), then he must have painted the kitchen.

                                                              The answer is A.

2.   Henrietta is Emma's daughter and Grace's mom. What is Emma to Grace?

Mother ⟶ Daughter / Mother ⟶ Daughter
Emma ⟶ Henrietta ⟶ Grace
Emma is Grace's grandmother.

The answer is C.

3.   Dan is Joshua's son and Guy's brother. Margaret is Guy's mother and Judy's daughter. Which of the statements below are true?

Judy is Margaret's mother. Margaret is Joshua's partner; therefore Judy is Joshua's mother-in-law. Dan and Guy are siblings, and therefore Margaret is also Dan's mother. Since Judy is Margaret's mother, she must be Dan's and Guy's grandmother. All of the statements are true.

The answer is D.

4.   John looked in the mirror and said, "the father of the person I see in the mirror is Simon's brother". Which of the statements below are true?

The person John sees in the mirror is himself. This means that John's father is Simon's brother, which makes Simon John's uncle.

The answer is D.

5. All Germans speak Italian. All Italian speakers ride bicycles. Which of the following statements must be true?

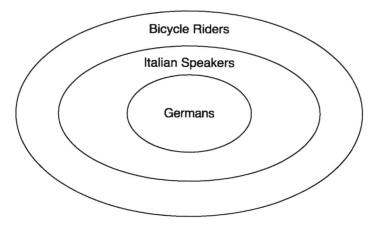

Based on the illustration, it's clear that all Germans are Italian speakers and that all Italian speakers are bicycle riders. Therefore, all Germans are bicycle riders.

The answer is C.

6. All owls have night vision, and birds that have night vision aren't black. Which of the following statements must be true?

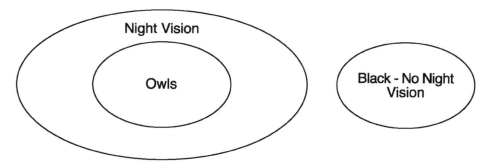

The illustration shows that black ravens don't have night vision; all owls aren't black and finally that black bird's lack night vision. All of the statements are true.

The answer is D.

7. All psychologists are scientists. All nice people are psychologists. Which of the following statements must be true?

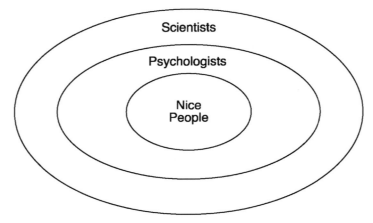

The illustration shows that the group of 'nice people' are included in the group of psychologists, which are included in the group of scientists. We can therefore conclude that all nice people are scientists.

The answer is C.

8. If there are no dancers that aren't slim and no singers that aren't dancers, then which statements are always true?

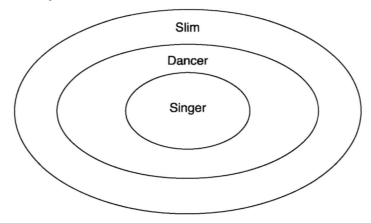

The tricky part of this question is that it is phrased negatively. This means that we have to identify the nature of each group initially and establish the relationship between the groups. Once the illustration is made, the relationship between the groups becomes clearer. The only true statement is that all singers are slim.

The answer is B.

9. All materials are degradable. Some materials are solid. Which of the statements below are true?

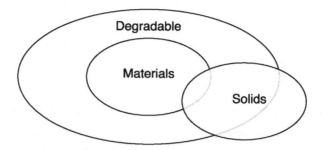

All materials are degradable and some materials are solid, but this doesn't mean that all materials are solid. Therefore only the solids that are also materials are degradable.

The answer is B.

10. If there are universal objects that are invisible and all universal objects are in space, then which of the statements below are true?

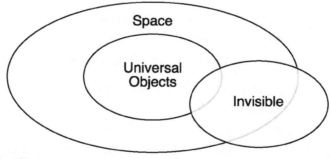

According to the diagram.   The answer is C.

11. If a person cannot testify on his/her own behalf and that person is appearing in court, then what is true?

According to the diagram.   The answer is A.

12. Danny discovered the following facts while working on his geography assignment: 30% of Georgia's inhabitants are Native-American, 50% of Georgia's inhabitants work in the service industry, 20% work in agriculture and 60% drink Coke. Danny drew four conclusions. Which of the four conclusions must be true?

The key to solving this problem is to figure out the sums (percentages) for each statement. If the results are greater than 100%, we can identify an overlap between categories.

A. Half of Georgia's coke-drinking inhabitants are Native-American.
If 60% of inhabitants drink Coke, then the Native-American inhabitants that drink Coke make up 30% of Georgia's total population. And 30% of Georgia's inhabitants are Native-American, so the sum of the two groups is 60% (i.e. 30%+30% = 60% < 100%) of the population. There isn't a definite overlap between the categories.

B. One-third of Georgia's coke-drinking inhabitants work in agriculture.
60% of Georgia's inhabitants drink coke. The percentage of people working in agriculture is 20%. We can therefore conclude (without calculating how many coke drinkers in Georgia make up the 1/3) that there isn't necessarily an overlap between the two categories (i.e. 20%+60% = 80% < 100%).

C. In Georgia, there are more Native-American people working in the service industry than in the agricultural industry.
There is no information that allows us to determine that this is true.

D. Some of Georgia's service industry employees drink Coke.
We know that 60% of Georgia's inhabitants drink Coke and 50% work in the service industry. We can then calculate that 50%+60% = 110% > 100%. So there's at least a 10% overlap between inhabitants of Georgia that both work in the service industry and drink coke.

The answer is D.

13. This is data supplied by the cabbage growers union report for 2007: 80% of cabbages collected were heavy (over 0.5 kg), 10% of cabbages were green, 60% were red and 50% were big (having a diameter of over 10 cm). Which of the following statements must be false?

You should approach this question in the same way we approached the previous question. You have to check the authenticity of each statement.

A. All red cabbages weren't big.
    We know that 60% of cabbages picked were red and only 50% were big, therefore, there is an overlap (60%+50% = 110% > 100%). The statement must be false, so this is the correct answer. There's no real need to check the rest of the statements, but we've provided an explanation in any case.

B. 30% of red cabbages were big.
    We know that 60% of cabbages were red and 50% were big, so there must be an overlap of at least 10% (60%+50% = 110% > 100%). However, we don't know the extent of the overlap. This statement may be true, but we don't know for sure.

C. There were no cabbages that were both green and big.
    We know that 10% of cabbages were green and 50% were big, so there may not be an overlap between the two (10%+50% = 60% < 100%). The statement can't be ruled out.

D. Half of the cabbages were small.
    We know that 50% (i.e. one half) of the cabbages are big, so the other half may be small. This would make this statement true.

The answer is A.

14. All airplanes that don't stop in Spain fly to India. The first airplane didn't stop in Spain. Which of the following statements are true?

All airplanes that don't stop in Spain fly to India. Since the first airplane didn't stop in Spain, it must have flown to India.

The answer is B.

15. People who play instruments don't sing. All singers play instruments. Which of the following statements must be true?

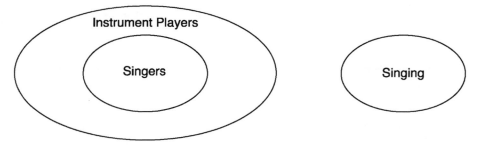

The illustration clearly illustrates that singers don't sing.

The answer is B.

16. Read the five statements below:
    1. Jennifer runs faster than Robyn, but slower than Grace.
    2. Emma is the slowest.
    3. Grace and Harriet run at the same speed.
    4. Harriet runs faster than Emma.
    5. Robyn runs faster than Andrea.

Which of the statements above are relevant to determine that Harriet runs faster than Andrea?

The first fact explains the relationship between Jennifer, Robyn and Grace. This is important, since Robyn and Andrea have a relationship that's explained further down.
The second fact explains Emma's ability, which is irrelevant to the question.
The third fact explains the relationship between Grace and Harriet, and allows us to position Harriet in relation to Jennifer and Robyn.
The fourth fact explains the relationship between Emma and Harriet, which is irrelevant to the question.
The final fact explains the relationship between Robyn and Andrea. This allows us to position Andrea in relation to Jennifer and Grace, and therefore in relation to Harriet as well due to the third fact. Facts 1, 3 and 5 are the only relevant pieces of information.

The answer is D.

17. Short basketball players don't exist. There are short football players. Which statements are true?

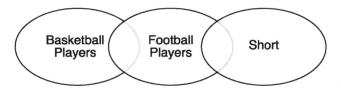

The illustration shows that there are football players that aren't basketball players.

<u>The answer is A.</u>

18. All birds with wings fly. There are black birds. Which statements are true?

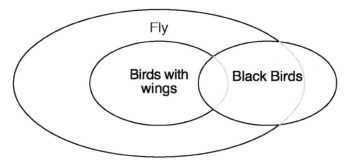

The illustration clearly shows that there are birds that are black and there are others types of birds as well. There are birds with wings, and black birds (not necessarily with wings) Not every bird with wings is necessarily black. Therefore none of the above statements are true.

<u>The answer is D.</u>

Test 17 Verbal Application

The verbal application test is used to evaluate grammar, vocabulary, spelling and reading comprehension skills. This type of test is used for a range of jobs, but most commonly for administrative and office-based jobs.

Instructions:
For each question below, circle the combination of words that most suitably fills in the blanks.
You have 3 minutes to complete the test!

Good Luck!

1. The job applicants that have successfully _____ the selection tests will be _____ to take part in a group activity.
    A. completed, invite
    B. mastered, presented
    C. completed, invited
    D. completed, administered

2. The first step in selling a publication is making sure you have found an _____ distributor to stock and _____ the books to the appropriate stores.
    A. satisfactory, release
    B. accept, carry
    C. adequate, deliver
    D. acceptable, liberate
    E. sufficient, convey

3. Work-life balance schemes in the workplace have been _____ by employees and increase morale and _____ at work.
  A. commended, motivate
  B. celebrated, discourage
  C. condemned, inspiration
  D. applauded, motivation
  E. criticised, inspired

4. Viewers _____ the screening of the foreign film _____ the missing subtitles and the uncomfortable seats.
  A. enjoyed, despite
  B. enjoyed, although
  C. liked, notwithstanding
  D. enjoy, regarding
  D. enjoyed, regardless

5. _____ and colourful outfits were _____ by carnival participants in the main parade crossing the capital city.
  A. Reserved, shown off
  B. Flamboyant, worn
  C. Reserved, dressed
  D. Glimmer, wear
  E. Flaming, wore

6. _____ interest rates have affected the real estate market gravely, making it _____ than ever for first time buyers to hop on the property ladder.
  A. Reduced, easy
  B. Increase, harder
  C. Reduce, harder
  D. Increased, harder
  E. Increasing, easier

7. His initial plan is to _____ the local _____ market in the region prior to choosing a _____ for his new agency.
    A. access, recruit, location
    B. axis, recruitment, place
    C. assess, recruitment, location
    D. appraise, recruit, locomotion
    E. excess, recruitment, location

8. Meteorologists _____ whether global warming will eventually _____ temperatures or induce a new ice age that will cause temperatures to _____ significantly.
    A. deliberate, drop, raise
    B. disputed, elevate, plunge
    C. disputing, inflate, drop
    D. debating, plunge, rise
    E. debate, raise, drop

Test 17 Answers:

1. The job applicants that have successfully **completed** the selection tests will be **invited** to take part in a group activity.

    The answer is C.

2. The first step in selling a publication is making sure you have found an **adequate** distributor to stock and **deliver** the books to the appropriate stores.

    The answer is C.

251 ■ Part 2   Aptitude Test Preparation

3. Work-life balance schemes in the work place have been **applauded** by employees and increase morale and **motivation** at work.

                                                            The answer is D.

4. Viewers **enjoyed** the screening of the foreign film **despite** the missing subtitles and the uncomfortable seats.

                                                            The answer is A.

5. **Flamboyant** and colourful outfits were **worn** by carnival participants in the main parade crossing the capital city.

                                                            The answer is B.

6. **Increased** interest rates have affected the real estate market gravely, making it **harder** than ever for first time buyers to hop on the property ladder.

                                                            The answer is D.

7. His initial plan is to **assess** the local **recruitment** market in the region prior to choosing a **location** for his new agency.

                                                            The answer is C.

8. Meteorologists **debate** whether global warming will eventually **raise** temperatures or induce a new ice age that will cause temperatures to **drop** significantly.

                                                            The answer is E.

Test 18 Word Relationships

The Word Relationships Test assesses your ability to logically comprehend and analyse relationships between words, and apply this logic to other word relationships. While it's categorised as a verbal test, it has an added logical dimension to it and therefore, organisations utilise it in verbal as well as logical reasoning tests. This test is not as commonly used as other verbal tests. It's aimed at a wide range of positions that require both verbal analysis and logical reasoning skills, ranging from administrative, junior management and technologically-affiliated posts.

Instructions
For each question, you must identify the relationship that exists between each pair of words and determine which of the additional four word pairs maintains the same logical relationship.
You have 10 minutes to complete 20 questions.

Good Luck!

1. brakes : car
    A. diet : fat
    B. dam : river
    C. spring : blossom
    D. traffic light : truck

2. team : coach
    A. car : mechanic
    B. cooking : chef
    C. musicians : conductor
    D. fruit : grocer

3. vehicles : motorcycle
    A. flower : tree
    B. chair : closet
    C. clothes : shirt
    D. houses : garden

4. flower : bouquet
    A. soldier : company
    B. bread : cookies
    C. magazine : cover
    D. tap : water

5. engine : airplane
    A. dog : legs
    B. road : drive
    C. oar : boat
    D. engine : bumper

6. smart : genius
    A. cute : adorable
    B. big : huge
    C. ugly : pretty
    D. spontaneous : sensitive

7.   short : tall
     A.   red : pink
     B.   sit : lie
     C.   running : walking
     D.   light : dark

8.   wolf : howl
     A.   dog : bitch
     B.   dog : bark
     C.   person : running
     D.   cat : meow

9.   decrease : increase
     A.   stretch : enlarge
     B.   beauty : ugliness
     C.   sitting : walking
     D.   square : triangle

10. vineyard : grapes
     A.   laboratory : bacteria
     B.   field : mango
     C.   wild : wolves
     D.   orchard : oranges

11. sand : glass
     A.   cotton : wool
     B.   tree : paper
     C.   seed : flower
     D.   stove : oven

12. distance : kilometre
     A.   radius : diameter
     B.   orange : colour
     C.   weight : pounds
     D.   speed : kilometre

13. government : minister
     A.   choir : singer
     B.   conductor : orchestra
     C.   teacher : pupil
     D.   restaurant : waiter

14. evolution : Darwin
     A.   Blair : Labour
     B.   Bell : telephone
     C.   quantum : Einstein
     D.   apple : Newton

15. bear : bare
     A.   crazy : lazy
     B.   hare : hair
     C.   dust : must
     D.   prize : praise

16. long : long run
     A.   dirty : dirty dancing
     B.   soul : soul mate
     C.   cold : cold feet
     D.   groom : bridegroom

17. taste : food
     A.   touching : feeling
     B.   paint : painter
     C.   eyesight : colour
     D.   hear : sound

18. week : day
     A.   square : angle
     B.   block : apartment
     C.   car : wheel
     D.   furniture : chair

19. beetle : butterfly
   - A. dog : cow
   - B. crocodile : chicken
   - C. ant : tiger
   - D. crow : horse

20. youth : old age
   - A. grace : ugliness
   - B. blossoming : withering
   - C. older : younger
   - D. neighbourhood : park

Test 18 General Tips:

Always pay attention to the <u>order</u> of the words in each pair. If more than one pair seems to apply, they may be in a different order than the original pair of words.

Example:

daughter : family
- pack : wolf
- flowers : garden
- pitcher : team
- producer : director

Daughter is to family as pitcher is to team but NOT as pack is to wolf. If the words pack and wolf were in reverse order, then the same logical rule would apply. The order of the words is significant.

Test 18 Answers:

1.   brakes : car

Brakes stop the car from moving and a dam stops the river from flowing. A Diet does not stop fat but rather stops the process of fattening. Brakes are to car as dam is to river.

The answer is B.

2.   team : coach

A team is managed/trained by a coach and musicians are managed/trained by a conductor. None of the other word pairs have a similar relationship.

The answer is C.

3.   vehicles : motorcycle

A motorcycle is a type of vehicle. A shirt is made of a type of cloth (belongs to the group clothes) and therefore has the same relationship. None of the remaining word pairs have a similar relationship.

The answer is C.

4.   flower : bouquet

A bunch of flowers make up a bouquet. The only pair of words that have a similar relationship are soldier and company. A group of soldiers make up a company.

The answer is A.

5.   engine : airplane

The engine makes the airplane run just as an oar makes a boat move. It's also true that a dog moves with its legs, however, in this case, the order of the words is reversed.

The answer is C.

6.   smart : genius

Genius is the highest degree of smart just as huge is the highest degree of big. The words cute and adorable can't be measured, and they aren't necessarily relative to each other.

The answer is B.

7.   short : tall

Short and tall are opposites, just like light and dark. None of the remaining word pairs are opposites.

The answer is D.

8. wolf : howl

    A wolf howls just like a dog barks. A cat makes a meow sound when it wails or
    yowls. However, meow isn't a verb that describes the way a cat communicates.

    <u>The answer is B.</u>

9. decrease : increase

    Decrease and increase are verbs that are opposites. Beauty and ugliness are nouns
    that are opposites. However, these are the only pairs of opposites, because sitting is
    not the opposite of walking.

    <u>The answer is B.</u>

10. vineyard : grapes

    Grapes grow in a vineyard just as oranges grow in an orchard. Mangos don't grow
    in a field, but rather in a grove or orchard. Bacteria may grow in a laboratory, but
    they are also present in a host of other environments.

    <u>The answer is D.</u>

11. sand : glass

    Sand is processed and turned into glass just as trees are processed to make paper. A
    flower grows from a seed, but there is no artificial processing involved

    <u>The answer is B.</u>

12. distance : kilometre

    Distance can be measured in kilometres just as weight can be measured in pounds.
    Speed can't be measured in kilometres; it can only be measured in kilometres per
    hour.

    <u>The answer is C.</u>

13. government : minister

Ministers form a government just as singers form a choir. A waiter doesn't form a restaurant and a conductor conducts an orchestra.

The answer is A.

14. evolution : Darwin

Evolution is the key word in Darwin's theory of evolution. Bell invented the telephone, which is not a theory. In addition, the word order is reversed. The apple symbolises the development of Newton's theory of gravitation, but apple isn't a key word in the theory. Einstein developed theories of quantum physics, and the word relationship in this case is similar.

The answer is C.

15. bear : bare

Bear and bare sound similar, but they have different meanings and are spelled differently. Crazy and lazy and dust and must rhyme, but they don't sound the same. Prize and praise don't sound the same. The words hare and hair have the same relationship as the words bear and bare.

The answer is B.

16. long : long run

Long is present in the term long run, and their meanings are related. The word soul is in soul mate and their meanings are also related. Groom and bridegroom have the same meaning rather than a related one. Cold and cold feet aren't related in meaning.

The answer is B.

17.   taste : food

Food is what we taste just as sound is what we hear. Feeling and touching have a different relationship. Colour is an aspect of eyesight, but colour isn't the only thing we see.

The answer is D.

18.   week : day

A week is made up of seven days. A chair is a piece of furniture, but not the only piece. A car has a wheel, but is also made up of other components. A block of apartments is made up of a number of apartments.

The answer is B.

19.   beetle : butterfly

The word pairs in this question are all animals. However, the beetle and the butterfly belong to the same class of animals – arthropods (insects). The crocodile is a reptile and the chicken is a bird, the ant is an arthropod and the tiger is a mammal, the crow is a bird and the horse is a mammal. Only the dog and the cow belong to the same class – mammals.

The answer is A.

20.   youth : old age

Youth and old age are opposite ends of the lifecycle. Grace and ugliness may be considered opposites, but neither has a time component. Older and younger are opposites and related to time, but their order is reversed. Blossoming and withering are opposites, related to time and in the same order as the original pair.

The answer is B.

4

SPECIALITY TESTS

At this point, we have covered the three main categories of aptitude tests: verbal, numerical and abstract. While these make up the vast majority of tests on the market, certain fields and positions require higher level and/or additional skills from the ones we have reviewed so far. To assess these skills, a wide variety of specific tests have been developed. These tests are usually administered in addition to the ones already covered. Each test targets a specific skill for a specific position or field. In this section, we will present a sample of these tests to provide you with a holistic and comprehensive picture of the job testing process on the whole. Each group of tests targets a different field, so if you aren't applying for a job in one of these areas, you may wish to skip this section. If you want, you can do these practice tests regardless. They will give you the chance to improve your abilities.

Test 19 Following Instructions

This test is as straightforward as it sounds; it assesses your ability to follow instructions accurately. The test is given to administrative staff, technical trainees and people in positions that are very hands-on, but it is often given to all job applicants. There are a number of versions of this type of test. Some are multiple choice and some are open-ended (free text).

Instructions:
- Choose **one** correct answer for each question.

Remember

Work as quickly and as accurately as you can.

You have 5 minutes to complete 10 questions.

Good Luck!

1. What is the 16th letter of the alphabet?
   A. R
   B. S
   C. O
   D. P
   E. Q

2. How many times does the letter l appear in the following sequence?
   Hjyhfljvnfhlvuvlludnbchftejsltyhfiulrdhcylbtluobl.
   A. 5
   B. 6
   C. 9
   D. 8
   E. 10

3. What's the last letter of the word describing where the sun sets?
   A. T
   B. H
   C. W
   D. E
   E. S

4.   If 356 plus 483 is smaller than 820, choose the first two digits of the sum. If not, choose the last two digits.
   A.   83
   B.   39
   C.   20
   D.   82
   E.   85

5.   Which letters are most commonly found last in the names of the months in the Gregorian calendar?
   A.   s and t
   B.   g and l
   C.   r and e
   D.   y and t
   E.   r and y

6.   Which word can be made by combining the letter before S in the alphabet, followed by the letter that comes two letters before W followed by the letter that comes two letters after L?
   A.   SUN
   B.   SUM
   C.   RUN
   D.   PUP
   E.   TUN

7.   Choose the word that has a single letter appearing more than once.
   A.   black
   B.   blue
   C.   pink
   D.   brown
   E.   purple

8.   Choose the second digit from the right of the smallest number below.
   2,869   5,748   2,854   2,965   3,257
   A.   5
   B.   6
   C.   7
   D.   8
   E.   9

9. Put this list of words in alphabetical order and choose the third letter of the second word.

cow   horse   dog   cat   lion   goat   tiger
A.   W
B.   O
C.   C
D.   T
E.   G

10. Choose the last digit of the number that includes at least two similar digits.

248,597   353,687   587,942   697,541   285,974
A.   4
B.   5
C.   6
D.   7
E.   8

Test 19 Answers

1.   The 16th letter of the alphabet is P.

The answer is D.

2.   Simply count the number of times that the letter l appears.

The answer is C.

3.   The sun sets in the west, and the last letter in the word west is t.

The answer is A.

4.   356+483 = 839, and 839 > 820. Select the last two digits of the number 839, which are 3 and 9.

The answer is B.

5.   January, February, May and July all end in y' and September, October, November and December all end in r'. Therefore y' and r' are the two letters most common as last letters of the Gregorian calendar months names.

The answer is E.

6.   The letter before s in the alphabet is r, the letter that is two letters before w in the alphabet is u and the letter that is two letters after l is n. These letters combine to create the word RUN.

The answer is C.

7.   In the word purple, the letter p appears twice.

The answer is E.

8.   The smallest number is 2,854, and the second digit from the right is 5.

The answer is A.

9.   The order of the words in alphabetical order: cat, cow, dog, goat, horse, lion, tiger. The second word in this list is cow and the third letter of the word cow is w.

The answer is A.

10.   The only number that has two similar digits in it is 353,687 (the number 3). The last digit in this string is 7.

The answer is D.

Test 20 Computer Checking

This test assesses your attention to detail and your ability to work quickly and accurately. There are several formats on the market, and they differ slightly in content depending on the fields and positions they are aimed at. Tests using symbols resembling programming languages are used to assess people in the IT industry. For administrative positions, the content of the test may include items such as budget charts and personal details. The sample test below is administered to candidates mainly in the IT industry, or to people working with computers.

Instructions
For each question, identify the two sets of characters that are identical.
Remember
You have 3 minutes to complete 20 questions.

Good Luck!

	A	B	C	D	E
1.	QSIO9#%	QSO9#%	QSO9#%	QS09#	QS9O#%
2.	693$, 50	639$: 50	693$: 50	693$: 50	639$; 50
3.	I.I.M..O	I.I.M..O	I.I:M.O	II.M.O	I.1.M.O
4.	RSQR&O	RSQR0&O	RS8Q&O	RSQR&O	RSQS&O
5.	(7ADYE!))	(7ADYE)!	(7ADYE!)	(7ADYE!!)	(7ADYE!)
6.	52 + & ^05	52 + &^5	53 + &^5	52 + &^5	52 + &!5
7.	GPS : = 7W	GPS : = 9W	GPS ; = 7W	GPS , = 7W	GPS : = 7W
8.	LP=51	LP#59	PL#59	LP5#9	LP#59
9.	SR,no:20,NR	SR,20,no,NR,	SR,no,20,NR	SR,no,20,MR	SR,no,20,NR
10.	RAMGAUKER	RAGMAUKER	ROMAGAUKER	RAMGAUKER	RAMAUKER
11.	L ^ > N <	L ^ < M >	L ^ < N >	L < ^ N >	L ^ < N >

	A	B	C	D	E
12.	~ ! BJ { 7 }	~ ! BJ { 7]	~ ! BJ { 7]	! ~ BJ { 7]	~ ! BJ { 1]
13.	BFRRRIL**\	BFRRIL*\	BERRIL**\	BFRRIL**\	BFRRIL**\
14.	GB HOUSE 9-	GB HUOSE9_	GB HOUSE9_	GB HOUSE9_	GSHOUSE9_
15.	(82 : LMK : 30)	(82 : LMK : 30)	(82 : LMK : 38)	(82 ; LNK : 30)	(83 : LMK : 30)
16.	(SJ * - C)	(SJ - * C)	(JS * - C)	`)JS * - C (	(JS * - C)
17.	(?45Z)9K	(?48Z)9K	(?48Z)9R	(?48Z)19K	(?48Z)9K
18.	36395508	36395503	36305508	36395508	33695508
19.	100&@co.uk	100%@co.uk	100%@co.uk	100%@CO.UK	100%@couk
20.	IF ? = 4 > B	IE ? = 4 > B	IF ? = 4 < B	IF ? = 4 > B	IF ? = 4 > 8

Test 20 Answers:

	A	B	C	D	E
1.	QSIO9#%	QSO9#%	QSO9#%	QS09#	QS9O#%
2.	693$, 50	639$: 50	693$: 50	693$: 50	639$; 50
3.	I.I.M..O	I.I.M..O	I.I:M.O	II.M.O	I.1.M.O
4.	RSQR&O	RSQR0&O	RS8Q&O	RSQR&O	RSQS&O
5.	(7ADYE!))	(7ADYE)!	(7ADYE!)	(7ADYE!!)	(7ADYE!)
6.	52 + & ^05	52 + &^5	53 + &^5	52 + &^5	52 + &!5
7.	GPS : = 7W	GPS : = 9W	GPS ; = 7W	GPS , = 7W	GPS : = 7W
8.	LP=51	LP#59	PL#59	LP5#9	LP#59
9.	SR,no:20,NR	SR,20,no,NR,	SR,no,20,NR	SR,no,20,MR	SR,no,20,NR

	A	B	C	D	E
10.	RAMGAUKER	RAGMAUKER	ROMAGAUKER	RAMGAUKER	RAMAUKER
11.	L ^ > N <	L ^ < M >	L ^ < N >	L < ^ N >	L ^ < N >
12.	~ ! BJ { 7 }	~ ! BJ { 7]	~ ! BJ { 7]	! ~ BJ { 7]	~ ! BJ { 1]
13.	BFRRRIL**\	BFRRIL*\	BERRIL**\	BFRRIL**\	BFRRIL**\
14.	GB HOUSE 9-	GB HUOSE9_	GB HOUSE9_	GB HOUSE9_	GSHOUSE9_
15.	(82 : LMK : 30)	(82 : LMK : 30)	(82 : LMK : 38)	(82 ; LNK : 30)	(83 : LMK : 30)
16.	(SJ * - C)	(SJ - * C)	(JS * - C)	`)JS * - C (	(JS * - C)
17.	(?45Z)9K	(?48Z)9K	(?48Z)9R	(?48Z)19K	(?48Z)9K
18.	36395508	36395503	36305508	36395508	33695508
19.	100&&@co.uk	100%@co.uk	100%@co.uk	100%@CO.UK	100%@couk
20.	IF ? = 4 > B	IE ? = 4 > B	IF ? = 4 < B	IF ? = 4 > B	IF ? = 4 > 8

Test 21 Basic Checking – Numbers

Like the Computer Checking Test, this test also assesses your ability to work accurately and quickly. However, it's designed for job applicants that are interested in administrative positions. Your aim when taking the test should be to strike a balance between working speed and accuracy. As a rule of thumb, if you complete half the test within the given time limit with up to three mistakes, you will receive an average score.

Instructions

Review the following two lists of numbers and put a tick next to each pair of numbers that are similar.

Remember

You have 2 minutes to complete the test.
Work as quickly and as accurately as you can.

Good Luck!

Number 1	Tick Box	Number 2
7671671487	☐	7671671467
13549870	☐	13549860
657911414	☐	657911414
235875457543	☐	235875457545
5560165410	☐	5560165410
5688846517	☐	5688846517
568774775	☐	568774775
13498777	☐	1349877
256216488	☐	256216448
688445725	☐	684445725
132455758	☐	132455758
865652767	☐	865652767

Number 1	Tick Box	Number 2
532466761	☐	53266761
6654477869	☐	66544777869
465788665	☐	465788865
568510536570	☐	568510536570
85641604	☐	85641064
875450566	☐	875450566
465776510	☐	465756510
568901545	☐	568901454
9065564455	☐	9065564555
1576434125	☐	1576434115
87145641546	☐	87145641546
0654054091	☐	0654050491
257404545	☐	257404545
5566668545	☐	5566668545
7748559452	☐	77485594502
097652323	☐	097654323
756874651	☐	7568674651
65889256	☐	65889256
45686876	☐	45686876
356235587	☐	356235587
43545685947	☐	43545675947
44558424765	☐	44558324765
558443547	☐	558443547
224658716	☐	2246587161
8846574567	☐	8846554567
6572278971	☐	6572278971

Number 1	Tick Box	Number 2
669945576715	☐	669945576715
56884488942	☐	56884488942
03489755234	☐	034897555234
65798716	☐	65797816
32487555	☐	32487555
4488610112	☐	4488612112
465710077	☐	463710077
56888154102	☐	56888144102
135700886	☐	135700786
8686986468	☐	8686986488
564687014	☐	564687014
578911008	☐	57891108
6576576577	☐	6576576557
866546664	☐	866546664
4567888641	☐	4567888641
6574869	☐	6574869
565658898	☐	565658898

Test 21 Answers:

Number 1	Tick Box	Number 2
7671671487	☐	7671671467
13549870	☐	13549860
657911414	☑	657911414
235875457543	☐	235875457545

Number 1	Tick Box	Number 2
5560165410	☑	5560165410
5688846517	☑	5688846517
568774775	☑	568774775
13498777	☐	1349877
256216488	☐	256216448
688445725	☐	684445725
132455758	☑	132455758
865652767	☑	865652767
532466761	☐	53266761
6654477869	☐	66544777869
465788665	☐	465788865
568510536570	☑	568510536570
85641604	☐	85641064
875450566	☑	875450566
465776510	☐	465756510
568901545	☐	568901454
9065564455	☐	9065564555
1576434125	☐	1576434115
87145641546	☑	87145641546
0654054091	☐	0654050491
257404545	☑	257404545
5566668545	☑	5566668545
7748559452	☐	77485594502
097652323	☐	097654323

Number 1	Tick Box	Number 2
756874651	☐	7568674651
65889256	☑	65889256
45686876	☑	45686876
356235587	☑	356235587
43545685947	☐	43545675947
44558424765	☐	44558324765
558443547	☑	558443547
224658716	☐	2246587161
8846574567	☐	8846554567
6572278971	☑	6572278971
669945576715	☑	669945576715
56884488942	☑	56884488942
03489755234	☐	034897555234
65798716	☐	65797816
32487555	☑	32487555
4488610112	☐	4488612112
465710077	☐	463710077
56888154102	☐	56888144102
135700886	☐	135700786
8686986468	☐	8686986488
564687014	☑	564687014
578911008	☐	57891108
6576576577	☐	6576576557
866546664	☑	866546664
4567888641	☑	4567888641
6574869	☑	6574869
565658898	☑	565658898

Test 22 Basic Checking – Words

This test is another version of the Basic Checking Test, using words instead of numbers. It is also designed to assess job applicants seeking administrative positions, and your aim should also be to strike a balance between working speed and accuracy. Once again, as an indication of performance, if you complete half the test within the given time limit with up to three mistakes, you will receive an average score.

Instructions
Review the following two lists of words and put a tick next to each pair of words that are similar.
Remember
You have 2 minutes to complete the test.
Work as quickly and as accurately as you can.

Good Luck!

Word 1	Tick Box	Word 2
Joshua Smith	☐	Joshua Smith
Tom Patel	☐	Tom Patel
Tim Jonson	☐	Tim Johnson
Tom Bercovic	☐	Tom Bercovic
Tyrone Nile	☐	Tyrone Neil
Lucy Kim	☐	Lucia Kim
Gerhardt Roehn	☐	Gerhart Roehn
Garcio Marx	☐	Garcia Marx
Sue Silverberg	☐	Sue Silberg
Joey Trib	☐	Joy Trib
Omar Mahmood	☐	Omar Mahmoud
Denn Dunn	☐	Denn Dumn

Word 1	Tick Box	Word 2
Ki Min Chi	☐	Ko Min Chi
Rupert Trevo	☐	Rupert Trevo
Jill Wayne	☐	Jill Wayne
Tamara Richardson	☐	Tamara Richardson
Lowelli Lin	☐	Loweli Lin
Olaf Johansson	☐	Olaf Johanssen
Jorgen Jorg	☐	Jorjen Jorj
Joe Bloggs	☐	Joy Bloggs
Bert Smit	☐	Bert Smiths
Joy Joyce	☐	Joy Joyce
Grace Minolito	☐	Grace Minolito
Thorsten Schmidt	☐	Torsten Schmit
Jacky Jonson	☐	Jacky Jomson
Jeremiah Inch	☐	Jeremia Inch
Isabelle Oui	☐	Isabelle Ouiu
Roy Umni	☐	Roy Umni
Bill Geffen	☐	Bill Geffen
Katja Schindler	☐	Katia Schindler
Sean O'Connoly	☐	Sean O'Connoly
Craig Abram	☐	Craigg Abram
Richie Caribaldi	☐	Richie Carribaldi
Jon Demio	☐	Jo Demio
Line Jensen	☐	Line Jensen
Joshua Goodfellow	☐	Joshue Goodfellow
Joop Cremers	☐	Joop Kremers

Word 1	Tick Box	Word 2
Harry Lin	☐	Harrie Lin
Hans Utrecht	☐	Hand Utrecht
Criston Nikos	☐	Cristos Nikos
Bernardo Luigi	☐	Bernardo Luigi
Lee Chen	☐	Leee Chen
Aci Coen	☐	Avi Coen
Don Brake	☐	Don Brake
Jay McGregor	☐	Jay MacGregor
Tom Jones	☐	Ton Jones
Linda Black	☐	Linda Black
Ahmed Sharif	☐	Ahmed Sharif
Jenny Parker	☐	Jenmy Parker
Lili Lu	☐	Lila Lu
Britney James	☐	Brittney James
David March	☐	David March
Hillie Berger	☐	Hillie Berger
Aristo Totlus	☐	Aristo Totls
Jim Green	☐	Jin Green

Test 22 Answers:

Word 1	Tick Box	Word 2
Joshua Smith	☑	Joshua Smith
Tom Patel	☑	Tom Patel
Tim Jonson	☐	Tim Johnson

Word 1	Tick Box	Word 2
Tom Bercovic	☑	Tom Bercovic
Tyrone Nile	☐	Tyrone Neil
Lucy Kim	☐	Lucia Kim
Gerhardt Roehn	☐	Gerhart Roehn
Garcio Marx	☐	Garcia Marx
Sue Silverberg	☐	Sue Silberg
Joey Trib	☐	Joy Trib
Omar Mahmood	☐	Omar Mahmoud
Denn Dunn	☐	Denn Dumn
Ki Min Chi	☐	Ko Min Chi
Rupert Trevo	☑	Rupert Trevo
Jill Wayne	☑	Jill Wayne
Tamara Richardson	☑	Tamara Richardson
Lowelli Lin	☐	Loweli Lin
Olaf Johansson	☐	Olaf Johanssen
Jorgen Jorg	☐	Jorjen Jorj
Joe Bloggs	☐	Joy Bloggs
Bert Smit	☐	Bert Smiths
Joy Joyce	☑	Joy Joyce
Grace Minolito	☑	Grace Minolito
Thorsten Schmidt	☐	Torsten Schmit
Jacky Jonson	☐	Jacky Jomson
Jeremiah Inch	☐	Jeremia Inch
Isabelle Oui	☐	Isabelle Ouiu
Roy Umni	☑	Roy Umni

Bill Geffen	☑	Bill Geffen
Katja Schindler	☐	Katia Schindler
Sean O'Connoly	☑	Sean O'Connoly
Craig Abram	☐	Craigg Abram
Richie Caribaldi	☐	Richie Carribaldi
Jon Demio	☐	Jo Demio
Line Jensen	☑	Line Jensen
Joshua Goodfellow	☐	Joshue Goodfellow
Joop Cremers	☐	Joop Kremers
Harry Lin	☐	Harrie Lin
Hans Utrecht	☐	Hand Utrecht
Criston Nikos	☐	Cristos Nikos
Bernardo Luigi	☑	Bernardo Luigi
Lee Chen	☐	Leee Chen
Aci Coen	☐	Avi Coen
Don Brake	☑	Don Brake
Jay McGregor	☐	Jay MacGregor
Tom Jones	☐	Ton Jones
Linda Black	☑	Linda Black
Ahmed Sharif	☑	Ahmed Sharif
Jenny Parker	☐	Jenmy Parker
Lili Lu	☐	Lila Lu
Britney James	☐	Brittney James
David March	☑	David March
Hillie Berger	☑	Hillie Berger
Aristo Totlus	☐	Aristo Totls
Jim Green	☐	Jin Green

Test 23 Clerical Checking

This test assesses your ability to work quickly and accurately when checking detailed information. There are a host of tests that simulate tasks where employees are required to complete activities like filling in expense forms, completing time sheets and writing out cheques. Usually the job applicant is asked to check for spelling mistakes, missing information and the use of incorrect codes where applicable.

This test is mainly used to assess people interested in administrative positions and supporting roles.

Instructions

Check that the information in the expense form below uses the correct codes, and that all the required fields have been filled in correctly.

-   Each claim must have a name.
-   Each claim must have a claim description.
-   For each claim made, the cost and an associated code must be provided.
-   All dates must be written in **dd/mm** format (e.g. 05/06).
-   Car mileage and destinations for train and bus travel must be provided for related claims.
-   The time the claim was made must be written in am/pm format (e.g. 11:45 am).

For each question identify the field or fields in the form that have been incorrectly completed or are missing, and circle the letter/s next to each question that represent mistake(s) in the following manner:

•   Mark **A** if the name of the claimant is missing.
•   Mark **B** if the claim description is missing or incorrectly completed.
•   Mark **C** if the claim is coded incorrectly or if the code is missing.
•   Mark **D** if the date is missing or completed incorrectly.
•   Mark **E** if the time the claim was made is missing or completed incorrectly.
•   Mark **F** if the travel destination and/or mileage is missing or incorrectly completed.
•   Mark **G** if the cost is missing or written in the wrong column.
•   Mark **I** if there are no errors on the expense form.

Remember

You have 3 minutes to complete 15 questions.

Good Luck!

No	Name	Claim Description	Code	Date	Time	Travel		Mileage		Hotel Costs	Meal Costs
						Dest	Cost	KM	Cost		
1	Jamie	Business Lunch	219	25/02	12:00am						26.35
2	Ron	Car Travel	215	30/02	11:00am			39	25.00		
3	Louise	Train Travel	217	11/26	12:38am	Paris			12.56		
4	Kam	Business Lunch & Hotel	219		11:38am					115.00	25.00
5	Jeff		215	12/27	10:25am			115	42.00		
6		Car Travel	215	12/03	09:58am			78	35.00		
7	Danny	Hotel	219	02.06	18:12						85.00
8	Graham	Lunch & Dinner	219	26/07 and 27/08	01:12pm & 08:00pm						25.00, 42.00
9	Ken	Car Hire & Car Travel	215, 220	12.12	08:00am	253	215.00				
10	Melanie		218	13/28	9:58am					152.00	
11		Dinner & Train and Bus Travel	216, 219	22/07	12:40pm	London	46.00 2.60				36.00
12	Joy	Car Travel	215	15/08	11:58am			269	75.00		
13	Jason	Hotel and Bus Travel	218, 216	12/04		Single fair	2.50			98.00	
14	Brian	Bus and Car Travel & Hotel	215, 216, 218	10/5	17:25	Berlin	5.20	75	36.00		165.00
15	Hillary	Lunch	219	8/05	08:26am						32.00
Codes	CarTravel - 215 Bus Travel - 216		TrainTravel - 217 Hotel - 218			Meals - 219 Other - 220					

1. A.   B.   C.   D.   E.   F.   G.   I.
2. A.   B.   C.   D.   E.   F.   G.   I.
3. A.   B.   C.   D.   E.   F.   G.   I.
4. A.   B.   C.   D.   E.   F.   G.   I.
5. A.   B.   C.   D.   E.   F.   G.   I.
6. A.   B.   C.   D.   E.   F.   G.   I.
7. A.   B.   C.   D.   E.   F.   G.   I.
8. A.   B.   C.   D.   E.   F.   G.   I.
9. A.   B.   C.   D.   E.   F.   G.   I.
10. A.   B.   C.   D.   E.   F.   G.   I.
11. A.   B.   C.   D.   E.   F.   G.   I.
12. A.   B.   C.   D.   E.   F.   G.   I.
13. A.   B.   C.   D.   E.   F.   G.   I.
14. A.   B.   C.   D.   E.   F.   G.   I.
15. A.   B.   C.   D.   E.   F.   G.   I.

Test 23 Answers:

1. The time of the claim is incorrect. It should be 12:00 pm.

The answer is E.

2. Every detail was filled in correctly.

The answer is I.

3. The date was written incorrectly (**mm/dd** instead of **dd/mm**) and the cost was written under the Mileage column instead of the Travel column.

The answers are D and G.

4. The hotel expense claim code is missing (218) and so is the date

The answers are C and D.

5. The claim description is missing (i.e., car travel) and the date was written in the wrong format (**mm/dd** instead of **dd/mm**).

The answers are B and D.

6. The name of the claimant is missing.

The answer is A.

7. The code is incorrect (it should be 218) and the date was written in the wrong format (**dd.mm** instead of **dd/mm**). The time was written using the 24 hour clock rather than am/pm, and the hotel costs were noted in the wrong column.

The answers are C, D, E and G.

8. Every detail was filled in correctly.

The answer is I.

9. The date was written in the wrong format (**dd.mm** instead of **dd/mm**). The car mileage and associated costs were written in the wrong columns.

The answers are D, F and G.

10. The claim description is missing (i.e., hotel) and the date was written in the wrong format (**mm/dd** instead of **dd/mm**).

The answers are B and D.

11. The name of the claimant is missing, and so is the code for Train Travel.

The answers are A and C.

12. Every detail was filled in correctly.

The answer is I.

13. The time of the claim is missing, and the bus travel destination was filled in incorrectly.

The answers are E and F.

14. The date was written in the wrong format (it should be 10/05 instead of 10/5). In addition, the time was written using the 24 hour clock rather than am/pm. The hotel costs were also written in the wrong column.

The answers are D, E and G.

15. The date was written in the wrong format (it should be 08/05 rather than 8/05).

The answer is D.

Test 24 Spatial Reasoning

Spatial reasoning tests measure your ability to visualise and manipulate two and three-dimensional objects that are presented in two-dimensional form. These tests are usually used to assess people in IT, engineering and any field that requires design skills, such as architecture and graphics. Spatial reasoning tests measure abstract abilities.

Spatial Reasoning

On this test, you are given a three-dimensional figure in two-dimensional form. Your task is to visualise and manipulate the form in your mind to determine the correct answer. This test is one of the most common types of spatial reasoning tests, and is at a fairly high level. It is aimed at IT developers, engineers, architects and designers that use graphics software. Another version of this test presents an open and unfolded cube. You are asked to fold back the cube in your mind and visualise how it should appear from various perspectives.

Instructions

On each question there is a cube with three visible sides, each with its own design.

Each side has its own design on a given cube. Rotate the cube in your mind until you find a match between the cube in the main diagram and **one** of the cubes in the answer options.

Example:

Which of the four options shows the cube on the left from a different perspective?

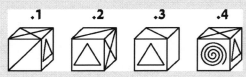

Solution:

- The first option can be eliminated, because the diagonal should appear on the back (hidden) side rather than on the front, in relation to the triangle.
- The second option can be eliminated because if the X is on the right-hand side of the cube, the triangle should be pointing to the right, towards the X, rather than up.
- The third option can be eliminated because the triangle is pointing up, towards the diagonal. The diagonal should be on the right-hand side in relation to the triangle.
- The fourth option is correct, and it shows the hidden left side.

Remember

You have 6 minutes to complete 8 questions.

Good Luck!

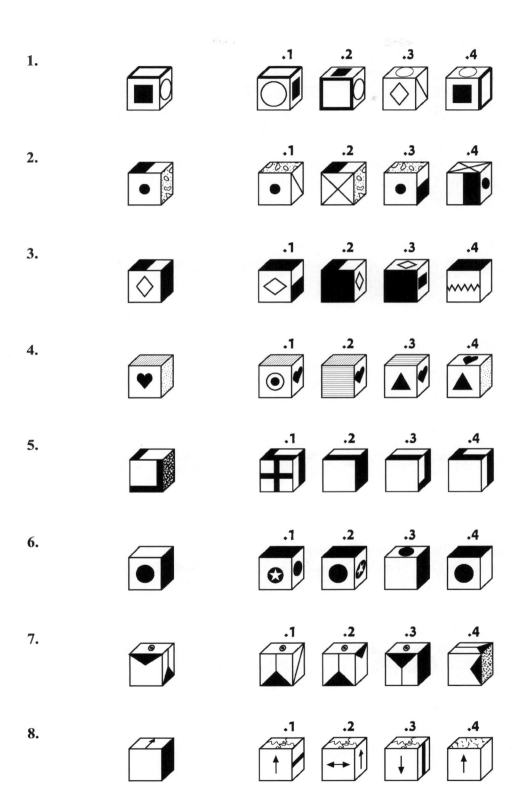

Test 24 Answers:

1.

- The first option can be eliminated because the black square and the white circle have swapped locations. When the cube is flipped over, the empty facet should be on the bottom rather than on top, as shown.
- The second option can be eliminated because the circle should be on the left side of the black square, rather than on the right.
- The third option is correct, because we now see two new designs that were hidden in the main diagram.
- The fourth option can be eliminated because the blank facet should be on the left side of the cube in relation to the black square and the white circle, rather than on the right.

The answer is 3.

2.

- The correct answer is the first option, which exposes the facet at the bottom of the cube in the main diagram - a diagonal.
- The second option can be eliminated because the cube hasn't rotated and the front facet has changed into an X instead of a black circle.
- The third option can be eliminated because the facet that is half black and half white is supposed to appear on the left instead of on the right, in relation to the other two visible facets.
- The fourth option can be eliminated because the circle should be on the top facet, in relation to the half black/half white facet.

The answer is 1.

3.

- The first option can be eliminated because the half black/half white facet should be on the left in relation to the diamond, rather than on the right.
- The second option can be eliminated because the half black/half white facet should be at the bottom of the cube.
- The third option can be eliminated because the facet on the right should be half black/half white rather than a black square.
- The fourth option is correct, and it reveals two hidden facets.

<u>The answer is 4.</u>

4.

- The first and second options can be eliminated because if we rotate the cube so that the heart is on the right, the top lines should be horizontal rather than vertical in relation to it.
- The third option can be eliminated because the design on the top facet has changed in relation to the heart.
- The fourth option is correct, and it reveals the hidden facet, a triangle, that is on the bottom in the main diagram.

<u>The answer is 4.</u>

5.   .1   .2   .3   .4

- The first option can be eliminated because the facet that has a black and white wallpaper pattern on it should be facing the front, instead of the facet with the black cross.
- The second option can be eliminated because the facet on the right-hand side should depict a reverse L shape rather than a black facet.
- The third option is correct, and reveals a blank facet that was hidden in the main diagram.
- The fourth option can be eliminated because the facet facing the front should be the black and white wallpaper pattern rather than a blank facet.

The answer is 3.

6.   .1   .2   .3   .4

- The first option can be eliminated because the facet facing the front should be white.
- The second option is correct, and reveals the bottom facet of the cube that was hidden in the main diagram.
- The third option can be eliminated because the white facet should be in back of the cube, rather than in front.
- The fourth option can be eliminated because the white facet should be on the left side, rather than on the right.

The answer is 2.

7.

- The correct answer is the first option, which indicates a left rotation and reveals the facet in back of the cube in the main diagram.
- The second option can be eliminated because if the triangle is on the right, the funnel should be in back rather than in front in relation to it.
- The third option can be eliminated because the circle should be on the bottom rather than on top of the cube, in relation to the funnel facet.
- The fourth option can be eliminated because the facet with the triangle and the facet with the funnel are misplaced in relation to each other.

<u>The answer is 1.</u>

8.

- The first option can be eliminated because the black facet should be on the right side of the cube.
- The second option is correct, revealing two hidden sides: the back and left sides of the cube in the main diagram.
- The third option can be eliminated because the white facet should be on top of the cube.
- The fourth option can be eliminated because the black facet should be on the right side of the cube.

<u>The answer is 2.</u>

Test 25 Mechanical Reasoning

Mechanical reasoning tests measure your aptitude for mechanics. They test your understanding of the basic principles of mechanics and mechanical physics. To succeed on these types of tests, you must have both the ability to visualise the movement of objects through space and an understanding of cause and effect relationships. They are designed to assess those in technical and engineering positions, as well as people in any type of hands-on position.

Instructions
The following test will assess your knowledge of basic mechanical and physical principles.
In each exercise, a question will be followed by a related figure(s). For each question, select only one answer from the three options listed.
Remember
You have 5 minutes to complete the 10 problems on the test.

Good Luck!

1.   Three axes are turning, and they are attached to each other by straps. Which axis will turn faster?

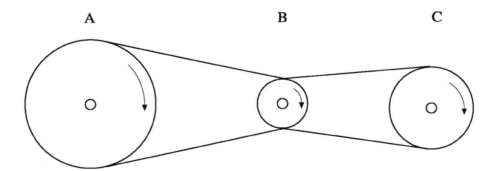

        1.   A
        2.   B.
        3.   C.

2.   In which situation would you have to exert more force to lift the weight?

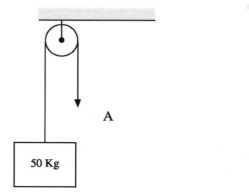
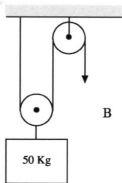

1.   A
2.   B
3.   You would have to exert equal force in each case.

3.   Which shelf can carry more weight?

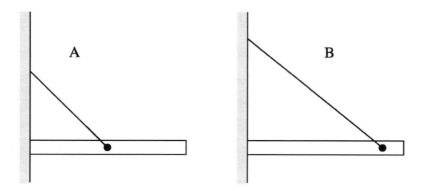

1.   A
2.   B
3.   Both shelves can carry an equal amount of weight.

4. Which car has to drive faster to stay in line with the other car when taking the turn?

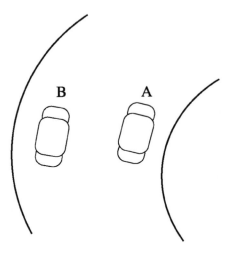

1.   A
2.   B
3.   They would have to drive at the same speed.

5. The three cogwheels are joined and are moving very quickly. Which wheel is moving faster than the others?

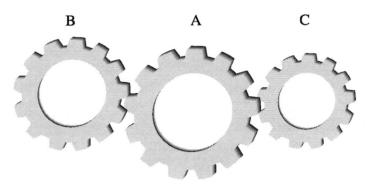

1.   A
2.   B
3.   C

6. Which figure depicts the right trajectory of the bomb being dropped?

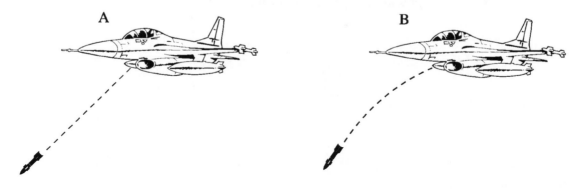

1. A
2. B
3. Both are correct.

7. Which cart is more likely to flip over during a turn?

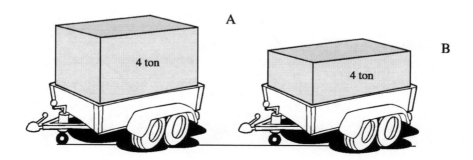

1. A
2. B
3. No difference.

8. If the cogwheel on the left moves in the direction the arrow is pointing to, then which direction will the right wheel turn towards?

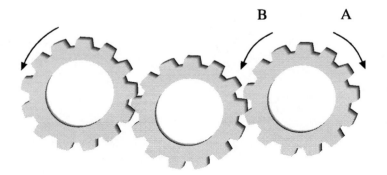

1. A
2. B
3. The wheel won't turn.

9. Which side of the road will the car slide towards when it takes the turn?

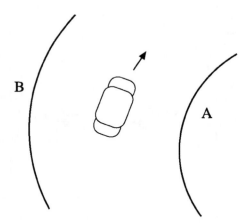

1. A
2. B
3. Neither side.

10. Which point on the wheel will rotate faster when the wheel is in motion?

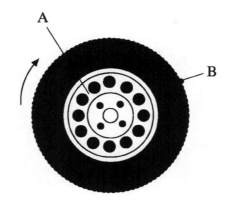

1. A
2. B
3. Both points will rotate at the same speed.

Test 25 Answers:

1. Three axes are turning, and they are attached to each other by straps. Which axis will turn faster?

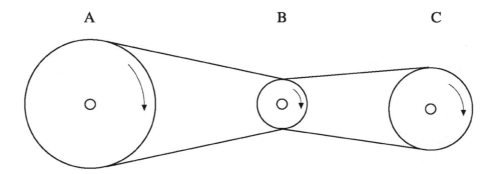

The smaller the wheel diameter surrounding the axis, the faster the axis will turn. Wheel B has the smallest wheel diameter and therefore, the axis will turn faster.

The answer is 2.

2.   In which situation would you have to exert more force to lift the weight?

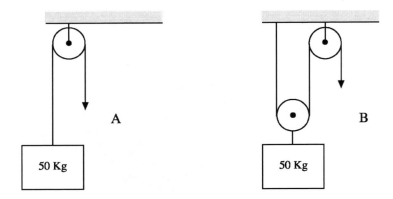

The double pulley block in figure B makes it easier to lift the weight, therefore you would use more force to lift the block in figure A.

<u>The answer is 1.</u>

3.   Which shelf can carry more weight?

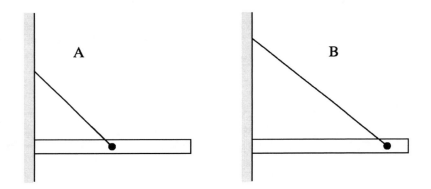

The anchor point in figure B is more distant from the wall, therefore the shelf in figure B can carry more weight.

<u>The answer is 2.</u>

4.   Which car has to drive faster to stay in line with the other car when taking the turn?

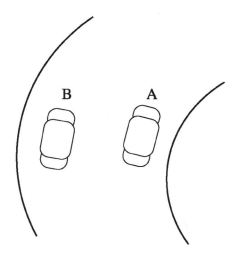

Because car B is driving on the outer side of the rim, it has to travel a greater distance. Therefore, it has to drive faster at the turn to stay aligned with car A.

<u>The answer is 2.</u>

5.   The three cogwheels are joined and are moving very quickly. Which wheel is moving faster than the others?

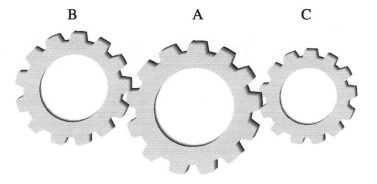

Wheel C is smallest in diameter, so it will move more quickly than the others.

<u>The answer is 3.</u>

6. Which figure depicts the right trajectory of the bomb being dropped?

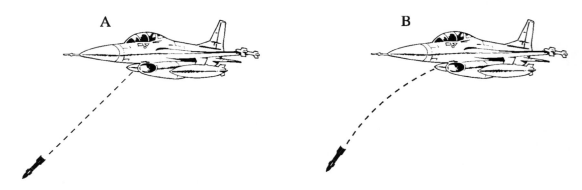

No drop is completely straight, without a ballistic curve.

The answer is 2.

7. Which cart is more likely to flip over during a turn?

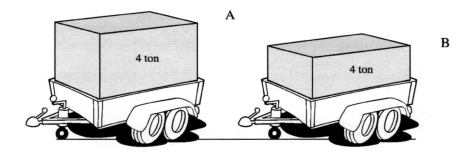

Because the load in cart A is higher up than the one in cart B, its centre of gravity is also higher. This makes it more likely to flip over during a turn.

The answer is 1.

8. If the cogwheel on the left moves in the direction the arrow is pointing to, then which direction will the right wheel turn towards?

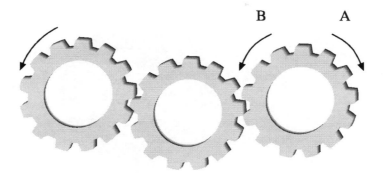

The cogwheels turn in opposite directions. When the left wheel turns in the direction of the arrow (anti-clockwise), the middle wheel will turn to the right (clockwise). This will cause the right wheel to turn anti-clockwise in direction B.

<u>The answer is 2.</u>

9. Which side of the road will the car slide towards when it takes the turn?

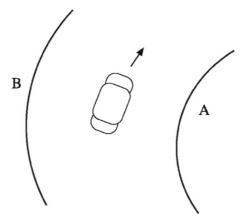

When a car takes a turn, the centrifugal power pulls from the centre outwards. Therefore, the car will slide towards the outer rim (B).

<u>The answer is 2.</u>

10.   Which point on the wheel will rotate faster when the wheel is in motion?

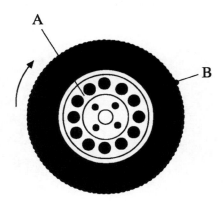

Point B, on the outer rim, will travel faster than point A. Point A is closer to the centre, and it has to travel the smaller distance.

The answer is 2.

Test 26 Fault Finding

Fault finding tests assess your ability to follow a logical sequence of events and make the deductions required to detect faults. These tests are designed to assess candidates in the IT industry who are applying for posts in programming, debugging and software engineering. Certain tests in the Abstract Series such as Diagramming and Diagrammatic Thinking also assess your ability to follow a logical sequence and identify the shape, form or sequence produced, and indeed they are given to applicants in the same fields. But apart from assessing your ability to follow a logical sequence, fault-finding tests analyse your ability to identify faults in a sequence.

There are a number of versions of this test on the market. On all of them, a key is provided detailing what each shape, switch or rule does, and you are asked to detect which of the shapes, switches or rules in the sequence are dysfunctional. On some of the tests, a dysfunctional shape, switch or rule performs a different action than a functional one, making fault detection even trickier. The practice test provided is one such example.

Instructions
On this test you have to follow sequences made up of a number of switches, and <u>determine which of the switches are dysfunctional.</u>

There are three kinds of switches:
1. Those that let the black/shaded shapes within them pass through.
2. Those that only let certain shapes through.
3. Those that are present at junctions, and that either do or don't let all shapes through depending on the type of switch.

Each switch reacts differently when it is dysfunctional. For the full list of switches and their respective functions, please see the switch key card.

Switch Key Card:

Switch	▲▷□○◆	⋈	⧓	◁▷	△▽	⊖	⊘	▲□○◇
Functional	Transfers the shaded shapes	Transfers only the triangle and square	Transfers only the circle and diamond	Transfers only the square and circle	Transfers only the triangle and diamond	Transfers shapes coming from two directions	Transfers only those shapes that appear once when coming from two directions	Presents the final outcome at the end of the process
Dysfunctional	Does not transfer any shape	Transfers all shapes	Transfers all shapes	Transfers all shapes	Transfers all shapes	Does not transfer any shape	Transfers all shapes	

Each switch affects the sequence differently, depending on whether it's functioning properly or not. It is of utmost importance that you know what a switch does when it is and isn't intact

Remember

There's only one correct answer to each problem.

You have 5 minutes to complete the 10 problems on the test.

Good Luck!

1.

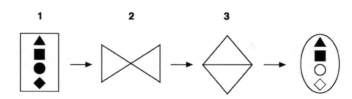

A. 1   **C.** 3
B. 2

2.

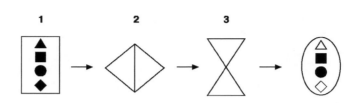

A. 1   **C.** 3
B. 2

3.

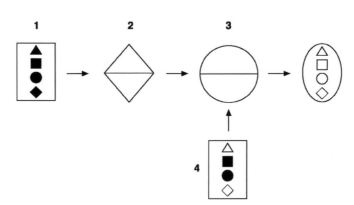

A. 1   **C.** 3
B. 2   **D.** 4

4.

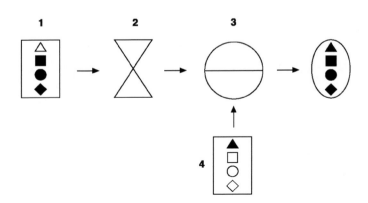

A. 1   **C.** 3
B. 2   **D.** 4

5.

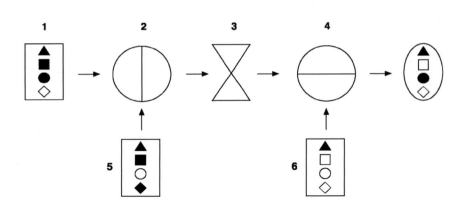

A. 1   **D.** 4
B. 2   **E.** 5
C. 3   **F.** 6

6.

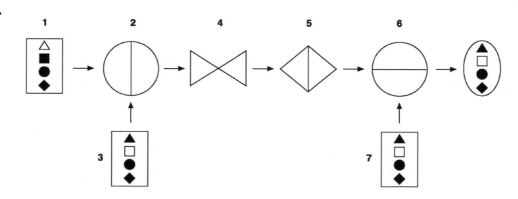

A. 1	**E.** 5
B. 2	**F.** 6
C. 3	**G.** 7
D. 4	

7.

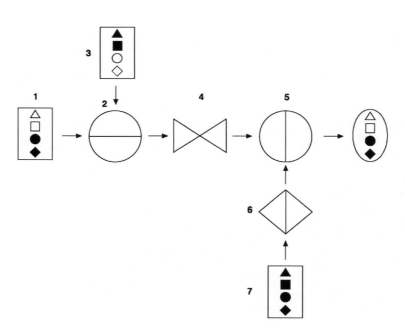

A. 1	**E.** 5
B. 2	**F.** 6
C. 3	**G.** 7
D. 4	

8.

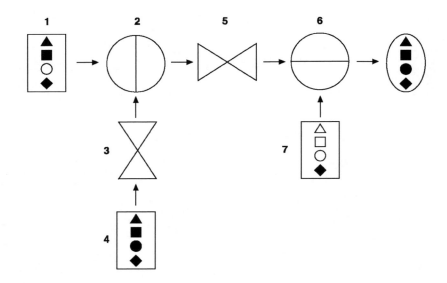

A.	1	E.	5
B.	2	F.	6
C.	3	G.	7
D.	4		

9.

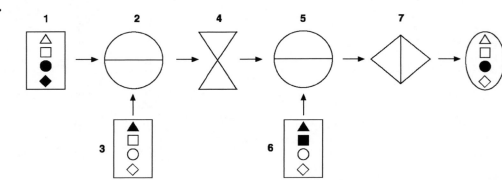

A.	1	E.	5
B.	2	F.	6
C.	3	G.	7
D.	4		

10.

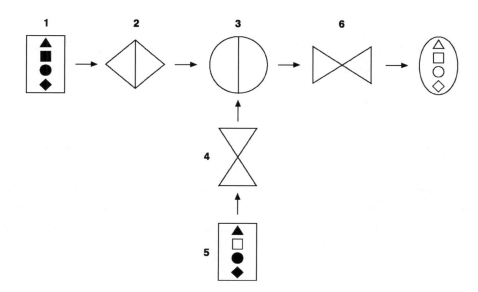

A. 1   **D.** 4
B. 2   **E.** 5
C. 3   **F.** 6

Test 26 Answers:

1.

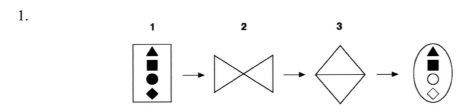

Switch 1, when dysfunctional, shouldn't allow any shapes to pass through it. However, we can see that at the end of the process some shapes managed to get through, so switch 1 must be intact. Switch 2 should only let the triangle and the square through, which it did, so it must be intact. Switch 3 should only let the triangle and the diamond through, but because it allowed the square through, it must have a fault. Therefore the dysfunctional switch is number 3.

The answer is C.

2.

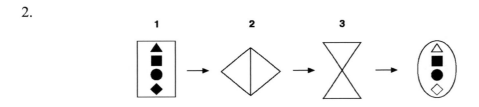

Switch 1, when dysfunctional, shouldn't allow any shapes to pass through it. We can see that at the end of the process some shapes did manage to get through, so switch 1 must be intact. Switch 2 should only let the square and the circle through, which it did, so it must be intact. Switch 3 should only let the circle and the diamond through, but because it let the square through it must be dysfunctional.

The answer is C.

3.

In diagrams that have switches coming from a number of directions, it is often wise to start searching for faults at the junctions. In this problem, switch 3 should let all the shapes through from all directions at the junction. Because it didn't allow any shapes through, it must be dysfunctional.

The answer is C.

4.

Switch 3 should let all of the shapes through, which it did. This also means that switches 1 and 4 let all of the shapes through, so they must also be intact. Switch 2 should only let the circle and the diamond through, but because it also allowed the square through it must be at fault.

The answer is B.

5.

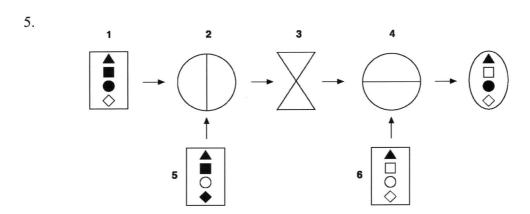

Switch 2 should only allow the circle and the diamond through, therefore the triangle and squares in switches 1 and 5 should be blocked. However, at the end of the process there is a triangle and circle. If switch 1 were dysfunctional, however, it would have blocked all of the shapes. This is not the case, since we see that there's a circle at the end of the process. If switch 5 were dysfunctional, it would have blocked all shapes within in the transfer, which it did, and that is why switch 2 let all of the shapes from switch 1 through.

<u>The answer is E.</u>

6.

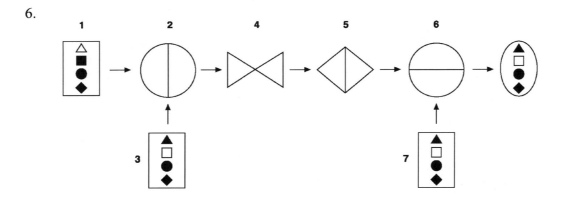

If all switches were intact, the square (currently missing at the end of the process) would have made its way from switch 1 through the entire process, and at the very end all of the shapes would be in place. However, since switch 1 is at fault, it did not allow any of the shapes through. This is why the square is missing at the end.

<u>The answer is A.</u>

7.

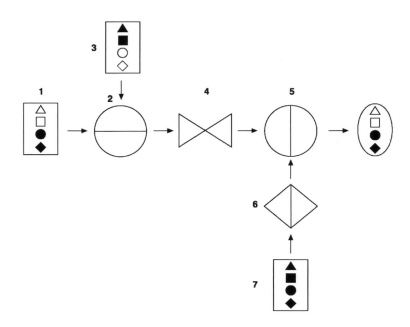

Switch 6 is dysfunctional. If it were intact, switch 6 would have allowed only the square and the circle through instead of all the shapes. The diamond at the end of the process clearly did not originate in switch 1, since switch 4 only allows triangles and squares through. Switch 4 must be intact, otherwise it would have let all the shapes through. The diamond would then have been blocked by switch 5.

The answer is F.

8.

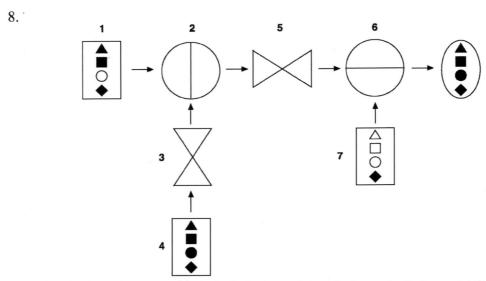

Switch 4 is the only one with a circle in it, and the circle made it through all the way to the end of the process. Switch 5 should only let the triangle and the square through, so it is at fault because it allowed the circle through as well.

The answer is E.

9.

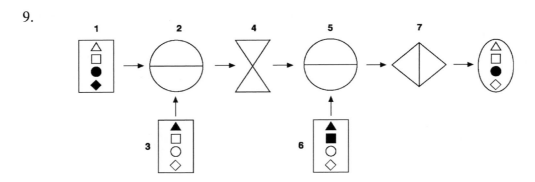

Switch 1 must be intact, because the circle made it through to the end of the process. Switches 2 and 5 must be intact, otherwise they would have blocked any shape coming across. Switch 7 must be intact otherwise it would have let the square through from switch 6 and blocked the triangle. However, neither the square nor the triangle made it. The only possible explanation is that switch 6 is dysfunctional, so it blocked both the triangle and the square.

The answer is F.

10.

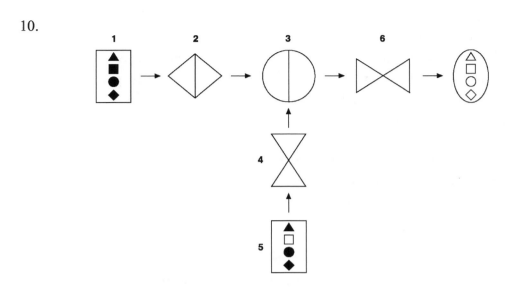

If all switches were intact, a square would have made it to the end of the process. Therefore, the fault must lay in switches 1 or 2 where the square originated. However, if switch 2 were at fault, it would have let all the shapes from switch 1 through. This would have ultimately resulted in a triangle and a square at the end of the process. This means switch 1 is at fault, because it blocked the way for all shapes within.

The answer is A.

Final Words

In the Aptitude Test Preparation part of the book you had the chance to familiarize your self with a multitude of tests – abstract, numerical, verbal and specialty tests.
A battery of aptitude tests is integral to most recruitment selection processes. This should not deter you; on the contrary!

You've learned that proper practice can dramatically improve your performance. Seeing the type of tests and formats of questions prior to taking the actual tests contributes to your success. In addition, learning the key rules and strategies underpinning each test significantly improves your success rate.

Do not accept the notion that your performance on these type of intelligence tests is determined from the outset; you have the ability to improve your scores dramatically! As you probably know, there are courses and books that prepare you for psychometric tests such as the GMAT and GRE. These tests are intelligence tests yet students that have prepared themselves for these tests have managed to raise their scores significantly – this is an undisputed fact.

The key to success is in your hands. With proper practice, you have all the reasons in the world to feel confident and relaxed on the day of the test.

We wish you all the very best on your big day.
For more practice on aptitude tests, visit our website at: **www.jobtestprep.com**

Good Luck!